Electric Salome

Loie Fuller in early publicity photograph, circa 1893, Bibliothèque
Nationale de France

Electric Salome

Loie Fuller's Performance of Modernism

❧

Rhonda K. Garelick

PRINCETON UNIVERSITY PRESS

Princeton and Oxford

Copyright © 2007 by Princeton University Press
Published by Princeton University Press, 41 William Street, Princeton, New Jersey 08540
In the United Kingdom: Princeton University Press, 3 Market Place,
Woodstock, Oxfordshire OX20 1SY

Library of Congress Cataloging-in-Publication Data

Garelick, Rhonda K., date.
Electric Salome : Loie Fuller's performance of modernism / Rhonda K. Garelick.
  p.   cm.
Includes bibliographical references and index.

ISBN: 978-0-691-14109-1

1. Fuller, Loie, 1862–1928. 2. Dancers—United States. 3. Modern dance. I. Title.
GV1785.F8G37 2006
792.8′028092—dc22
[B]
2006036908

British Library Cataloging-in-Publication Data is available

This book has been composed in Goudy

Printed on acid-free paper. ∞

press.princeton.edu

Printed in the United States of America

1 3 5 7 9 10 8 6 4 2

To my father, Milton,
to whom I owe my love of music and dance, and

To my late mother, Shirley,
who taught me to see the drama in people's stories

Contents

∽

Illustrations

Acknowledgments

I AM GRATEFUL TO THE KNOWLEDGEABLE, kind, and attentive staffs at the Bibliothèque de l'Arsenal in Paris and at the New York Public Library for the Performing Arts—particularly to Pat Rader and Tom Lisanti. Curator Betty Long-Schleif of the Maryhill Museum was generous with her collection and understanding when I needed materials quickly. Hélène Pinet-Cheula granted me access to the Musée Rodin archives. At a very early point in this project, I benefited from conversations with the late Philippe Néagu, curator of photography at the Musée d'Orsay, as well as with Giovanni Lista and with dancer and critic Brigyda Ochaim. I am grateful to film historian Nicholas Villodre of the Cinémathèque Française for permitting me a private screening of *Le Lys de la vie*, and to the Smithsonian Institute for providing me with a copy of some very rare footage of Loie Fuller in a film by Georges Méliès. I am also endebted to the superb Getty Research Institute, particularly its department of Special Collections, as well as to my assistant while at the Getty, Rebecca Karni of UCLA.

Over the years, this project has received funding from the American Association of University Women, the National Endowment for the Humanities, and the Gilbert Chinard Foundation, all of which has been greatly appreciated. I would also like to acknowledge the administration of Connecticut College for its support for summer research, as well as for its generosity toward me in all professional matters. At Princeton University Press, Mary Murrell was instrumental in shaping the project at its inception, Hanne Winarsky has helped see it through to its conclusion, and Jodi Beder provided knowledgeable and careful copyediting.

April Alliston and Julie Stone Peters have both offered helpful suggestions of many kinds. And for his keen critical eye and astute readings of every chapter, I am very grateful to Richard Halpern.

George Jagatic, Candida Scott Piel, and Jody Sperling graciously shared their thoughts and talents with me. Melanie Hawthorne and Stacy Wolf each offered thoughtful comments on the manuscript. I am grateful also to Christopher Braider, Mary Ann Caws, Georgiana Colvile, Julia Frey, Joseph Roach, and Richard Stamelman for their support at different key moments over the years.

For continually redirecting my thinking in surprising ways, and for his vibrance and what can only be described as gentle exuberance, I am most grateful to my husband, Jorge Daniel Veneciano.

Unless otherwise indicated, all translations from both archival and published sources are my own.

Parts of chapter 2 appeared as "Electric Salome: Loie Fuller at the Exposition Universelle of 1900," pp. 85–103 in *Imperialism and Theatre: Essays on World Theatre, Drama and Performance*, edited by J. Ellen Gainor, Routledge, 1995.

Electric Salome

Introduction

⤗

IN 1892, LOIE FULLER (NÉE MARY-LOUISE FULLER, in Illinois) packed her theater costumes into a trunk and, with her elderly mother in tow, left the United States and a mid-level vaudeville career to try her luck in Paris. Within days of her arrival, she had secured an interview with Edouard Marchand, director of the Folies-Bergère. Alighting from her carriage in front of the theater, she stopped short at the sight of the large placard depicting the Folies' current dance attraction: a young woman waving enormous veils over her head, billed as the "serpentine dancer." "Here was the cataclysm, my utter annihilation," Fuller would later write, for she had come to the Folies that day precisely to audition her own, new "serpentine dance," an art form she had invented in the United States (fig. I.1).[1] The woman already performing this dance at the Folies turned out to be one Maybelle Stewart of New York City, an acquaintance of Fuller's who had seen her perform in New York City and, apparently, had liked what she had seen a little too much.[2]

Told that Marchand could speak with her only after Stewart's matinee, a horrified Fuller settled in to watch her imitator. Although initially "trembling" and covered with "cold perspiration," she soon overcame her anxiety, determining that Stewart was no match for her. "The longer she danced the calmer I became. I could gladly have kissed her for her . . . inefficiency."[3] After the performance, Fuller put on her robes, took the stage in the now empty theater, and, with only one violinist left to accompany her, auditioned her own serpentine dance. By the end of the day, Marchand had granted Fuller a solo show of her own choreography and agreed to dismiss the imitator Stewart. However, since publicity for Stewart had already been circulated, and Marchand feared public protest, Fuller agreed to perform for the first two nights (October 28 and 29) under the name Maybelle Stewart, dancing her own imitation of Stewart's imitation of the serpentine dance. With this triple-layer simulation, worthy of an essay by Baudrillard, Loie Fuller launched her career as a modernist dance and performance artist. Although no one in Paris could have known it at the time, it was an ironically perfect beginning for

[1] Loie Fuller, *Fifteen Years of a Dancer's Life* (Boston: Small, Maynard & Co. Publishers, 1913), 53.

[2] Sally Sommer, "Loie Fuller," *Drama Review* 19, no. 1 (1975): 61.

[3] Fuller, *Fifteen Years*, 54.

Figure I.1. Loie Fuller in early "Serpentine" costume, Bibliothèque Nationale de France

someone destined to construct her career around self-replication, mirrored
images, and identity play.

On November 5, 1892, Loie Fuller, short, plump, and thirty years old, finally
premiered under her own name at the Folies, a venue known at the time for
its strippers, gymnasts, trapeze artists, and other circus-style, often bawdy acts.[4]

[4] During her time there, Fuller would cross paths with such well-known Folies performers
as Yvette Guilbert and the exotic dancer known as "La Belle Otéro." (See Richard Current
and Marcia Ewing Current, *Loie Fuller: Goddess of Light* [Boston: Northeastern University Press,
1997], 74.)

Swathed in a vast costume of billowing white Chinese silk that left only her face and hands visible, Fuller began her performance. Using rods sewn inside her sleeves, she shaped the fabric into gigantic, swirling sculptures that floated over her head. As she turned onstage, her arms lifted and molded the silk into undulating patterns. At the same time, rotating, colored spotlights dyed the silken images a variety of deep jewel tones. The audience saw not a woman, but a giant violet, a butterfly, a slithering snake, and a white ocean wave.[5] Each shape rose weightlessly into the air, spun gently in its pool of changing, rainbow lights, hovered, and then wilted away to be replaced by a new form. After forty-five minutes, the last shape melted to the floorboards, Fuller sank to her knees, head bowed, and the stage went black. The audience was silent for a few seconds. When the lights went back on, Fuller reappeared to the thunderous applause that signaled the beginning of her triumphant new career.

By the next morning, all of Paris was talking about this "priestess of pure fire" and the *danses lumineuses* that had "transformed the Folies-Bergère," in Marchand's words, creating a "success without precedence in this theatre."[6] Fuller would perform at the Folies for an unheard-of three hundred consecutive nights, well launched on what was to become an unbroken thirty-year reign as one of Europe's most wildly celebrated dancers.

But Fuller was an unlikely candidate for such stardom. She had had no formal training, and exhibited, frankly, little natural grace. There was nothing of the showgirl about her. "You should see her, she walks like a bird, but that bird is a duck," wrote one reviewer.[7] To say she was unglamorous is an understatement. Her round face, wide blue eyes, and short, stout body gave her a cherubic rather than sultry look. And at thirty, Fuller was nearly of retirement age for a music-hall dancer of that time. Offstage, she dressed haphazardly in oversized clothes, kept her hair in a tight bun, and wore little round spectacles. "She had a shapeless figure. She was an odd, badly dressed girl," recalled Eve Curie (daughter of Marie and Pierre).[8] "For heaven's sake, fix yourself up; you're

---

[5] Fuller's program for this first Folies-Bergère performance listed her dances as *Violet, Butterfly, The Serpentine,* and *La Danse blanche.*

[6] Marchand went on to describe Fuller's audience at the Folies: "Every night, the regular boulevard public is submerged in a crowd of scholars, painters, sculptors, writers, ambassadors. . . . All these people, forgetting their social rank and dignity, climb on tabletops like a group of kids" (qtd. in Giovanni Lista, *Danseuse de la Belle Epoque* (Paris: Editions Somogy, 1995): 133. See also Margaret Haile Harris, "Loie Fuller: The Myth, the Woman and the Artist," *Arts in Virginia* 20, no.1 (1979): 18.

[7] Qtd. in Loie Fuller, "The Walk of a Dancer," unpublished manuscript, Loie Fuller papers, New York Public Library for the Performing Arts (henceforth noted as NYPLPA).

[8] Qtd. in Frederic Grunfeld, *Rodin: A Biography* (New York: Henry Holt, 1987), 444.

a sight!"[9] chastised one journalist who interviewed her. But such remarks never bothered Fuller, who seemed to take curious pride in her own ungainliness. She even begins her autobiography with a description of herself as a badly dressed infant, a "poor little waif" partially clad in a meager "yellow flannel garment." She goes on to write, "I have likewise continued not to bother much about my personal appearance."[10] Despite her many decades in France, Fuller's French (as attested to by her voluminous correspondence in the language) remained garbled and fractured all her life. To complete the picture, she never went anywhere without her ailing mother, whose dour countenance and austere dress conjured the pair's hardscrabble past in the American Midwest so distant in every way from the music halls of fin-de-siècle Paris.[11]

In other words, Fuller's stardom owed nothing to the sexual glamour that, to this day, usually comprises the appeal of female performing artists. Fuller even managed to be openly lesbian while evoking virtually no titillation or disapproval in her public. Contemporary journalists tended to describe her personal life as "chaste," and "correct," writing often of her relationship with her mother and rarely even mentioning her live-in female companion of over twenty years, Gabrielle Bloch, a Jewish-French banking heiress who dressed only in men's suits.

Nevertheless, when she stepped onstage, this overweight, ungraceful American woman vanished, replaced by her sequences of ephemeral sculptures. Routinely hidden by hundreds of yards of silk, Fuller manipulated her voluminous robes into swirling shapes above her head, transforming herself by turns into lilies, butterflies, raging fires, even the surface of the moon. Audiences were left breathless. What so captivated them was the unique amalgam of Fuller's human agency, the creativity and force she exhibited as she wielded the enormous costumes; the power of her technology, the innovative stagecraft that she had designed and patented herself; and the oneiric, ephemeral landscapes evoked by this combination of body and machine, the disembod-

---

[9] Qtd. in Loie Fuller, "Dead Ashes," unpublished manuscript, Fuller collection, NYPLPA.

[10] Fuller, *Fifteen Years*, 18–19.

[11] "And then there's her mother," wrote an acerbic Jean Lorrain in a review, "yes, in a little ermine jacket . . . rigid, erect, upright, who comes every night and sits right in front of the stage with an entire coterie of clergymen . . . you would think it was the Salvation Army. And there she is, pale, grey-lipped, . . . nearly ghostly, following Loie's dances with her two big vacant eyes. . . . And, at the end, Loie, who dances only for her, leans over in her long white robes and from her high pedestal blows kisses to her mother. Isn't that touching? Yes, a regular chapter out of Dickens." Jean Lorrain, *Poussières de Paris* (Paris: Société d'Editions Littéraires et Artistiques, 1902), 195.

ied, rising and falling silken shapes. "She acquires the virginity of un-dreamt-of places," wrote Mallarmé in his famous essay on Fuller.[12]

Fuller had invented an art form balanced delicately between the organic and the inorganic, playing out onstage a very literal drama of theatrical transformation. Unlike actors playing theatrical roles or costumed dancers portraying swans, fairies, or gypsies, Fuller hardly ever "played" or "portrayed." Rather, in the vast majority of her performances she *became* the forms she described in silk, subsuming her physical self within them. Her work, therefore, drew upon and exaggerated a very deep aspect of performance: the magical, undecidable doubleness implied in any theatrical mimesis, what Diderot called the actor's paradox: "One is oneself by nature; one is another by imitation; the heart you imagine for yourself is not the heart you have."[13]

Contemporary reviews bear out the fact that Fuller's power derived from her thrilling enactments of metamorphosis. Her capacity to merge with the realm of the nonhuman or the supernatural attracted the most critical attention. While most music-hall stars of the era garnered praise for their singing or dancing, their charm, or their beauty, Fuller earned accolades for her nearly supernatural transcendence of self. She was "Herculaneum buried beneath the ashes . . . the Styx and the shores of Hades . . . a terrifying apparition, some huge pale bird of the polar seas," rhapsodized Jean Lorrain.[14] Another reviewer imagined her as "something elemental and immense, like the tide or the heavens, whose palpitations imitated the most primitive movements of life . . . the vibrations of the first cell."[15]

Virtually nothing about Fuller's dowdy offstage persona or her physical self ever crept into her performances, but when occasionally something did, reviews could be unforgiving. Her 1895 dance-pantomime version of *Salome*, for example, met with critical failure—largely because it failed to keep an overweight and visibly sweating Fuller under wraps or at a suitable distance from the audience. In other words, although she would become famous as a "*Salome moderne*" for her veil-like costumes, Fuller failed to impress audiences as an in-character Salome, having "lost that aura of unreality, ineffability, and

[12] Stéphane Mallarmé, "Les Fonds dans le ballet," *Oeuvres complètes* (Paris: Editions Gallimard, 1979), 308.

[13] Denis Diderot, *Selected Writings on Art and Literature*, trans. Geoffrey Bremer (London: Penguin, 1994), 141. (Original entitled "Le Paradoxe du comédien," written in 1773, first published in 1830).

[14] Qtd. in Philippe Jullian, *The Triumph of Art Nouveau*, trans. Stephen Hardman (New York: Larousse, 1974), 89–90.

[15] Francis Miomandre, *Danse* (Paris: Flammarion, 1935), 15.

mystery" on which her appeal depended.[16] Biographer Giovanni Lista refers
to the problem as the "collapse of magic into the banal."[17] But so long as Fuller
kept her somewhat graceless self out of sight, and centered her performance
on her technological genius, she dazzled her crowds, succeeding as more of an
Electric Salome than a biblical one.

Since her offstage self did not jibe with her onstage appeal, Fuller never
achieved the convergence of life and art that would come to mark the age of
media stardom. This is not to say, however, that her personality did not play
a crucial role in her career. On the contrary, Fuller's offstage persona, with its
odd admixture of magical child and unthreatening matron, only helped endear
her to the public. She was perceived as a kind of whimsical, female version of
Thomas Edison, a mad lady scientist, known as "la fée éléctricité." She lent her
face and name to soap and perfume advertisements. Her costumes were copied
and sold as streetwear at the Bon Marché and Louvre department stores.
Women bought "Loie" skirts and scarves; men sported "Loie ties." Bar patrons
sipped "Loie cocktails." Fuller, a savvy businesswoman, even sold likenesses of
herself in theater lobbies, in the form of lamps, figurines, and other household
objects. Later in her career, she tried her hand at the newest and most powerful
form of mass culture—cinema—and made several films, working with luminaries such as Pathé, the Lumière brothers, and Georges Méliès.

Fuller managed then, to reify herself offstage, commodifying her image by
marketing and multiplying her persona, just as onstage she transformed her
physical body into countless, reproducible shapes. In this way, she qualifies as
a direct forerunner of today's modern media celebrities. She cannily created
both an art form and a commercial business that exploited her era's fascination
with the alchemy inherent in the union of human and machine. Indeed,
Henry Adams might have been thinking of Fuller's effect on audiences when
he explored, in The Virgin and the Dynamo, the nearly religious ecstasy that
technology inspired during the late nineteenth century. Fuller was neither
entirely human, not entirely machine, but an onstage enactment of the fin de
siècle's—and modernism's—newly blurred boundaries between these realms.[18]

The fin de siècle dismantled also much of the boundary between high and
low or popular culture; and Fuller's career typified this new fluidity as well.
She was what we would call today a "crossover artist," poised between the

[16] Current and Current, Loie Fuller, 80.

[17] Lista, Danseuse, 192.

[18] "Modern technology collapsed the vault of heaven. Never before . . . did the heavens seem
to be so close or so accessible, a place . . . for human bodies in manmade machines." Stephen
Kern, The Culture of Time and Space 1880–1918 (Cambridge, MA: Harvard University Press,
1983), 317. See also Mark Seltzer, Bodies and Machines (New York: Routledge, 1992).

music hall and the concert or recital stage and devoting her life to bringing increased respect and status to dance as an art in itself.[19] She succeeded, to a large extent, in bridging both social and artistic chasms. The working-class cabaret audiences loved her; but she was equally beloved of the aristocracy. Europe's wealthy and powerful flocked to see her at the Folies, as well as on the stages of the Odéon, the Olympia, and the Athénée. These luminaries made for unfamiliar customers in such populist venues. A journalist for *L'Echo de Paris* wrote: "There is nothing so curious as the . . . change . . . in the clientele of the Folies Bergère. One now sees black dress coats . . . carriages decorated with coats of arms; the aristocracy is lining up to applaud Loie Fuller."[20] And the upper class's interest in Fuller extended beyond the theaters. The Vanderbilts, the Rothschilds, and even Queen Marie of Romania sought her out as a friend and frequent houseguest, inviting Fuller to use their villas and manicured gardens as stages for her works.

Along with the aristocracy, European high culture embraced "la Loie" and used her often as an object of aesthetic contemplation. Mallarmé and Yeats wrote of her; René Lalique, Emile Gallé, and Louis Comfort Tiffany fashioned her image in glass and crystal objects; Pierre Roche sculpted her in marble. Massenet and Debussy composed music for her; Whistler painted her; and her close friend Auguste Rodin made bronze casts of her hands. Fuller even fascinated the world of academic science, gaining the admiration and friendship of Marie and Pierre Curie, as well as of astronomer Camille Flammarion, all of whose laboratories she regularly visited. Flammarion even arranged for Fuller to become a member of the French Astronomical Society for her investigations into the physical properties of light.[21] In 1924, the Louvre itself honored Fuller, with a 24-piece exhibition of her work, focusing on her experiments with light and fabric.[22]

Given this degree of celebrity and wide sweep of artistic influence, one might have expected Loie Fuller to remain in the cultural imagination long after her

---

[19] Lynn Garafola, *Diaghilev's Ballets Russes* (New York: Da Capo Press, 1989), 16, 44. Also, Sally Banes, *Writing Dancing in the Age of Postmodernism* (Hanover, NH: University Press of New England, 1994), 90.

[20] Unsigned review, *L'Echo de Paris*, 26 Nov. 1892.

[21] Bud Coleman, "The Electric Fairy: The Woman behind the Apparition of Loie Fuller," in *Staging Desire: Queer Readings of American Theater History*, ed. Kim Marra and Robert A. Schanke (Ann Arbor: University of Michigan Press, 2002), 314.

[22] The exhibition was called "Retrospective on Studies in Form, Line and Color for Light Effects, 1892–1924," and featured costumes worn by Fuller, some of which were on loan from the private collections of Rudolph Valentino and the Baron de Rothschild (Current and Current, *Loie Fuller*, 302).

death in 1928. But this did not happen. Although Fuller would choreograph
128 dances between 1892 and 1925 and die a wildly famous woman, she quickly
faded from popular consciousness. Today, it is largely only scholars who are
familiar with her work. The general, educated public has lost sight of her.

The factors depriving Fuller of lasting fame are the very factors that made
her such a household name during her lifetime: her whimsical but unglamorous persona, her technical genius, and the uncategorizable nature of her art
itself. By not fitting into established and narrow parameters for female performers, by branching out into such overwhelmingly male fields as stage design, mechanical invention, and filmmaking, and by straddling both music-
hall and "high" culture concert dance, Fuller left no ready "hook" on which
to hang memories of her. While too different not to be noticed in life, Fuller
may have also been too different to be noticed after she was gone.

And then there is the work itself. What made the crowds gasp when Fuller
was onstage was never Fuller as a recognizable individual. They gasped, rather,
at the conversion of her physical self into pure aesthetic form. In essence,
Fuller made a career of staging her own immateriality, dissolving into light
projections on fabric. While this lent a definite proto-cinematic quality to her
stage work, and while she did make several films, even Fuller's proximity to
cinema did little to keep her fame alive. Like her stage work, Fuller's films
never emphasized her individual identity. They consisted mostly of Fuller —
and later, sometimes troupes of young dancers she gathered—performing in
much the same way she did on stage, with dissolving shapes and shifting shadows rendered even more effective through the magic of the camera. In the
end, perhaps, it should not surprise us that an artist who took such pleasure
in playing at disappearance should vanish so effectively after her death.

Fuller does, however, retain a reputation among scholars, some of whom
have done important work in reconstructing her career. Among these, Sally
Sommer and Giovanni Lista stand out for their thorough and painstaking
archival work. Lista in particular has produced an impressive scholarly volume
that reconstructs Fuller's entire career and lays out compelling arguments for
her influence on and proximity to movements and aesthetic forms as wide-
ranging as Art Nouveau, Futurism, Surrealism, Japanese line drawing, and
even American transcendentalism. Margaret Haile Harris and Hélène Pinet-
Cheula have each put together beautiful exhibitions and catalogues of Fuller's
work; and Richard and Marcia Current have written a highly readable, gen-
eral-interest biography of Fuller.

In addition to the few individual studies on her, virtually all histories of
modern dance devote a preliminary page or two to Fuller, usually describing

her as a forerunner of more famous dancers.[23] Theater scholars mention her
as an inventor who prefigured much of the modernist stage theory and practice
to come, including the work of E. Gordon Craig, Adolphe Appia, Ernst Stern,
Filippo Marinetti, and Enrico Prampolini.[24] In other words, critics tend to
relegate Fuller to "pioneer status"; that is, they regard her as the earliest manifestation of a vast array of modernist developments including performing recital dance with no balletic technique, discarding constricting costumes and
elaborate stage sets, using classical music for cabaret dance, downplaying narrative, working with light and shadow onstage in proto-cinematic fashion,
and incorporating electricity and technology into her onstage work. Such observations are, of course, accurate. Fuller was indeed a progenitor of modern
dance and an interdisciplinary artist stretching well beyond the confines of
dance and into the realms of visual art, mechanical reproduction, stage design,
and film. I shall address many of these contributions later.

But enumerating Fuller's innovations is insufficient. Nor is it enough merely
to point to similarities between her work and that of subsequent artists. Such
cataloguing of comparisons reduces the history of performance to a simplistic
and linear narrative of "modernism" in which stage sets become steadily more
mechanized or geometric and performers move in increasingly "free" or "abstract" fashion. Furthermore, within such a paradigm, Fuller ranks consistently
as "precursor" and little more, receiving attention only for having anticipated
the modernist flourishes of later, more famous artists. Of her contributions to
stage lighting, for example, the *Larousse Encyclopédie du théâtre* declares Fuller
"no more than a point of departure."[25] Such contextualizing criticism fails to
attend closely enough to what Fuller was actually *doing* with these modernist
trappings, or how she used them to confront, on many subtle levels, such key
issues as the dialogue between dance and dramatic theater, the changing role
of psychological character in modernism, politics and ethnic identity, and
sexuality. By the same token, little has been written about Fuller's relationship

---

[23] See, for example, Marcia Siegel, *The Shapes of Change: Images of American Modern Dance*
(Boston: Houghton Mifflin, 1979); see also Garafola, *Diaghilev's Ballets Russes*; Banes, *Writing
Dancing*; and Julia Foulkes, *Modern Bodies: Dance and American Modernism from Martha Graham
to Alvin Ailey* (Chapel Hill: University of North Carolina Press, 2002).

[24] See Giovanni Lista, "Prampolini scenografia," in *Prampolini: Dal futurismo all'informale*
(Rome: Edizioni Carte Segrete, 1992), 108–44; Denis Bablet, *Esthétique générale du décor du théâtre
de 1870 à 1914* (Paris: Editions du Centre de la Recherche Scientifique, 1965); and Jacques Baril,
La Danse moderne (Paris: Editions Vigot, 1977).

[25] Paul Léon, "Art du théâtre," in *Encyclopédie du théâtre*, section 10, *Photographie et Cinématographie* (Paris: Editions Larousse, 1955), 26.

to what came before her, namely *earlier* dance history, specifically ballet, of which her work is seen—incorrectly—as a total rejection.

More interesting work on Fuller has been done of late by those who explore her status as a "queer" artist, finding lesbian subtexts in her ostensibly chaste and bodiless performances. "Fuller . . . staged a presence that was specifically lesbian. . . . Audiences were never sure, in all the lights and swirls of fabric, exactly what her body was doing, where it was, or even exactly how many bodies were on stage," writes Tirza True Latimer.[26] "Fuller resembles a witch or a sorcerer far more than a seductress," observes Sally Banes; "perhaps partly because she was an openly identified lesbian, she shunned the provocative female representation of enticement so closely identified with 'the dancing girl.' "[27] And Julie Townsend writes: "[Fuller's] experience and representation of her body as transformative could instead be read as a strategy with lesbian implications. By constructing herself as Other (insect, serpent, butterfly, etc.), Fuller removed herself from the realm of gender altogether."[28] Such readings of Fuller's work are overdue, since until recently scholars have been curiously accepting of Fuller's apparent sexlessness. Her occulting of her physical body and her eschewal of overt eroticism have led critics to disregard wrongly the powerful bodiliness that nonetheless existed in Fuller's performances. For this reason, Fuller's work cries out to be "queered." Scholars such as Townsend and Latimer clearly perform important interpretive work, for they are putting the sexual body back into an art form seemingly hell-bent on its disappearance. Yet it is limiting to look only for lesbian or gay subtexts when studying a performer like Fuller whose appeal was so widespread and long lasting. Fuller's queerness comprises but one part of the unspoken physicality of her work. Furthermore, some of these approaches to Fuller seem oddly to dismantle their own goal, rediscovering Fuller's sexuality only then to subtract the body yet again, equating queerness—at least in the case of *lesbian* queerness—with the suppression of the body. To say that Fuller performed lesbian sexuality by virtue of removing her fleshly self from the stage is to err on two counts. First, it suggests that Fuller's body actually had no part in the construction of her performances or in the powerful appeal they held. Second, it makes of lesbian sexuality an absence, a refusal of eros rather than an alternative expression of it.

---

[26] Tirza True Latimer, "Loie Fuller: Butch Femme Fatale," in *Proceedings of the Society of Dance History Scholars, 22nd Annual Conference* (Albuquerque: University of New Mexico Press, 1999), 86.

[27] Banes, *Writing Dancing*, 74.

[28] Julie Townsend, "Alchemic Visions and Technological Advances: Sexual Morphology in Loie Fuller's Dance," in *Dancing Desires: Choreographing Sexualities on and off the Stage*, ed. Jane C. Desmond (Madison: University of Wisconsin Press, 2001), 76.

Perhaps the most interesting work on Fuller has been that of Felicia McCarren, whose 1998 book, *Dance Pathologies*, locates Fuller in the interstices of nineteenth-century poetics and medical and psychoanalytic practices. McCarren looks at Mallarmé's use of Fuller as performer of his modernist notion of the disembodied "idea"; she then uses Fuller to place Mallarmé within the context of the psychoanalytic theatricalization of the "pathological" (hysterical) female body. McCarren accomplishes this by uncovering the resonances between Mallarmé's discussion of Fuller's multiplicity (of onstage shapes and offstage personae) and the discourse of hypnosis, in which multiple, "alternative" and unconscious selves were placed in medical mises-en-scène:

> Fuller's subjectivity hinges on her movement between an onstage and an offstage persona, and her dance allows that doubleness to multiply. She produces . . . a series of constantly changing images . . . not because she pretends to be them . . . but because her stage image makes it possible for the viewer to imagine them. In Mallarmé's writing, Fuller becomes an "inconsciente révélatrice" of his mystical literary system, of the visual but invisible "idée" and of the subjectivity that system presupposes: "unconscious" because onstage she becomes a Sign, unaware of her literary potential and unable to manipulate language herself "knowing no eloquence other" than her steps.[29]

For McCarren, Fuller's art form partakes of the nineteenth century's discovery of "visual knowledge of the body" (the term is Foucault's), and she sees in Fuller's onstage floating funnel-like shapes "uncanny resemblance to . . . illustrations of a uterus."[30] For McCarren: "Fuller's work de-anatomizes femininity, redefining it as movement rather than structure." In Fuller's movement away from structure and toward motion, McCarren finds an analogue to Charcot's theories on hysteria, which similarly moved away from an anatomical view of hysteria's etiology (the wandering uterus theory) to a dynamic, decorporealized explanation.[31]

[29] Felicia McCarren, *Dance Pathologies* (Stanford, CA: Stanford University Press, 1998), 155.
[30] Ibid., 166.
[31] "[Fuller's] dance parallels Charcot's shift from the traditional 'uterine' theory of hysteria to a neurophysiological one, in which physiological processes are not governed by hidden anatomical structures and hysteria is not corporealized in the womb (ibid., 166). Curiously, Frank Kermode, in his very lyrical (and not particularly psychoanalytic) essay on Fuller, "Loie Fuller: Poet and Dancer before Diaghilev," draws a parallel similar to McCarren's. After noting that the Parisian music hall was "as important in the early history of modern art as folk music and primitive painting," he goes on to recall that Jane Avril, the famous cabaret singer, was once a patient of Charcot's at the Salpêtrière, noting that this famous hospital "was used as a kind of alternative to

McCarren also reminds us that Fuller's use of electricity further allied her with the practices of early, pre-Freudian psychoanalysis while also gesturing toward Freud's later practices:

> Fuller's work responds to the medical and cultural linking of dance and hysteria by using the clinician's tools: hypnosis and electricity. Although her work thus asks to be read in the context of Charcot's cures, and she uses, significantly, those techniques that Freud would discontinue in psychoanalysis, she uses them to such radically different ends that her goals seem more closely to resemble those that Freud will adopt. . . . Fuller can make into art what is, in the psychiatric hospital, only symptom; she can express what the hysterical patient represses. . . . Loie Fuller's dancing can be understood . . . as a successful or healthy theatricalization of what Freud calls early on "double conscience" or "hysterical dissociation" (the splitting of consciousness).[32]

Reading Fuller's work in light of psychoanalytic inquiry makes sense. Her performances problematized the desiring female body, recreating it aesthetically and questioning the objectifying gaze of the spectator. And, as McCarren also mentions, Fuller was aware of her own proximity to hypnosis, and remarked often on the hypnotic effect of her dancing. But McCarren's book ends its chapter on Loie Fuller with the announcement (quoted above) of Fuller's proximity to Freud—a provocative yet insufficient observation. Furthermore, McCarren suggests that Fuller somehow resolves, through dance, the splitting of the hysteric subject, that Fuller's dance physically enacts the Freudian ideal of a fully narrativized conflict. For McCarren, Fuller performs a "working through," a "healthy theatricalization," as she calls it.

Leaving off here ties up Fuller's—and Freud's—loose ends a little too neatly. Fuller may successfully perform, as McCarren suggests, a "healthy" version of the nineteenth-century hysteric ("what the hysterical patient tries and fails to say"), but that is not the end of the story. McCarren's work partakes of a curious phenomenon that pervades studies on Fuller: the propensity to see her as an "antidote" of one kind or another. From the beginning of her career, Fuller managed to inspire critics of every stripe to view her as a correction of various—sometimes totally contradictory—ills. We can see this impulse in McCarren's version of Fuller as a "healthy hysteric" and in Townsend's or

---

music-hall." (Frank Kermode, "Loie Fuller Poet and Dancer before Diaghilev," *Salmagundi*, 33–34 (Spring–Summer, 1976): 28–29; an earlier, shorter version appears in *Theatre Arts*, September 1962, 6–22.) McCarren does not mention Kermode in her book.

[32] McCarren, *Dance Pathologies*, 168–69.

Latimer's "queered" Fuller. The former reading restores power to the victimized hysteric; the latter reading restores a kind of sexual truth, and undoes the injustice of historical closeting. In all cases, though, Fuller represents a desired restitution of some kind of sexual health or authenticity.

For some reviewers of her own time, Fuller offered an opposite yet equally antidotal model: for them, she provided chaste correction for the *louche* tastes of French cabaret audiences, a salutary *re*-closeting, that is, of an overly free sexuality. Journalist Paul Adam, for example, wrote of Fuller: "Nothing bestial remains. Here may die then the *gaudriole* and the *bon esprit gaulois*. How wonderful that these vulgar souls don't tire of [Fuller], and though drawn by the hope of erotic poses, they are satisfied with higher things. In this way debauchery marches toward its redemption."[33] "Miss Fuller has done wonders in improving the public taste, and proving that dancing is not an art that degrades," wrote another journalist in approval of Fuller's onstage modesty.[34]

On the other hand, not all contemporary critics applauded Fuller's bodily restraint. Some welcomed what they saw as her liberation of the body. For them, she was the antidote to the artificial constraints of ballet, a pure return to nature. Jules Clarétie declared of Fuller: "She no more learned to dance than she learned to breathe."[35] In 1922, one critic wrote, "No need to look here for the virtuosity of pointe work or leaps . . . this is a new rite of dance"[36] "To the devil with the turnouts, *entre-chats*, and *jetés*," wrote another enthusiastic reviewer.[37] And then there were the centrists, for whom Fuller was a kind of savior Goldilocks who rejected both the too-hot dances of the music hall and the too-cold ones of the ballet: "she delivers dance from both the cancan and the tutus," wrote Michel-Georges Michel, for example.[38]

For yet a different camp of critics, Fuller provided an even more dramatic "antidote." For these, she pried open a window of transcendence, representing escape from the greatest constraint of all: mortal, fallen human life. Her life-

[33] Paul Adam, review of Loie Fuller, *Le Courrier de la Presse*, 13 February 1893, 6, Musée Rodin archives.

[34] Mrs. M. Griffith, "Loie Fuller: The Inventor of the Serpentine Dance," *Strand Magazine*, Winter 1894, 540.

[35] Jules Clarétie, review of Loie Fuller, Fuller papers, NYPLPA.

[36] Marcel Rieu, "Miss Loie Fuller inaugure des ballets fantastiques," 10 June 1922, Fuller papers, NYPLPA.

[37] Louis Vauxcelles, "L'Art de Loie Fuller," 10 May 1914, Collection Rondel on Loie Fuller, Bibliothèque de l'Arsenal, Paris (hereafter, Collection Rondel).

[38] Qtd. in Lista, *Danseuse*, 294. See also Silvagni who writes, "There were only two kinds of dance before Loie Fuller: classical and Toulouse-Lautrec, one is stiff, the other degrading." (Silvagni, "L'Etonnante vie de la fée de la lumière," *Pour Tous*, 20 September 1953, Musée Rodin Archives).

long friend and admirer, critic Claude Roger-Marx, saw Fuller as a "glimpse of the ideal, removed from time and place."[39] Another contemporary critic believed: "she is not a human being."[40] Camille Mauclair exulted: "Loie Fuller tears us away from . . . everyday life and leads us to purifying dreamlands."[41] Watching Fuller dance, Paul Adam felt he had experienced "a return to Eden."[42]

If we divide critical responses to Fuller into two main camps, the interpretive-theoretical (exemplified by McCarren) and the scholarly-historical (exemplified by Banes or Lista, for example), we see that even the latter group demonstrates this tendency to view Fuller as "antidote," in this case, the bracing antidote of "newness," the turning over of a new theatrical leaf. These scholars, of course, seek neither a metaphoric return to psychical health nor an edenic purity in her dances. Instead, they see in Fuller's work a line of demarcation, or a clearly pivotal moment where ballet disappears and modern dance begins.

Susan Foster, for example, tells us that Fuller "introduced radical new movement vocabularies and . . . detonated the ballet stage."[43] Elizabeth Kendall views Fuller as a "doorway to revolution," one of the rare individuals who spark radical change.[44] Other critics go even further, making of Fuller the symbol of an entire century. Recalling Fuller's prominence at the World's Fair of 1900, the great Jean Cocteau wrote:

> I retain only one vibrant image from the *Exposition Universelle* . . . Mme Loie Fuller . . . a fat, ugly American woman with glasses atop a pedestal maneuvering great waves of supple silk . . . creating innumerable orchids of light and fabric unfurling, rising, disappearing, turning, floating. . . . Let us all hail this dancer who . . . created the phantom of an era.[45]

Even as recently as 1988, one enthusiastic French journalist opined that "By the end of the nineteenth century, Loie Fuller had already invented everything . . . cinematic art . . . electric art . . . abstract art, [and] 'all-over' art."[46]

---

[39] Claude Roger-Marx, "Loie Fuller," *Les Arts et la Vie*, May 1905, 3.

[40] Miomandre, *Danse*, 16.

[41] Camille Mauclair, *Idées vivantes* (Paris: Librairie de l'Art Ancient et Moderne, 1904), 104.

[42] Adam, *Le Courrier de la Presse*, 6.

[43] Susan Foster, *Choreography and Narrative* (Bloomington: Indiana University Press, 1998), 261.

[44] Elizabeth Kendall, "1900: A Doorway to Revolution," *Dance Magazine*, January 1999, 81.

[45] Jean Cocteau, *Souvenirs* (Paris: Editions Flammarion, 1935), 5.

[46] Untitled article on Loie Fuller, *Libération*, 22 September 1988 (Musée d'Orsay collection of documents on Loie Fuller).

What is it then that prompts so many of Fuller's critics to cast her in such light? How does she manage to occupy the apparently paradoxical position of "fat, ugly American woman" and founding mother of a century of modernism? For an answer, we should perhaps look to the specifics of Fuller's art form. Essentially what she did was swath her body in white silks and then shine images upon them. In other words, she became a projection screen. But the screen functioned as more than just a site for the images and lights beamed down by Fuller's electricians. It served also as hypnotic tabula rasa for her spectators, prompting the countless descriptions of her work as "sorcery" or "magic" and inducing that initial hushed silence at the end of her performances. In this sense, Fuller's dances seem to have offered audiences a metaphoric screen on which to project their own unconscious fantasies, hypnotizing with a power akin to that of rushing ocean waves or the dancing flames in a fireplace.

This hypnotic effect finds a counterpart in the claims about Fuller by critics and scholars. To see Loie Fuller as the "phantom of an era," "a dead yet perfect being," the inventor "of everything," or even as a "detonator" of ballet, is to fall a bit under her hypnotic spell. Fuller's genius lay in appearing radically "other" than her plump, dowdy self, in the dazzling obscuring of human effort behind the ephemeral shapes and colors. Perhaps, had she not been matronly but sleek and sylphlike instead, and therefore less "transformed" onstage, Fuller would have been less successful, for her magic depended upon beautiful forms emerging (seemingly) out of nowhere, with no logical provenance. Consequently, her critics sometimes see *Fuller herself* as arising from nowhere, floating down to earth to do away with past forms of theater or dance or to inaugurate a hundred different art forms. Critically hypnotized, they project radical newness onto Fuller, severing her from her context. The same is true for those who find "correction" or "antidote" in Fuller's work. They are projecting onto her blank screen their own critical desires, be they for uplifting chastity, freer bodily movement, staged psychoanalytic success, or coded lesbian performance. (Some critics and scholars fall prey to several of these tendencies at once.)

It would be comically wrong-headed here (but so easy) to claim that *Electric Salome* will wipe clean the slate of prior interpretations of Fuller, rousing the field at last from this critical trance. Obviously, such an approach would only reproduce the problem, using Fuller yet again to turn a page or mark some new definitive transition. Furthermore, I do not wish to imply that scholarly work on Fuller has been wrong. All of the critics mentioned above have made valuable contributions, grounded in careful study. But in attributing to Fuller so much radical newness or "correction," these writers tend to exempt her from critical dialogue with other artists and genres. By demonstrating both Fuller's radical otherness—however they define the term—and (somewhat paradoxically) Fuller's close proximity to so many movements, scholars have managed to overlook her deep *connectedness* to and relationship with dance and theater history, not as "detonator" or "pioneer," but as interlocutor.

Taking a step back to look at Fuller in a broader context, we might see that the history of all modernism is replete with the same kinds of narratives of rupture that subtend Fuller's career. We know and retell so many stories of shocked art critics (such as those first viewers of Manet's *Déjeuner sur l'herbe*), or scandalized theater patrons (at the opening of *Ubu Roi*, for example). We imagine cultural chasms between Petipa and Duncan or between Scribe and Pirandello. But, we also know of course that modernist art forms did not just spring autochthonously to life to exile all that had preceded them. Rather, they evolved out of earlier art forms, even while occasionally causing shock in spectators. Loie Fuller affords us a unique opportunity to see played out in microcosm several of the key transitions to modernist performance, because *she embodies them.* Careful attention to her work reveals, for example, that she performed the transition from ballet to modern dance, retaining and trans-forming elements of each and thereby revealing the profound connections between the two genres. In fact, Fuller's work allows us to witness the ongoing conversation between ballet and modern dance. Similarly, although she is rarely discussed in this context, Fuller acted out onstage much of the problem-atics of modern European drama: the struggle between breaking or main-taining the coherence of characters, the question of how or whether to portray psychological depth, the dilemma of the "fourth wall," the debate over ac-knowledging the audience, and the role of costume and the body onstage.

Accordingly, *Electric Salome* will place Fuller in deeper, more critical dia-logue with dance and drama, proceeding first from an examination of the element most often ignored in her work: what I shall call her secret "danci-ness." I refer here to Fuller's profound yet largely unexamined relationship to actual, bodily dancing, to onstage bodily reality and, by extension, to certain contemporaneous developments in modern theater, beyond those in stagecraft alone. I intend to demonstrate how Fuller helps us understand the way in which different genres of modernist performance "speak" to one another.

With these goals in mind, I shall devote myself largely to examining Fuller in a series of critical relationships. After an introductory first chapter ex-plaining the bases of Fuller's art, chapter 2 addresses her work within the context of a major movement of nineteenth- and early twentieth-century en-tertainment: Orientalist performance, with its crucial subtext of French impe-rialism. As a "modern Salome" who staged and starred in two different productions of the biblical story (in 1895 and again in 1907), Fuller partook heavily of her era's Orientalism. But critics have rarely examined the political ramifications of this aspect of her work, viewing Fuller's Orientalism as a kind of sanitized "borrowing." In part, this is because Fuller seems too high-tech, too asexual, too white, and too "unforeign" to be compared to such "exotic" and scantily clad dancers as the era's popular Algerian troupe, the Ouled-Nayl. But despite her modernist and ostensibly chaste trappings, Fuller does not eschew the mess of politics or history. On the contrary, as we shall see, Fuller responded to and reinterpreted certain key racial, national, and sexual complexities of her moment in popular culture. This chapter focuses particularly on Fuller's place at the heavily imperialist Paris World's Fair of 1900, where, I believe, her apparent political neutrality helped further the French government's colonialist aims.

Chapter 3 moves on to Fuller's relationship to Romantic ballet. This discussion involves reassessing what counted as body and muscle in Fuller's performance. I shall argue, in fact, that one must begin by reading her thin, pointed batons and the attached billowing veils as prosthetic inversions of the ballerina's legs on pointe and the Romantic tutu. Once we see the startling analogy between Fuller's onstage physical structure and that of the ballerina, we can see how, rather than "detonate" the ballet stage, Fuller embraced and reworked it.

From Romantic ballet, I shall move on to the other end of dance spectrum: high modern dance. Specifically, chapter 4 situates Fuller's work in the context of Martha Graham's revolution. Here once again, Fuller's odd position between high modernist art and "low" popular or mass culture has deterred critics from studying the real, artistic relationship that exists between her work and that of more "serious" artists. As I have noted, critics generally content themselves with citing Fuller as a precursor to modern dance (both Graham's and others'), but rarely examine her choreography very closely. This chapter juxtaposes one of Fuller's later works, *The Sea*, with Graham's landmark work, the mournful and haunting *Lamentation* (1930). *The Sea* is a group work performed by Fuller's troupe of young dancers, and is one of a series of pieces that involved the use of a vast collective silk veil that entirely concealed all of the dancers' bodies. Completely invisible beneath the material, Fuller's dancers used their bodies to mold the fabric from beneath into a series of mutating sculptural shapes, forcing the audience to view the enormous veil as an animate, dancing being. In Graham's *Lamentation*, the dancer remains encased from head to toe in an elasticized fabric tube, against which she struggles to extend her limbs and delineate three-dimensional forms. Placed side by side, these two works not only reveal the significant parallels between Fuller and

Graham, but also shed new light on the role of gravity, space, and even physics in modern dance.

This pairing of Fuller and Graham serves as a departure point for chapter 5, which treats Fuller's largely unexamined relationship to modern drama, particularly the work of such artists as Ibsen, Strindberg, and Pirandello. Just as Fuller's work deeply engaged the physical body she appeared to spurn, so was it especially invested in the notions of dramatic character that it ostensibly rejected. While Fuller often receives scholarly acknowledgment for her influence on modernist theorists and stage designers, no one has examined how she prefigures and performs certain key developments in modern drama, including the dismantling and reconfiguring of "character," the new use of stage space, and naturalism. Looking, for example, at the projected slides of human cancer cells that Fuller used to "decorate" her costumes, we can find a version of modern drama's quest to stage the interiority of the physical self, new ways to reveal bodily truth. And when Fuller installed a wall of transparent glass between herself and the audience, dancing behind it as if unaware of its presence, did she not succinctly sum up the whole debate about the theater's "fourth wall"?

Finally, in the Afterword, *Electric Salome* looks at Fuller's continuing influence and legacy in the contemporary arena. Here, I shall consider recent choreography by a young artist named Jody Sperling who uses Fuller's dances as a springboard for her own postmodern fantasies, as well as an underground party entertainment known as "flagging," which is uncannily reminiscent of Fuller's work.

Chapter One
The Evolution of Fuller's Performance Aesthetic

I assure you that there is nothing original in me.

FROM HER EARLIEST DAYS, Fuller founded her aesthetic upon denial, displacement, and disavowal. She habitually insisted, for example, upon the accidental nature of her discoveries, brushing aside her own agency, hard work, and vast experimentation. By the age of thirty, she had developed a disingenuously chaste offstage persona, bypassing any overt sexual presentation of her body or life, while onstage she appeared to deny her body altogether, dissolving its physical presence via myriad tricks of light and costume. And while her mature style owed a great deal to her early career in burlesque and cabaret, Fuller preferred to ignore those roots, glossing over the evolutionary process of her work with narratives of accident and epiphany to explain her aesthetic choices.

At the same time, though, amid all this disingenuousness, Fuller claimed great theatrical power for herself. She spoke repeatedly of having a nearly supernatural effect on audiences, describing her effect in otherworldly terms. This perception was not pure fantasy, either. For over thirty years, Fuller regularly received acclaim for just such mystical powers, and was compared to a "wizard," a "goddess," a "fairy," or a "hurricane." To reconcile these disparate facets of her self-presentation—her professed innocence and her hypnotic control over crowds—we must consider that they are actually two sides of the same phenomenon. We must consider that the sheer force of Fuller's denials and displacements wound up resurfacing in her work under the guise of mystical power. After all, those elements denied by Fuller—the body, sexuality, her own history—would require great effort to shunt aside. The powerful force of this denial, of this shunting aside, seems matched by the force felt by her

Loie Fuller to Gabrielle Bloch, February 1892, NYPLPA.

audiences. Ultimately, it is possible that Fuller's profound effect on spectators, their feeling of being enraptured and under her spell, resulted from their sensing that beneath her fairytale purity lay a potent, bodily, sexual, historical self constantly being beaten back by those whirling veils.

Sometimes, the force of this denial carried with it a kind of suppressed violence, an aggressiveness perceptible in certain pieces. Occasionally, we can sense this violence in the thematics of Fuller's performance, as in her productions of *Salome* with its plot of cruelty, fire, and bloody decapitation. Sometimes, we can find a *visual* violence in Fuller's work, in her use of surprisingly unlovely, harsh, or morbid images. At other times, we can perceive a striking albeit displaced violence in the way she directs and manipulates her spectator's gaze, transforming it into a transgressive instrument, a prurient weapon intruding into the closed and pristine space she erects onstage. As we shall see, Fuller's tacit violence was also imbued with a modernist sensibility, for it anticipated the starkness, scientificism, and jagged forms common to such movements as Futurism, Russian Constructivism, and Cubism.

In order to understand these powerful but less evident currents within Fuller's work, one first must understand the arc of her long career: where and how she performed early on, what elements from her past remained with her, and the mechanics of her later, developed style. Accordingly, this chapter has two sections. The first focuses on Fuller's early years in the United States, and the second on the signature style that she developed once in Paris, including her innovations in stagecraft and costuming. Throughout, I shall indicate how the various components of Fuller's performances fit within the conceptual framework of what we might call an aesthetics of disavowal.

That disavowal, finally, shall be my point of entry into a discussion of the political ramifications of Fuller's work, specifically her relationship to empire. Did the suppressed violence and sexuality of Fuller's work fit within a larger political drama? What did it mean that at the height of its imperial expansion, France adopted as a cultural icon this odd American woman with the disingenuous persona, this "modern Salome?" While these questions are addressed at length in chapter 2, here, in this chapter's second half, I shall introduce them via an examination of the technological, scientific, and even medical gaze staged by Fuller in her performances, a gaze that plays a role in the construction of empire.

Early Years: Awareness and Unconsciousness

Ma très peu consciente ou volontairement inspiratrice[1]

---

[1] Mallarmé on Loie Fuller, "Les fonds dans le ballet," 308.

Loie Fuller did not begin her career as an Electric Salome, or indeed as any kind of modernist innovator. She began, instead, in venues easily open to a young American girl with no formal training, from the Sunday school stage to burlesque shows. In her autobiography, Fuller claims that her theatrical debut occurred at the age of two and a half when she spontaneously mounted the stage of the Chicago Progressive Lyceum (where her "freethinker" parents attended Sunday services) and recited her bedtime prayers. The episode delineates with exceptional clarity the paradoxical themes that would underlie Fuller's entire career: insistence upon her own mystical, nearly superhuman power over an audience and an equal insistence upon her total innocence and lack of forethought in performing. This description of her earliest stage experience, therefore, sets the tone for a lifetime of similar anecdotes:

> "What! Said the president [of the Lyceum to Loie's mother], "haven't you heard that Loie recited some poetry last Sunday? and she was a great success too. . . . During an interval between the exercises, Loie climbed up on the platform . . . and . . . recited a little prayer. . . . After that Loie arose, and saluted the audience once more. Then immense difficulties arose. She did not dare to descend the steps in the usual way. So she sat down and let herself slide from one step to another until she reached the floor . . . the whole hall laughed loudly at the sight of her . . . petticoat and her copper-toed boots. . . ."
>
> The following Sunday I went as usual to the Lyceum with my brothers. My mother came too . . . [and then heard a woman say,] "And now we are going to have the pleasure of hearing our little friend Loie Fuller recite a poem entitled: 'Mary had a little Lamb.' " My mother, absolutely amazed, *was unable to stir or to say a word.* She merely gasped: ". . . She will never be able to recite that. She has only heard it once."
>
> In a *sort of daze* she saw me rise from my seat, slowly walk to the steps and climb upon the platform. Once there I turned around and took in my audience. I made a pretty courtesy, and began in a voice which resounded throughout the hall. I repeated the little poem in so serious a manner that, despite the mistakes I must have made, the spirit of it was intelligible and impressed the audience. I did not stop once. Then I courtesied again and everybody applauded wildly. I went back to the stairs and let myself slide down to the bottom, as I had done the preceding Sunday. Only this time no one made fun of me. When my mother rejoined me . . . she was still *pale and trembling.* She asked me why I had not informed her of what I was going to do. I replied *that I could not let*

her know about a thing that I did not know myself. "Where have you learned this?" "I don't know mamma."[2]

While many performers can recall such pivotal moments when first seduced by the thrill of applause, Fuller's account is striking for two reasons. First, it insists oddly on her mother's exaggerated and very physical shock; and second, it lays rather disingenuous claim to the child Loie's own "unconsciousness" in performance.

Fuller describes her mother as "unable to stir," "gasping" "dazed," "pale," and "trembling,"—all peculiarly *dire* responses to hearing a child recite "Mary Had a Little Lamb." But this reported incongruity of response is telling; it bespeaks Fuller's long-standing notion of herself as not just a performer, but a *hypnotizer*, a supernatural force. Here, for example, in another passage from her autobiography, she describes young spectators' reactions upon seeing her (the adult Fuller) dance. Fuller attributes to the children responses nearly identical to her mother's thirty years prior: "The unearthly appearance of my dances . . . enraptured . . . children, caught under the spell of my art. [One little girl was] fascinated and dazed. She did not say a word, did not make the slightest noise, hardly dared to stir. I seemed to have hypnotized her."[3] Children appear frequently in Fuller's descriptions of her own hypnotic power, used perhaps to reinforce her public persona as wholesome, family entertainer. At the same time, children occupy a powerful, liminal space between innocence and knowledge, the boundary upon which was poised Fuller's entire aesthetic.

However hubristic her self-descriptions, Fuller was indeed regarded as a supernatural theatrical power, capable of inspiring awe and disbelief. Decades of contemporary reviews attest to her mystical reputation. The Lyceum anecdote does demonstrate, however, how willingly Fuller embraced this view of herself, and how invested she was in naturalizing her theatrical power, "finding" it even in her two-year-old self. (It is not incidental that in the story, the toddler Loie manages to eclipse a Sunday religious service with her poem.)

The second striking aspect of this anecdote is Fuller's insistence that she was not only mesmerizing at the Lyceum, but also utterly spontaneous, performing without prior intention. "I could not let [my mother] know about a thing that I did not know myself." Yet we know this cannot be. This was not the first, but the *second* time the toddler Loie (or rather, "Mary-Louise," although, tellingly, Fuller uses her adult stage name in the anecdote) had mounted those stage stairs, the second time she had bounced endearingly back down again on her

---

[2] Fuller, *Fifteen Years*, 22–23. Emphasis added.
[3] Ibid., 137–38.

bottom. In fact, the whole episode smacks less of spontaneity than of premeditation, of a very precocious understanding of rehearsal and performance. As Richard Schechner has famously observed, "performance means: never for the first time. . . . Performance is 'twice-behaved' behavior."[4] Nonetheless, as an adult, Fuller imposes unconsciousness on the scene, even though that unconsciousness is disproved by the story itself. In other words, this childhood memory performs a kind of retroactive or staged innocence—a quality that will prove essential to both Fuller's art form and her own explanations of it.

Fuller never stopped performing after that toddler debut. Between the ages of four and thirty, she dabbled in myriad genres of popular performance: dramatic readings, western-themed burlesque, operetta, Orientalist cabaret, and risqué dance hall numbers. And while she would later eschew most traditional stage conventions, Fuller spent these early years dressed in countless "period" costumes, performing in the most hackneyed plots, and contending with the elaborate backdrops and props typical of vaudeville and cabaret. Moreover, a brief look at these early stage experiences reveals that Fuller never completely abandoned her roots. However "purified" her later aesthetic, traces of these costumed melodramas and burlesque acts reappear (albeit highly transformed) in much of Fuller's mature work.

Fuller performed her first dramatic role *en travesti* when, at four, she played the little boy Reginald in *Was He Right?* at Chicago's Academy of Music. At thirteen, she expanded her theatrical repertoire, becoming a Shakespearean "reader" as well as a temperance lecturer in her dry hometown of Fullersburg.[5] In the latter capacity, young Mary-Louise used what was known as the "horrible example" method, finding the town drunk and hauling him onstage to serve as a repellent reminder of alcoholism. Her other scare tactic involved showing the audience color illustrations of cirrhotic livers, taken from medical textbooks. (This interest in dramatizing biology would resurface in her later work, as we shall see.) In 1878, at sixteen, Mary-Louise changed her name to the more glamorous "Loie," moved to New York City with her mother and brother Burt, and began her vaudeville and burlesque career in earnest.

Through the late 1870s and 1880s, based in New York, Fuller traveled with a long list of theater companies, acting in light dramas and musicals. In addition to a number of cross-dressed, boys' roles, she frequently played soubrettes, and occasionally kicked up her exposed legs to do the racy "tights dance."[6]

---

[4] Richard Schechner, *Between Theatre and Anthropology* (Philadelphia: University of Pennsylvania Press, 1985), 36.

[5] The town, named for Fuller's pioneer ancestors, is known today as Hinsdale, Illinois.

[6] She had a part, for example, in *The Shaughraun* (1878), a comic melodrama by the popular Irish playwright Dion Boucicault. She traveled with Dave Henderson's Imperial Burlesque, which

In 1883, Fuller went on tour with the world-famous pageant known as William "Buffalo Bill" Cody's *Wild West Show*, playing "Miss Pepper, a deserted waif" in *The Prairie Waif*.[7] The play was one in the series of open-air melodramas that comprised the *Wild West Show*, all of which featured highly detailed tableaux of western life, shooting displays (Annie Oakley was a star attraction), and stories about American expansionism and the colonizing of Native American lands by white settlers. Joseph Roach has written of the "double nature" of the *Wild West Show* (particularly its parades), "falling somewhere between a folklore procession . . . and a military parade."[8] Insistent upon a kind of ethnological authenticity, Cody not only hired United States cavalry veterans to recreate battles such as Little Big Horn and Wounded Knee, he succeeded in hiring Sitting Bull and Geronimo to play themselves as well. Marketed as an educational exhibition, *The Wild West Show* was essentially a social-Darwinist project that portrayed Native Americans as ruthless savages obstructing civilization and progress. Theater programs doubled as political pamphlets and featured essays such as "The Rifle as an Aid to Civilization."

The *Wild West Show* also appealed to audiences beyond the United States. While Fuller only traveled within the United States with Cody, throughout the show's thirty-year history, it was seen by over fifty million people in North America and Europe. Cody's Manichean worldview and ethnologically justified imperialism were widely attractive, particularly in those countries with their own imperial stories. As John Blair has written, "Cody managed to make this show seem the epitome of the whole of Western colonization—not just the domination of North America but a world-scale suppression of native, nonwhite peoples."[9] Queen Victoria loved *The Wild West Show* so much that she summoned Cody for a command performance on the occasion of her golden jubilee in June of 1887.

Traveling with Buffalo Bill, then, Fuller was exposed to this highly mythologized and exportable version of Americana—a subgenre of popular theater whose bonhomie barely masked its militant nationalism and even genocidal

---

even produced one of her own early plays, *Larks*. Fuller also studied singing briefly and performed in a popular version of Gounod's *Faust* in Chicago. In 1886 she became a full-time contract actress with the Miles and Barton's Burlesque at New York's Bijou Theater, playing soubrettes and, once again, cross-dressing to play men's roles. See Sommer, "Loie Fuller"; Current and Current, *Loie Fuller*; Lista, *Danseuse*.

[7] Current and Current, *Loie Fuller*, 15.

[8] Joseph Roach, *Cities of the Dead* (New York: Columbia University Press, 1996), 203.

[9] John G. Blair, "First Steps toward Globalization: Nineteenth-Century Exports of American Entertainment Forms," in *Here, There and Everywhere: The Foreign Politics of American Popular Culture*, ed. Reinhold Wagnleitner and Elaine Tyler May (Hanover: University Press of New England, 2000), 23.

overtones. In her later career, Fuller's repertoire was devoid of any such overt political resonances, and her status as a white American woman seemed to grant her little more than the awkward charm of the outsider. Nonetheless, a subtle imperial politics would persist in Fuller's later work, despite its careful occulting of historical or social references. That she spent time within Buffalo Bill's showcase of violent exoticism confirms, at the very least, Fuller's exposure to and awareness of the myths surrounding America's own brand of domestic colonialism. I shall return to this in chapter 2.[10]

While *The Wild West Show* exoticized Native Americans, some of Fuller's other early engagements partook of alternative strains of Orientalism common to late nineteenth-century cabaret: those showcasing North African, Indian, or Middle Eastern themes. Years before her own *Salome* productions of 1895 and 1907 in France, Fuller appeared in a variety of Orientalist entertainments in the United States. In 1887, for example, she played "Ustane, the singing slave girl" (fig. 1.1) in a production of *She*, a novel by the popular Victorian adventure writer H. Rider Haggard[11] Steeped in elaborate descriptions of ancient legends and mystical rituals, *She* recounts an English explorer's travels to Africa and his encounters there with an Arab-speaking tribe and their mysterious white queen known as "she-who-must-be-obeyed."[12]

That same year (1887), Fuller continued her habit of cross-dressing onstage, assuming the title role in *Aladdin's Wonderful Lamp*, Alfred Thompson's pantomime adaptation of the Orientalist classic *Thousand and One Nights*, produced at New York's Standard Theater. *Aladdin's* set consisted of luminous caves and grottos that appeared and disappeared in dreamlike fashion thanks to a "magic lantern"—the popular nineteenth-century cabaret device that created changeable backdrops by projecting images of light onto gauze fabric. *Aladdin's* fourteen dance numbers included an Indian "nautch" dance in which

[10] See Lista, *Danseuse*; Sommer, "Loie Fuller." See also Richard Slotkin, "Buffalo Bill's 'Wild West' and the Mythologization of the American Empire," in *Cultures of United States Imperialism*, ed. Amy Kaplan (Raleigh, NC: Duke University Press, 1993), 164–81. Buffalo Bill's *Wild West Show* was seen by fifty million people in over twelve countries. A master showman, Bill Cody embarked on his first European tour with a cast including 97 American Indians, 180 horses, and 18 buffalo.

[11] Haggard had published *She* that same year, 1887, just one year after the appearance of his highly successful novel, *King Solomon's Mines* (1886), a similarly Orientalist adventure tale. (The stage production of *She* was likely a bastardization of Haggard's novel, given that Ustane is not a slave in the original text.) Fuller later said that it was not talent that won her the role of Ustane, but her willingness to roll down the prop pyramid stairs "harder and further" than any other actress would for ten dollars per show.

[12] See Ann McClintock's *Imperial Leather* for a discussion of the relationship between Haggard's life and the imperialism of his work. (Anne McClintock, *Imperial Leather: Race, Gender, and Sexuality in the Colonial Contest* [New York: Routledge, 1995]).

Figure 1.1. Fuller in costume as Ustane (not the heroine "She," as the caption indicates) in Haggard's *She*, Billy Rose Theatre Collection, New York Public Library for the Performing Arts, Astor, Lenox, and Tilden Foundations

women wore filmy, transparent costumes, a "Veil of Vapor Dance," performed (by Fuller) behind a translucent "curtain" of steam over which colored lights were projected, and a "Crypt of the Crimson Crystals" number in which a "switchboard of electric lights" created a twinkling, jewel-like background.[13] Although Fuller never admitted it publicly, it would become clear that both

[13] The Indian nautch dance was popular in American vaudeville from 1881 through the first decades of the twentieth century, as Indian women dancers came to the United States. The graceful hand gestures of these dances later entered the modern dance canon via Ruth St. Denis

the role of Aladdin and its attendant technical experience deeply influenced her later experiments in creating veil dances and ephemeral light-based back-drops with her own magical lamps.

In addition to performing in dramas informed by exoticism and empire, Fuller had occasion to see some of Europe's colonies for herself when, in 1889, she formed her own company and embarked on a Caribbean tour. Her company and its travels were financed by her new husband, a certain Colonel William Hayes, cousin to President Rutherford B. Hayes and a very wealthy man in his own right. Almost immediately upon marrying Hayes, Fuller saw fit to gather a troupe and take off for Bermuda, Haiti, Jamaica, and the Antilles, performing light plays and operettas. She did not see fit, however, to invite Hayes along. Fuller's company soon foundered badly as a disgruntled Hayes withdrew his support. Both the touring company and the marriage disbanded quickly (the marriage quite acrimoniously) and Fuller went back to work as a contract player.[14] Fuller would not form another company until 1908, when she founded Les Ballets Loie Fuller with a group of young girls.

After her brief marriage, Fuller (and her mother) spent several months of that same year, 1889, in London, where she worked at the Gaiety Theatre, home of the famed Gaiety Girls and their "skirt dance." For this engagement, Fuller replaced skirt dancer Letty Lind in the role of Mercedes in a play called *Carmen up to Date*. Like the French cancan, the skirt dance was a lighthearted, slightly racy confection that involved dancers throwing their lightweight, pleated skirts up over their heads to expose stockinged legs and frilly panta-loons.[15] Fuller did not dabble long in skirt dancing, but one can easily see the way in which her later work reinterpreted and aestheticized this genre, suppressing the fleshly body underneath and setting the skirt whirling end-lessly around an absented physical dancer. As Carl Van Vechten observed of

---

and Maud Allen (Sommer, "Loie Fuller," 55). For more on the nautch dance, see also Malek Alloula, *The Colonial Harem*, trans. Myrna Godzich and Wlad Godzich (Minneapolis: University of Minnesota Press, 1986; and Nancy Reynolds and Malcolm McCormick, *No Fixed Points: Dance in the Twentieth Century* (New Haven: Yale University Press, 2003), 4.

[14] When Hayes grew tired of bankrolling his absent wife, Fuller countered by suing him for bigamy, a charge that might have been accurate, although the details remain murky to this day. Hayes countersued, accusing Fuller of "immoral" behavior, basing his charges on some early nude publicity photos of her that he had somehow procured as well as on his own suspicions of her lesbianism. Both parties agreed to drop their charges once Fuller made a one-time payment to Hayes of $10,000.

[15] Sally Sommer, "Loie Fuller," in *International Encyclopedia of Dance*, vol. 3, ed. Selma Jeanne Cohen (New York: Oxford University Press), 91, and Lista, *Danseuse*, 72–74.

Fuller's *Fire Dance* in 1896, "She borrowed the skirt of the Skirt Dance [and] exaggerated it to insane proportions."[16]

The Skirt Dance is but one of the many early experiences with costuming, lighting, and stagecraft that formed a theatrical lexicon from which Fuller would later build her own signature stage language. Fuller, though, rarely acknowledged the influence of these early years, probably because she sought to distance herself from her populist origins. Typically, she chose instead to tell a story of artistic epiphany, of having discovered her life's work in a moment of thrilling serendipity onstage. This pivotal moment came, according to Fuller, in 1891 while she was appearing in *Quack, M.D.* (by Fred Marsden, produced by Charles Hoyt). Fuller played Mrs. Imogene Twitter, a young widow hypnotized by Dr. Franck Drake, the punningly named "quack" of the title. The part was so small that Fuller's name did not appear in the program, she had to provide her own costume, and she was left to devise her own brief dance number. For her dress, she decided to sew together a large thin white silk skirt and several yards of white gauze, creating a costume similar to many she had worn before. As for the choreography, Fuller claimed that, once onstage opening night in Holyoke, Massachusetts, she decided to dance as she imagined a hypnotized patient might:

> I endeavoured to make myself as light as possible. . . . [Dr. Drake] raised his arms. I raised mine. Under the influence of suggestion, entranced— so at least it looked—with my gaze held by his, I followed his every motion. My robe was so long that I was continually stepping on it, and, mechanically I held it aloft, all the while I continued to flit around the stage like a winged spirit. There was a sudden exclamation from the house: "It's a butterfly! A butterfly!" I turned . . . running from one end of the stage to the other, and a second exclamation followed: "It's an orchid!" To my great astonishment sustained applause burst forth. . . . At last, transfixed in a state of ecstasy, I let myself drop . . . completely enveloped in a cloud of light material.[17]

While reviewers panned the play, the nameless hypnotized dancer won raves. Fuller's "serpentine dance"—the basis for all her future groundbreaking work— had been born. *Quack, M.D.*—a play about hypnosis and unconscious behavior—offered Fuller the perfect setting for "discovering" her power over an audi-

---

[16] Carl Van Vechten, "Terpsichorean Souvenirs," *Dance Magazine*, January 1957, 16.

[17] Fuller, *Fifteen Years*, 31.

ence.[18] Her account, furthermore, turns the play into an obvious precursor of her later onstage play with mirrors and mirroring effects. First, within the fiction of the play, "Imogene" mirrors her hypnotist's motions; next, the spectators serve as mirror for Fuller, reflecting back to her verbally what they believe they are seeing in her moving costume; finally, in response to the audience's delight, Fuller herself falls under some kind of *deuxième degré* hypnosis: she holds her skirts "mechanically" and then, "transfixed in a state of ecstasy," falls to the floor. The playacted hypnotic state has become uncannily real.

This description recalls the account of her mother's reaction to watching her little Loie recite a poem at the Lyceum. Both episodes begin lightheartedly—a toddler's first performance and a comic vaudeville skit—and then shift into tales of hypnotized reactions to a performance, either on the part of a spectator (Mrs. Lily Fuller, Loie's mother) or the actor (Fuller herself). Moreover, just as in the Lyceum anecdote, Fuller here maintains that her success was accidental. She insists paradoxically upon both her own inspired originality and her total lack of forethought or interpretation: it is the audience that interprets her performance by shouting out the shapes it sees, and applauding "to [her] great astonishment." Like her character Mrs. Twitter, who, under hypnosis, dances in unconscious imitation of Dr. Quack, Fuller dances, she claims, under a kind of enchantment, unmindful of the effect created. Thus does Fuller explain the founding moment of her career. In her telling, the "serpentine dance," soon to make her world-famous, is born when a vaudeville character's situation—being hypnotized—mysteriously affects the actress playing her and leads, uncannily, to a life-changing burst of creativity. It matters little how much of this anecdote is true. I would argue that the foundational moment of Fuller's aesthetic resides not in the actual performance of *Quack, M.D.* but in this written account of it—a story of staged unconsciousness, mirroring, unwitting artistry, and an uncanny, Pirandellesque merging of a (hypnotized) fictional character and the actor portraying her. [19]

---

[18] For an interesting discussion of the peculiarly close relationship between cabaret theater and nineteenth-century approaches to psychological illness and treatment, see Rae Beth Gordon, "From Charcot to Charlot: Unconscious Imitation in French Cabaret," *Critical Inquiry* 27, no.3 (Spring 2001): 515–49.

[19] Debora Silverman believes that Fuller "transformed the images released by the hypnotic trance into direct, irregular movements, which she expressed automatically, without conscious meditation," in other words, that Fuller was as unconscious as she claimed and thereby all the more authentic as a demonstration of "ideodynamism"—an Art Nouveau concept. I think Fuller was deeply related to these concepts, but a far more knowing manipulator of them. In so perceiving Fuller as an unconscious expression of anything, Silverman becomes yet another critic to fall

Fuller left the cast of *Quack, M.D.* in anger, having been refused a raise. Nevertheless, her association with the play continued to affect her life, provoking issues of doubled identity and imitation similar to those staged in its plot, and presaging many larger themes of Fuller's future career. To replace Fuller, the management of the Casino Theater hired dancer Minnie Renwood Bemis to play Mrs. Twitter. Bemis then appropriated all of Fuller's techniques for the "hypnosis" scene, thereby imitating Fuller's choreography of imitating Dr. Drake's movements onstage.[20] Then, in an attempt to maintain ticket sales, the Casino used a poster depicting Fuller to advertise Bemis's performance, using the image of the original to represent the imposter. An irate Fuller brought suit for copyright infraction.

This 1892 lawsuit, which Fuller lost, marks the beginning of her lifelong struggle to control her image and limit her many imitators. Furthermore, the verdict in this case reveals the degree to which Fuller's work was already challenging conventional notions of character onstage. "A stage dance," the judge wrote,

> illustrating the poetry of motion by a series of graceful movements combined with an attractive arrangement of drapery, lights and shadow but telling no story, portraying no character and depicting no emotion, is not a "dramatic composition" within the meaning of the copyright act.[21]

The judge's remarks offer a neat explanation of the difference between nineteenth-century narrative or character-based dance and its twentieth-century abstract, modernist descendant. The lawsuit, furthermore, throws into relief a paradox of Fuller's art: her dance seemed too impersonal to copyright, but

---

under Fuller's peculiar spell (Debora Silverman, *Art Nouveau in Fin-de-Siècle France* [Berkeley: University of California Press, 1991], 300).

[20] It is unclear whether the decision to imitate Fuller's dance was Bemis's or the producers'. In either case, it is clear that all parties wished to sustain the success Fuller had brought to the play.

[21] The judge's decision continues:

It is essential to such a composition that it should tell some story. The plot may be simple. It may be but the narrative or representation of a single transaction; but it must repeat or mimic some action, speech, emotion, passion, or character, real or imaginary. And when it does, it is the ideas thus expressed which become subject of copyright. An examination of the description of the complainant's dance . . . shows that the end sought . . . was solely the devising of a series of graceful movements, combined with an attractive arrangement of drapery, lights, and shadows. . . . The merely mechanical movements by which effects are reproduced on the stage are not subjects of copyright where they convey no ideas whose arrangement makes up a dramatic composition. [*Fuller v. Bemis*, Circuit Court, New York, *Federal Reporter* vol. 50, no. 929, 18 June 1892 (#5929), NYPLPA]

it was her image, her own persona that she was trying to protect. When the Casino Theater put Loie Fuller's likeness on that poster it was promoting not only a dance, but an identity, a new star's persona. Although Fuller's name had been omitted from the program, by the time Minnie Bemis had taken over the role, Fuller had become a trademark-worthy performer. At the same time, the very success of her dance in *Quack, M.D.* required an apparent evacuation of onstage identity, an imitative mechanicity that led the audience to imagine her transformed into nonhuman shapes. Fuller would long occupy this charged frontier between human and inhuman, dancer and dance, actor and character.[22]

Fuller continued to perform her "serpentine dance" in the United States for another year, earning good reviews.[23] Though born in vaudeville, the dance owed its appeal largely to shape and form, and so when Fuller performed it as a solo piece, she stripped it of all accompanying narrative and décor. For Fuller, her subsequent move to France in 1892 represented an analogous purification of her work, an opportunity to evolve from small-time performer into artist: "The notion of going to Paris possessed me. I wanted to go to a city where, as I had been told, educated people would like my dancing and would accord it a place in the realm of art."[24] With this goal in mind, upon arriving in France, Fuller would attempt first to perform at the loftiest venue she could find, the Opéra, home of the prestigious Académie Nationale de la Danse. When the Academie's director, Pedro Gailhard, offered her only a brief engagement, Fuller declined and moved on. Indignant but undaunted, she made her way to her second-choice theater: the Folies-Bergère, where, as we know, she ousted yet another imitator and embarked on a new life.[25]

---

[22] This ruling against Fuller continued to stand until 1976, affecting all choreographers wishing to obtain legal rights over nonnarrative dancers (Lista, *Danseuse*, 105).

[23] She performed it for example during the winter of 1891–92, as part of her role in a play called "Uncle Celestine" at the Parke Theater of Brooklyn, New York. The reviewer for New York's *Spirit of the Times* wrote: "The only artistic feature is the *Serpentine Dance*, introduced by Loie Fuller, whose name is not on the bills . . . she floats around the stage, her figure now revealed, now concealed by the exquisite drapery which takes forms of its own. . . . It is not a skirt dance, although she dances and waves a skirt. . . . She emerges from the darkness, her airy evolutions now tinted blue and purple and crimson, and the audience . . . insists upon seeing her pretty, piquant face before they can believe that this lovely apparition is really a woman" (qtd. in Sommer, "Loie Fuller," 57).

[24] Fuller, *Fifteen Years*, 19.

[25] Giovanni Lista estimates at least 37 different Fuller imitators. These women, who appeared both in the United States and abroad, include Mlle. Emilienne D'Alençon at "Menu-Plaisirs," Miss Matthews at the Ba-ta-Clas, Miss Any Feyton at Concert-Européen, and an American, Miss

The Evolution of a European Modernist

In Paris, Fuller began her life's work in earnest, distilling and refining many elements taken from her youthful career in the States and synthesizing them into a style that entranced the cabaret public, Europe's artistic and intellectual elite, the aristocracy, conservatives, and children. This wide-ranging appeal was due largely to Fuller's uncanny capacity to absorb and reflect myriad aspects of her artistic and cultural environment without appearing to be pandering or overly indebted to any one group or movement. Her style was a seamless blend of apparent opposites: a sleek, impersonal mechanomorphic modernism that endeared her to Mallarmé and the Futurists, for example, and a Romantic, dreamy, somewhat naïve painterliness incorporating motifs borrowed from nature, fairytales, mythology, and drama, which appealed more to dowagers and royalty.[26]

Once she reached Paris, Fuller took care to distance herself from most visible trappings of cabaret dance (although not from cabarets themselves). Leaving her Gaiety Girl days behind, she refrained from any kind of suggestive movement. "No more contortions or arched backs," wrote Claude Roger-Marx, "no pelvic rotations."[27] Indeed, Fuller refrained even from showing her body in any way again, rarely permitting spectators to see so much as her silhouette.[28] For the rest of her career, her figure would remain hidden beneath ever more voluminous costumes from which only her face and hands would emerge. Slowly, she transferred attention away from her physical self, allowing it to be subsumed by the lights and costumes.

Marie Leyton, at Tivoli in London. (Lista, *Danseuse*, 137 ff; see also H.C., review of Loie Fuller, *Revue Encyclopédique*, February 1893, 109, Collection Rondel.)

[26] Mallarmé praised what he called Fuller's "industrial accomplishment," and Marinetti found in Fuller an artist "free of mimicry, and without sexual stimulation," representing "pure geometry" (Filippo Marinetti, "Manifesto of Futurist Dance," 8 July 1917, http://futurism.org.uk/manifestos). To accompany her performances, Fuller used well-known classical piano music, including pieces by Mendelssohn, Grieg, Berlioz, Purcell, Wagner, Beethoven, and, after 1909, more modern composers such as Debussy, Scriabin, Stravinsky, and de Polignac. Fuller was among the first popular performers to pair dance in this way with serious piano music. Classical composers paired with dance would soon be popularized by Isadora Duncan and the Ballets Russes. See Foster, *Choreography and Narrative*; also Claire de Morinni, "Loie Fuller: The Fairy of Light," in *Chronicles of the American Dance: From the Shakers to Martha Graham*, ed. Paul Magriel, (New York: Da Capo, 1984), 203–20.

[27] Roger-Marx, *La Loie Fuller*, 10.

[28] The sole exception to Fuller's commitment to onstage modesty was her 1907 performance of *Salome*, in which she allowed her naked (45-year-old) body to appear briefly in silhouette.

As we have seen, this apparent chastity earned Fuller the moral approbation of many critics of her time. "Let us hope that the craze for high kicking, unnatural straining of the muscles, and the hideous short skirts and scanty bodice will become a thing of the past," wrote one critic with the ladylike by-line of Mrs. M. Griffith.[29] So chaste was Fuller's image at the Folies, in fact, that its management decided to feature her in their first-ever afternoon performances, designed to attract women and children. Fuller "changes the music-hall," proclaimed one contemporary review, "Mothers can now take their daughters, even their granddaughters to see Fuller. And I don't see why Father would not greatly enjoy these dances as well ."[30]

Fuller also eschewed both formal dance technique and displays of athleticism or flexibility. Having never studied *danse d'école* or ballet, she relied on simple steps of her own invention, designed to manipulate her enormous costumes and maximize her lighting effects. These movements consisted of raising and lowering her rotating arms; taking small jumps; kneeling with one leg outstretched; arching her torso; running downstage and upstage with small steps; turning with increasing speed in a small circle to gather momentum for the airborne shapes; and alternately turning her face toward and away from the audience.[31] Her onstage motion, in other words, was largely instrumental, designed purely to maximize the drama of the fabric's motion, for it was ultimately not Fuller's natural body dancing, but the one she constructed with her stagecraft.

It was this stagecraft, her many innovations in costuming and lighting, that inspired the adoration of cabaret audiences, even though Fuller studiously avoided nearly every predictable aspect of cabaret dance—narrative, décor, titillation, and standard choreography. Her experiments in stagecraft were original enough that Fuller received a series of patents for her apparatuses, both in the United States and abroad. But given the number of imitators she spawned, Fuller never fully trusted patents alone to protect her from theft and plagiarism. As a result, she insisted upon a culture of secrecy, closely guarding all the details of her costumes and lighting. She arranged, for example, to have her costumes painted in sections so that the artists working on them remained unaware of the intended final result. She also took the unusual step for a solo

---

[29] "The dancing of la Loie has so raised the reputation of the Folies-Bergère that now the most particular Parisian has no hesitation about taking his wife or lady friends there" (Griffith, "Loie Fuller: Inventor of the Serpentine Dance," 542).

[30] Giovanni Lista, in his biography of Fuller, argues that her modesty stemmed simply from her discomfort at being overweight.

[31] These movements are visible in the extant films of Fuller. See also Gay Morris, "La Loie," *Dance Magazine* 51, no. 8 (August 1977), 36–41.

performer of refusing to employ the in-house technicians of the many theaters in which she appeared. Instead Fuller hired and maintained her own independent crew of up to thirty electricians, headed by her brother, Burt Fuller. These workers traveled everywhere with her and were sworn to secrecy about their techniques. Fuller even refused to commit her lighting cues to paper, preferring to signal her technicians through a system of onstage heel taps.[32] While such guardedness may have been necessary to protect professional secrets, in maintaining this level of secrecy around her performances Fuller only enhanced her reputation as an unknowable "wizard" with mysterious powers.

In large part, Fuller maintained this aura of the magical via her many innovations in costumes, lighting, and stage design, many of which were designed to lend a supernatural ambiance to performances, appearing to dismantle fleshly reality or, sometimes, even to deny the laws of physics. At times, these apparatuses appeared to occult the body altogether; at other times, they served to disperse or fragment it. Overall, Fuller's inventions tended to dissolve the shape of her body into a whirl of fabric and light, devoid of most corporeal as well as social or historical specificity; she was no longer a dancer performing a role, or even a dancer dancing, but somehow a force of performativity itself, mutating into vast and ephemeral decorative forms.[33]

In so suppressing her relationship to the outside world, Fuller partook of a phenomenon that Fredric Jameson has labeled "the spell of the artistic commodity," in which modernist art works appear utterly outside of or beyond their context.[34] Indeed, Fuller's hypnotic brand of performance fits especially well into this category of the artwork that "[tries] to repress its referential content." Jameson cautions us to break that fetishizing spell, observing that "what is real is precisely not the isolated script or text itself but rather the work-in-situation." [35]

In the spirit of such demystification, this section seeks to contextualize Fuller's free-floating abstractions, to ask how they responded to and reinterpreted those early days in vaudeville, the art and cultural trends of Fuller's time, corporeal reality, and politics. In other words, I shall try to combat Fuller's own

[32] Kermode, "Loie Fuller: Poet and Dancer," 38 ff; Griffith, "Loie Fuller," 544; Current and Current, *Loie Fuller*, 98.

[33] "The dancing woman is not a woman who dances," wrote Mallarmé, "for these juxtaposed reasons that she is not a woman, but a metaphor, resuming one of the elemental aspects of our form, dagger, chalice, flower, etc. . . . and that she does not dance, suggesting with a corporeal writing . . . a poem detached from any scribe's implement" (Mallarmé, "Ballets," 304).

[34] Fredric Jameson, "Modernism and Its Repressed," in *The Ideologies of Theory* (Minneapolis: University of Minnesota Press, 1988), 180.

[35] Ibid., 178–79.

tendency to blot out referentiality, by explaining and contextualizing her most important performance techniques. I do not intend, however, to offer here a complete list or description of Fuller's lifetime total of 128 dances. Such a task falls beyond the purview of this book and has already been completed admirably by Giovanni Lista in his biography, *Loie Fuller: Danseuse de la Belle Epoque*.

The Costumes

The first element in Fuller's metamorphosis into a "supernatural being" or "a figure from one of Rodin's dreams" was her virtuosity with fabric. Having done away with most backdrops and scenery, Fuller darkened all space around her by draping the stage and its floor in black or deep blue velvet or chenille—focusing all attention on the dancer's moving body. The typical scenario, then, of performer gazed upon, enframed by, and explained by her space disappeared. Instead, the multiple functions usually served by scenery were subsumed by Fuller's costumes and lights. Mallarmé was particularly struck by this phenomenon: "The enchantress creates the ambiance," he wrote, "drawing it out of herself and then returning to it in a palpitating silence of crêpe de chine." [36]

At the outset of her solo career, Fuller had designed and worn cape-like circles of fabric bearing hand-painted depictions of her dance's various motifs: curved serpents, flowers, or the iridescent moiré of butterflies (fig. 1.2). Over time, however, the costumes underwent a kind of modernist streamlining. By 1895, Fuller had largely abandoned painted costumes in favor of vast robes of white silk which she then sculpted into colossal versions of the same images she had once painted upon them. Instead of referring to a butterfly, for example, via a costume whose colorful painted "wings" were hinged to her still-visible torso, Fuller became the butterfly itself, disappearing inside a much larger expanse of molded, unpainted silk whose colors came from electric lights projected from above (fig. 1.3). And with the advent of this new sculptural technique came a much greater occulting of Fuller's own body. Onstage, then, she replaced both her physical body and any enframing or explanatory stage space with the three-dimensionality of the costumes themselves, turning herself into the invisible occupant of a mutable theatrical space. Fuller was no longer performing on a stage set; she was not telling a story with dance. She had become, rather, both stage and performer, having taken upon her body both the image and the space in which the image appeared. [37] Later in

---

[36] Mallarmé, "Ballets," 308–09.

[37] Felicia McCarren describes the phenomenon thus: "Fuller's performances collapse the distinction between matter and the matrix space of the womb, merging the woman dancing with

Figure 1.2. Fuller in early butterfly costume, Bibliothèque Nationale de France

her career, in productions such as *The Sea* and *The Dance of the Opal*, Fuller would employ still larger expanses of silk, using them as collective veils to be sculpted by multiple dancers who remained partly or entirely hidden beneath the fabric they shaped with their hands and bodies.[38]

While she performed primarily in plain white silk, Fuller did not totally abandon the practice of painting fabrics. Instead, she tried to literalize her concept of "painting with light," by experimenting with the dye-like properties of phosphorescent salts, which she first encountered while visiting

---

the womb-like space in which she performs" (Felicia McCarren, "The Symptomatic Act," *Critical Inquiry* 21, no. 1 (1995): 758.

[38] See chapter 4 further discussion of these "collective veil" dances.

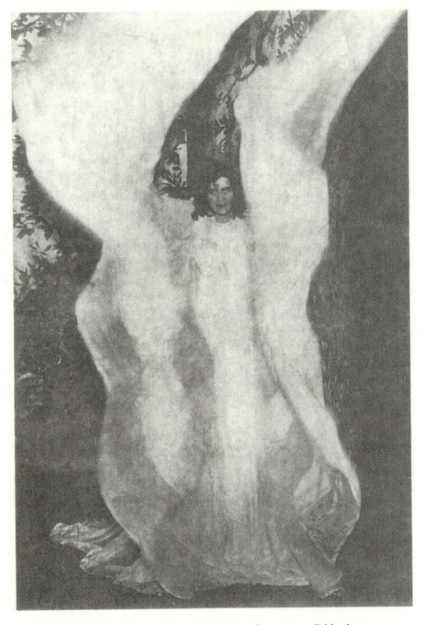

Figure 1.3. Fuller in later, more developed butterfly costume, Bibliothèque Nationale de France

Figure 1.4. Loie Fuller's costume for a version of *The Butterfly Dance* using phosphorescent paints, courtesy of the Maryhill Museum of Art

Thomas Edison's New Jersey laboratory in 1896. It was there, in Menlo Park, that Fuller discovered Edison's fluoroscope, an early version of an x-ray machine that made use of phosphorescence.[39] When Edison placed her hand inside the machine, she was thrilled to see her flesh turn translucent, to see her body's solidity dissolve. She imagined at once a theatrical application:

> Mr. Edison explained to me that the wall in the box [the machine] was covered with phosphorescent salts and these salts compressed the light as sand did water and that was why one could see the bones, they were outlined against the light because they were thick and solid and the flesh around the bones resembles matter like a veil. This curious stuff all aglow . . . held me spellbound. It suddenly occurred to me that if I could have a dress permeated with that substance it would be wonderful. I asked Mr. Edison if the salts would retain the luminousness when the lamp was gone. He hadn't thought of that so we tried it and lo and behold the light remained.[40]

Fuller procured some of the salts but, upon experimentation, found that they stiffened her fabrics too much, impeding her aerial sculpting technique. She therefore contented herself with dabbing on the salts in tiny drops, which created a "starlit" effect when illuminated by spotlights (fig. 1.4). These glow-in-the-dark silks provided the focal point for performances such as *The Phosphorescent Dance*, of which critic Julius Meier-Graefe wrote:

> She disappears and all is dark, but something moves in the darkness, it is tiny brilliant points that dance, it is a dance of lights glittering like stars. They form large, brilliant circles that merge into luminous mountains side by side, crisscrossing, nothing but these points of light dance, not an iota of human movement—it takes one's breath away. It is a mystical dance.[41]

[39] Fuller and Edison found each other equally fascinating. Fuller had declined an earlier request from Edison to be filmed by him. Consequently, in 1897, he made a film with one of her imitators, Annabelle Whitford Moore, performing a similar dance (*Trailblazers of Modern Dance*, prod. and dir. Merrill Brockner and Judy Kinber, Indiana University, 1977). In keeping with the way Fuller lent herself to imitation, Edison presented this film in 1894 at the Paris Cinétoscopes as *Danse de la Loie Fuller* (*Encyclopedia dello spettacolo*, vol. 5 (Rome: Unione Editorale, 1954), s.v. "Loie Fuller").

[40] Fuller, "Prelude to Light," unpublished lecture, 1911, NYPLPA.

[41] Qtd. in Lista, *Danseuse*, 328. In the course of her experiments, Fuller also managed to blow up her home in Paris, singe off her eyebrows, and have her insurance policy canceled (Fuller, "My Laboratory," unpublished essay, NYPLPA). Her helpers in these exploits were some of her young dance pupils. Sadly, it appears that exposure to the volatile chemical salts may have caused a number of them to develop cancer later in life, a possibility of which Fuller should have been

Underlying all the sculptural play with fabric was Fuller's system of hooked bamboo and aluminum rods that were sewn into the underside of the silk. These rods, patented in 1893 (fig. 1.5), essentially became extensions of the dancer's arms, allowing Fuller to hold a costume as far as ten feet from her body.[42]

The overhead shapes formed by the fabric and rods required considerable force and control on Fuller's part. Once aloft, the shapes spun partly out of centrifugal force, in the manner of clay pots taking shape on a spinning wheel. In the case of her 1895 *Dance of the Lily*, a costume of five hundred yards of thin white Chinese silk reached a height of twenty feet over her head. This 1896 review gives us an idea of the effect achieved:

> There is so much of the costume that Miss Fuller has to run all the while just as fast as she possibly can, and also to keep her arms in swift motion at the same time, to keep the voluminous gown under control. The wands used in this dress are very long and at the very end of the dance she forms a figure of a colossal white lily, such as could have lived and flourished only in the land of Munchausen. When the big lily wilts out of sight in the last dance she returns to her dressing room and sinks panting into a big chair . . . "do you know," she said, "I make that lily by sheer will force? . . . *Le Lys du Nil* is the hardest thing I do."[43]

For the French public of the 1890s, these gigantic costume lilies or butterflies, and indeed all of Fuller's curvilinear, flowing forms, recalled the decorative motifs of the reigning aesthetic movement, Art Nouveau. Accordingly, Fuller was hailed as an icon of Art Nouveau, a living embodiment of its "femme-fleur" and "femme-papillon" motifs, especially during the movement's apogee at the World's Fair of 1900. Leading artists of the movement, such as Pierre

---

aware. Her unpublished journals reveal that Edison spoke later to her of having abandoned his work with phosphorescent salts precisely out of fear for his employees' health. Fuller then goes on to describe her own continued experiments with these substances, never acknowledging that she was risking the health of children. Even after Fuller's death, her companion, Gabrielle Bloch, continued working with these salts, producing "ballets in black light" in Paris (Lista, *Danseuse*, 330 ff.) In Fuller's unpublished notebooks she describes blowing up her house in Paris in her experiments burning magnesium to illuminate salts of sulphur and calcium. Her insurance company thereafter canceled her policy (Fuller, "My Laboratory").

[42] "My invention," wrote Fuller in her patent application, "consists of certain improvements . . . which . . . assist the dancer in posing, and in causing, by movements of the body, the folds of the garment to assume variegated and fanciful waves of great beauty and grace. By use of wands . . . connected to the dress a double purpose is afforded. First it facilitates the creating of a waving motion in the folds of the garment, and second, it assists the dancer in performing statuesque poses and in imitating different styles of wings" (qtd. in Sommer, "Loie Fuller," 61).

[43] Fuller, interview, *New York Blade*, 11 April 1896.

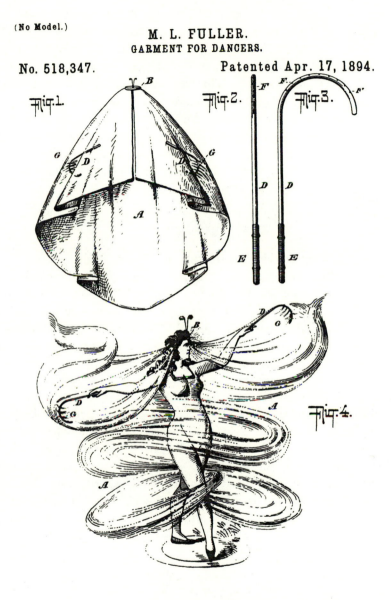

Figure 1.5. Patent drawing for Fuller's costume with wands

Roche, Emile Gallé, and Georges de Feure, all took Fuller as their model, and no catalogue of Art Nouveau fails to include multiple reproductions of Fuller, veils flying.[44] As Art Nouveau waned, though, in the years after 1900, so did Fuller's perceived connection to it, even while her style remained fairly constant. In Fuller's relationship to Art Nouveau, then, we find an excellent example of how her performances managed the apparently paradoxical task of appearing to exist in their own fantastical universe, a "land of Munchausen," while actually dovetailing perfectly with the reigning forces of the outside cultural world. Fuller seems to have had a curious spongelike quality in aesthetic matters, absorbing and embodying the influences around her, while remaining convincingly original and unshackled to any one label or category.

Lighting

Audiences and critics seemed most dazzled by the proto-cinematic effects obtained by the play of lights upon Fuller's ephemeral shapes. In performances such as *The Fire Dance*, *The Butterfly*, *The Violet*, and *The Chimeras* (1922, with music by Armande de Polignac), Fuller showered her mobile silk costume-sculptures in cascades of changing colored lights provided by another apparatus of her own invention: a projector reminiscent of the magic lanterns of the 1880s. Fuller's projector consisted of a platform of rotating pasteboard wheels positioned in front of searchlights. Each round piece of pasteboard (from twelve to sixteen inches across) was surrounded by a gelatin disk of either a solid color or a combination of colors. In front of some of these disks, Fuller would place a panel of glass which she had hand cut and painted with designs appropriate to her performance. She had also invented the process for obtaining these special pigments, which were dissolved in a gelatin emulsion. The lights would then be shined upon her as she danced, projecting colors and mutating abstract designs upon her face, hands, and costumes. In effect, she had moved from painting fabrics to painting the light itself. For each dance, Fuller used between fifteen and twenty of these projectors.[45]

---

[44] For Fuller's relationship to Art Nouveau, see Rhonda Garelick, *Rising Star* (Princeton: Princeton University Press, 1998); Lista, *Danseuse*, 26 ff. See also Brygida Ochaim, "Loie Fuller, The Soloist of the Dancing Color," *Parkett* 9 (1986): 115–19; Jullian, *The Triumph of Art Nouveau*; and Silverman, *Art Nouveau*. "An effigy of Loie Fuller whirling under the projectors should have crowned the [Fair's entrance]. . . . Her . . . quality of movement could be found in all the truly modern parts of the exhibition" (Jullian, *The Triumph of Art Nouveau*, 90).

[45] See Kermode, "Loie Fuller and the Dance before Diaghilev," 38; also Sommer, Loie Fuller." The *Dance of the Lily* began as a scene from the 1895 *Salome* but, like *The Fire Dance*, was later performed as an independent piece.

For the 1895 *Fire Dance*, performed to Wagner's *Ride of the Valkyries* and which began as a scene in her first production of *Salome*), Fuller made particularly striking use of this machine. To create the impression of dancing while engulfed by growing flames, Fuller swirled her robes under red and yellow rotating lights.[46] A contemporary critic described the effect this way:

> In the *Fire Dance* she appeared turning and twisting in a torrent of incandescent lava; her long tunic leaps about in the flames, curled in burning spirals, undulating and whirling, it suddenly explodes and then wilts slowly into a red blaze.[47]

Fuller held patents for a number of other stage apparatuses, all of which served to dematerialize the body onstage. She created and patented her "underlighting device" in 1893, while working at the Folies-Bergère. It consisted of a glass pedestal of approximately four feet in width and four feet in height. Set deeply into the stage floor, the pedestal was lit by a lamp hidden beneath it. With the rest of the theater darkened, Fuller would climb atop this pedestal and dance illuminated only from below. Under these conditions, the pedestal would, essentially, disappear, leaving for the audience only the sight of a woman suspended in midair, dancing four feet above the stage floor, unaffected by gravity, freed from bodily weight, disconnected from her physical context. For *Fire Dance*, for example, Fuller employed the underlighting pedestal to create the illusion of walking on fire.[48] (fig. 1.6).

That same year (1893) Fuller invented and patented another device designed to dematerialize with light: a backdrop that essentially transformed a lit stage into a bisected diamond. Having pierced the backdrop all over in a regular grid pattern, Fuller then inserted faceted glass "gemstones" into each pierced hole, suspended by wires. When hit with the intense rotating spotlights these faceted stones sprang to life, catching the light and flashing it back and forth among themselves prismatically in countless vectors.[49] This device recalls, of course, the "Crypt of the Crimson Crystals" in which Fuller danced during her vaudeville appearance as *Aladdin*. But when Fuller first used her version of this apparatus for her 1893 dance *Le Firmament* (also known as

---

[46] *Loie Fuller's Fire Dance: Reconstruction and Performance*, produced by John Mueller, performed by Jessica Lindberg (Columbus: Dance Film Archive, Ohio State University, 2003). See also Coleman, "The Electric Fairy," 319.

[47] Qtd. in Lista, *Danseuse*, 252.

[48] Ibid., 240. For the *Fire Dance*, Fuller dressed all in white, with a long white transparent scarf, and stood atop a glass square on the stage. The light alone lent the appearance of flames, ranging from blue through brilliant orange.

[49] See Ibid., 158.

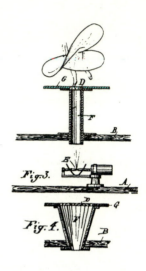

Figure 1.6. Patent drawing for underlighting pedestal

Bonne Nuit), she stripped away all visible traces of the original vaudevillian context: narrative, overt Orientalism, even the delineation of a body dancing. Paul Adam described the effect thus:

> In this . . . luminous dance, forms lose their precision. Nothing bestial remains. There is no object onto which desire may attach itself. One must follow the undulation of the lovely lines, be rocked in the waves made by these robes transfigured by ever-changing colored projections.[50]

We should note here that Adam's review focuses not only on the hypnotic beauty of Fuller's abstractions—"the lovely lines"—but also on the absence of other elements. He enumerates what is *not* in Fuller's performance: precision of forms, anything "bestial," an object of desire. While Adam is contrasting *Le Firmament* with other cabaret shows, his remarks suggest that in her zeal to remove those worldly aspects of the dance Fuller may have succeeded simply in creating their negative imprint. Adam's list of what is not in Fuller's dance suggests that the performance somehow conjured these elements anyway, that the bawdy, physical, and elaborately detailed world of a music-hall *Aladdin* somehow left its mark on Fuller's astral and sleek performance, if only in the starkness of its absence.

[50] Adam, untitled article in *Le Courrier de la Presse*.

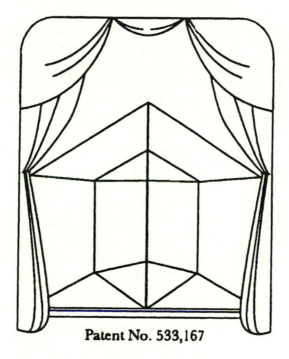

Patent No. 533,167

Figure 1.7. Patent drawing for the mirror room

In 1893 Fuller patented (in France) the first version of her "mirror room," another device that diminished the physical solidity of her body onstage. The mirror room was an octagonal backdrop, open in the front, made up of contiguously arranged mirrors illuminated by tiny electric lights installed in the interstices (fig. 1.7). This curving wall of lights and mirrors created multiple reflections of the dancer performing before it. Instead of one dancer, a small crowd of identical dancers appeared to be performing side by side, making it difficult for spectators to determine *which* of the many silk-covered moving forms was the real, flesh-and-blood Fuller. British writer Mrs. Griffith described the effect:

> By some mysterious arrangement, eight Loie Fullers appear to be dancing at the same time, and the whole stage is bathed in a flood of glorious tints, in which may be seen aerial forms, in cloudlike vestures, whirling and dancing as if they were the fabled victims of the Tarantula.[51]

The mirror room, in other words, both dissolved and reproduced Fuller's image, problematizing the whole notion of bodily reality onstage. Within the

[51] Griffith, "Loie Fuller: The Inventor of the Serpentine Dance," 545.

mirror room, Fuller was able both to be replicated and to fully control the performances of her "doubles," her myriad reflected selves. Griffith's reference to the deadly Sicilian "Tarantula"—or "tarantella"—dance further evokes the implied loss of identity created by the mirrors, since according to the dance's legend, when the poisonous tarantula attacked its female victims, they would become incoherent, hallucinate, and spin uncontrollably until they collapsed and died.[52]

The mirror room underwent several permutations, many of which were patented as well. Fuller's 1897 *Danse du miroir*, for example, used a semi-polygonal construction of mirrored walls supplemented by still more mirrors positioned on both the stage floor and "ceiling," affording spectators additional views of the dance from below and above. In 1898, Fuller patented yet another version which featured a frontal wall of transparent glass that both caught and created more reflections, effectively turning the room into a glass box, resembling an aquarium.[53] The audience could then watch Fuller as she performed inside a display case, as so much merchandise within a vitrine.[54] Furthermore, when the house lights were fully extinguished and the glass box most brilliantly lit from within, the glass wall was transformed into a one-way mirror, transparent to the audience, but a purely reflecting surface for the dancer within. In other words, Fuller had here again found a way to stage "unconsciousness": while audiences could see her clearly through her glass pane, Fuller could not see them; she saw only her own reflection and danced without acknowledging the audience. She danced before her own image, imposing a staged prurience, a transgressive gaze upon the spectators who were now espying a lady alone at her mirror. Thus did Fuller literalize and thereby parody the commodified nature of performance, becoming a "dancer-in-a-box." In this, she recalls Benjamin's remarks about the role of mirrors in the commodity culture of

---

[52] Griffith may also be recalling the feminist connotations of the tarantella. As a partnerless, unfettered dance with Mediterranean roots, it connoted sexual and social liberation for women. Ibsen's heroine Nora in *A Doll's House* rehearses a tarantella. Similarly, the daring, sexually mysterious heroine of Rachilde's 1900 novel, *La Jongleuse* (*The Juggler*), performs a provocative tarantella in full costume. In fact, in 1909, Fuller proved Griffith right and included Chopin's *Tarantella* in a group piece she performed in Washington, DC and New Jersey. Her star pupil, the ballerina, Rita Sacchetto, danced the piece, which was entitled *Dance to Death*. See Hélène Cixous and Catherine Clément, *The Newly Born Woman* (Minneapolis: University of Minnesota Press, 1986). Cixous and Clément see an analogy between the madwoman's tarantella and the contortions of Freud's hysterics, all "bombarding his mosaic status/Law of Moses with their carnal, passionate body" (p. 95).

[53] Lista, *Danseuse*, 259.

[54] For an excellent discussion of "vitrine" culture in late-nineteenth-century France, see Philippe Hamon, *Expositions* (Paris: José Corti, 1989).

Paris: "Paris is the city of mirrors. The asphalt of its roadways smooth as glass, and at the entrance to all bistros, glass partitions. A profusion of window panes and mirrors in cafés, so as to make the inside brighter and to give all the tiny nooks and crannies, into which Parisian taverns separate, a pleasing amplitude." For Benjamin, the lure of the mirror is inseparable from the flashy appeal of the marketplace: "One may compare the pure magic of those walls of mirrors which we know from feudal times with the oppressive magic worked by the alluring mirror walls of the arcades, which invite us into seductive bazaars."[55]

The multiply reflected images of Fuller dancing onstage in her mirror room found their own commercial, bazaar-like counterpart offstage in her habit of using theater lobbies to sell reproductions of herself in the form of "Loie" dolls, figurines, and lamps—a practice that nearly literalizes Benjamin view of commodity circulation as the "impassioned cult of similarity."[56]

Eventually, Fuller's zeal to reproduce her own image led her to organize troupes of young female students (first as informal extras and then in 1908 as Les Ballets Loie Fuller) who functioned largely as "Loie replicas" (fig. 1.8). Any discussion of Fuller's stagecraft must include a word about these young girls, for they were treated more as mechanical light projections of Fuller's body than as independent beings. Chosen partly for their physical resemblance to Fuller (and partly too for their families' wealth), they were nearly all blond and blue-eyed and required to wear their hair long like their teacher's. Fuller went so far as to issue them stage names in keeping with her aesthetic, such as Orchidée, Ange, or Buttercup, never permitting the girls' real names to be used in theater programs or public appearances. One journalist referred to the student dancers as Fuller's "cohorte anonyme."[57]

Fuller always insisted that she needed to protect the girls' identities in order to ensure their (often aristocratic) families' privacy. But she was also obscuring

[55] Walter Benjamin, The Arcades Project, trans. Howard Eiland and Kevin McLaughlin (New York: Belknap Press, 2002), 541.

[56] The infinite sameness of mirrored reflections and their connection to commodity culture has been treated by Benjamin in his discussion of "impassioned cult of similarity" inherent in the circulation of commodities (Walter Benjamin, Charles Baudelaire: A Lyric Poet in the Era of High Capitalism, trans. Harry Zohn (London: Verso, 1983), 206. Terry Eagleton, writing of this aspect of Benjamin, observes, "The exchange of commodities is at once smoothly continuous and an infinity of interruption: each gesture of exchange is an exact repetition of the previous one. each presents to the other a mirror which reflects no more than its own mirroring; all that is new in this process is the very flash and dexterity with which mirrors are interchanged" (Terry Eagleton, Walter Benjamin or Towards a Revolutionary Criticism [London: Verso Press, 1981], 28–29).

[57] Legrand-Chabrier, "La Loie Fuller: D'Une Exposition à l'autre," L'Art Vivant I (July–December, 1925): 28.

Figure 1.8. Fuller and her troupe members in outdoor performance, 1910, Billy Rose Theatre Collection, New York Public Library for the Performing Arts, Astor, Lenox, and Tilden Foundations

their identities in order to turn them more fully into reflections of herself.[58] Indeed, in 1910, when her most talented dancer, Vilma Banchi, known as "Orchidée" (fig. 1.9), tried to perform independently, under her own name, Fuller sought legal injunction against her.[59]

Such large-scale narcissism did not escape critics such as Francis Miomandre, who wrote:

> Fuller thought she might enhance the impact of her aesthetic by multiplying it. She created a school: a corps of young girls dancing around her in the same costumes and following the same rhythms. This invention allowed her to create effects of inconceivable grandeur. . . . A central nebula, she emits fragments of her image which immediately then revolve around her, according to the law of planetary attraction in the empyreum.[60]

[58] Harris, "Loie Fuller: The Myth, the Woman and the Artist," 25.

[59] The injunction prevented Orchidée from performing any similar choreography without her teacher (De Morinni, "Loie Fuller: The Fairy of Light," 206; also Lista, *Danseuse*, 644). Banchi later appeared in a 1926 film with Rudolph Valentino, *The Son of the Sheik*, in which she played the dancer Yasmin.

[60] Miomandre, *Danse*, 54.

Figure 1.9. 1910 photograph of dancer Vilma Banchi ("Orchidée"),
Billy Rose Theatre Collection, New York Public Library for the
Performing Arts, Astor, Lenox, and Tilden Foundations

(See fig. 1.10.) In a 1909 interview Fuller virtually confessed to her own curiously dehumanized view of the children. Asked about her future plans for the
young dancers, she replied, "Oh yes there are children this year; but no one
knows what may happen; perhaps we may reach a point where the children
will be optical delusions as well"[61] (fig. 1–10).

Not all critics found Fuller's various optical "delusions" delightful. Jean Lorrain, who was always brutally honest in his varying opinions of Fuller, found
the fragmentation of the mirror room particularly unsettling:

And so, "la Loie?" Her new dances! Who possibly could have advised
her to do that! One can easily see what she meant to do, create a ballet

[61] Qtd. in Sommer, "Loie Fuller," 61. The group known as the Ballets Loie Fuller disbanded
and reformed on a number of occasions. Observers noted that despite Fuller's protestations of
motherly love for the girls, they seemed to come and go very quickly.

Figure 1.10. Loie Fuller and two of her youngest pupils in stage
costumes modeled on Fuller's own. Bibliothèque Nationale de France

of Loies with all her gestures and attitudes repeated by the mirrors, but
she didn't realize that her dance is cut up, mutilated even by each mirror
and we see only amputated pieces of Loie, her hands, her arms, her
neck—all spinning infinitely in the compartments of an aquarium.
Aquarium! Yes, that's the word. I felt as though I were at the Jardin de
l'Acclimatation [The botanical and zoological park of Paris]. But the
aquarium at the Jardin is better.[62]

Like Griffith, then, who was reminded of the deadly tarantella, Lorrain sensed
violence in the mirror dances, imagining Fuller's body in amputated pieces.

---

[62] Lorrain, *Poussières de Paris*, 195. In an entry in her unpublished journals entitled "Chinese
Punishment," Fuller evinced a private delectation for images of amputation. She describes a newspaper account of the execution of a young thief in China. The boy's punishment, Fuller recounts,

While we might have assumed that the mirror room emphasized only the dancer's *immateriality*, given the multiple light reflections, it appears also to have had the opposite effect for these two (very different) critics. Both find echoes of mortality and corporeal, fleshly destruction in Fuller's myriad whirling forms. Their responses testify to audience awareness of Fuller's hidden bodiliness, and of the darker, less "pretty" side of her work lying just beneath its ethereal charms. Lorrain also seems to sense here Fuller's anticipatory modernism—his description of the "cut up" body parts strongly conjures Cubism.

Oddly, though, Lorrain assumes that Fuller was unaware of this effect: "she didn't realize that her dance is cut up." He is probably wrong. Given the meticulous planning and care that Fuller invested in her performances, it is likely that Fuller had simply once again succeeded in staging unconsciousness, creating the disturbing "amputation" effect while simultaneously disavowing it, appearing somehow too wholesome to have intended it.

Attending closely to Lorrain's remarks, we can see that their peculiar internal logic leads us to still another key aspect of Fuller's work. Lorrain first laments the amputated look of Fuller's body in the mirror dance; next, he compares the dance to the aquarium exhibition of the Jardin d'Acclimatation. In other words, he moves from complaining of having seen her body displayed as if surgically fragmented to complaining of having seen her body parts displayed like so many fish in a tank. The two complaints share more than their mean-spiritedness; both are responses to Fuller's scientific, exhibitionary quality, her very fin-de-siècle tendency to turn the stage into a laboratory or vitrine. Displays of amputated limbs and of undersea life both attribute to the spectator a highly scientificized gaze. To peer at a severed limb (or its facsimile) onstage is to assume a surgical gaze into the body's hidden connections, a gaze that wrenches apart organic wholeness. Similarly, to watch the antics of aquarium fish is to espy creatures reframed by science after being wrenched from their hidden ocean home. In both cases, the enjoyment is prurient and transgressive.

Much has been written, of course, about the late nineteenth century's fascination with such transgressive looking.[63] This intense preoccupation with vi-

---

was to be hacked to death while sedated with opium: "they cut out the muscular front of his two arms just above the elbow [and] cut off his legs at the knees."

[63] Benjamin writes of the unreturned gaze of a photographed subject as a prime example of the destruction of aura effected by mechanical reproduction, which he contrasts with the "auratic" experience of exchanging human gazes: "The camera records our likeness without returning our gaze. But looking at someone carries the implicit expectation that our look will be returned by the object of our gaze. Where this expectation is met (which in the case of thought processes, can apply equally to the look of the eye of the mind and to a glance pure and simple), there is an experience of aura to the fullest extent" (Benjamin, *Charles Baudelaire*, 147).

sion and visibility was propelled in part by what Mark Seltzer has called "machines of perception"—those technologies that extended the reach of the human gaze into the heavens as well as into the human body: the telescope, the fluoroscope, the microscope. By the turn of the century, such optical instruments had become common attractions at cabarets and theme parks. The Jardin d'Acclimatation, to which Lorrain refers, partook of this obsessive "desire to make visible, to embody, to open the inner states." Established in 1859 as a center for botanical and zoological study, it had by 1877 broadened its focus to include human beings, importing "natives" from a variety of colonized countries to display in recreated "natural habitats."[64] These exhibitions amounted essentially to human zoos, and illustrate well how the period's scientific-medical gaze melded with the colonial gaze. "The age of exhibition was necessarily the colonial age," as Timothy Mitchell has written.[65]

Jean Lorrain's acerbic remarks suggest, therefore, just how much Loie Fuller's work partook both of her era's scientific, prurient gaze and of its concomitant colonial gaze. Once we consider Fuller's scientifism alongside her frequent mise-en-scène of unconsciousness, we can begin to ask how such disavowal of the power of spectacle fits into the politics of imperialism. To answer this we must first consider one last aspect of Fuller's stagecraft, her use of projected images.

Screened Images, Projections, and Shadows

For all her talk about "freeing" the stage with light, and although she banished much conventional narrative, Fuller's work was neither austere nor wholly abstract. On the contrary, her work had a carnivalesque or theme-park quality which invited spectators to gaze upon marvels and espy new realms created via the canny manipulation of technology.[66] It is in her use of projected images that we most clearly see how Fuller created these alternative worlds.

[64] See Paul Greenhalgh, *Ephemeral Vistas* (Manchester: Manchester University Press, 1988), 86. In an 1883 edition of the Bulletin de la Société d'Anthropologie, Léone Manoeuvrier wrote, "At the Jardin d'Acclimatation what information can we obtain? These individuals . . . are transported to an environment where they can no longer, so to speak, be themselves. Everything is changed in their way of life; they must contend on the one side with the administration of the Jardin, on another with those who brought them, on another with the crowds of the curious, and on another side with a committee that comes out to examine and measure them by means of little trinkets" (qtd. in Greenhalgh, *Ephemeral Vistas*, 86).

[65] Timothy Mitchell, "Orientalism and the Exhibitionary Order," in *Colonialism and Culture*, ed. Nicholas Dirks (Ann Arbor: University of Michigan Press, 1992), 303.

[66] Bablet, *Esthétique générale du décor du théâtre*, 146: Fuller in an interview with André Rigaud: "The stage must be extremely free" (qtd. in Lista, *Danseuse*, 146).

By projecting painted illustrations or photographs onto her costumes, Fuller created a wide range of ephemeral backdrops. Some of these displayed her usual, decorative motifs: seascapes, flames, polar snowstorms, spring prairies, and once even the aurora borealis. But Fuller also regularly indulged a taste for wittier, edgier, or more "scientific" topics. In August of 1893, for example, during Fuller's first return to the United States, she appeared at New York's Garden Theater in a whimsically patriotic performance. Here, she projected stereoptic portraits of George Washington and incumbent president Grover Cleveland onto her silks, allowing the illustrations to float across her own body as she danced.[67]

Fuller's most compelling images, though, came from formerly unseen natural worlds which were yielding their secrets to the era's new apparatuses. The notion of seeing all possible facets of nature obsessed Fuller, who returned often to this subject in her personal journals. "One must come into contact with the elements of nature whether they are interior or exterior," she wrote in one undated entry. Indeed, Fuller seemed to find nearly divine revelation in the new vistas being opened by technology. "The microscope," she wrote, "revealed to me a world greater than the bible had told me about."[68] In 1911 Fuller delivered a lecture on radium in which she focused primarily on the substance's ability to render the invisible visible: "The Curies . . . had discovered something unseen and unseeable, something which had to do with those forces which hitherto had been looked upon as supernatural, insomuch as our eyes were inadequate to see them. . . . If radium can bring to our vision those things we cannot see, we cannot measure its influence."[69]

This love of seeing the formerly unseeable led Fuller to enhance her performances with glimpses into such realms as astronomy and biology. For the dances known as *Les Nuages*, *Le Firmament*, and *Land of Visions*, for example, Fuller used photographs of the moon, taken with the aid of a telescope. She then printed the photographs onto her glass slides, and danced as lunar images drifted across her body—a dazzling sight for the time. In her high modernist *Danse d'acier* (*Dance of Steel*, 1914, music by Florent Schmitt), Fuller used a

---

[67] Current and Current, 63; and Review of Loie Fuller, *New York Times*, 17 August 1893, 4.

[68] Loie Fuller, "Prelude to Light," NYPLPA, 19. It is not clear where Fuller gave this lecture, but aspects of it suggest that it was delivered to university students.

[69] Loie Fuller, "Radium," unpublished lecture, NYPLPA, 34. Given her special interest in the Curies' work, it is unsurprising that Fuller even tried to obtain a sample of radium for use in her 1904 "Dance of Radium." Equally unsurprising was the Curies' (cordial) refusal to lend out any radioactive material. In a letter, Fuller told the Curies that she wished to create "butterfly wings of radium" for her performance. She had to settle for using some of the phosphorescent salts on her costume. See De Morinni, "Loie Fuller: The Fairy of Light," 214.

large canvas backdrop onto which she projected abstract, geometric shapes (reminiscent of works being created during this time by artists such as Malevich) alongside laboratory photographs of cancer cells and the skeletons of fish, all awash in silver light. The use of bodily interiors—particularly images of cell pathology—recalls the curiously morbid biologism of the young girl who punched up her temperance lectures with diagrams of a diseased liver.[70] They also display an ingenious sleight of hand, for at the same time that Fuller was denying audiences even a glimpse of her own body occupying the interior of her vast costumes, she was inviting them to peer at far more hidden and private natural spaces, belonging to other living bodies—spaces that she wore as a second skin.

In addition to projecting light images over her costumes, Fuller later experimented with versions of shadow play, elaborating on a technique used for "ombres chinoises," an entertainment popularized by Rodolphe Salas's famous cabaret, Le Chat Noir, and the Tanagra-Théâtre of Léon Huret, who worked with light play and marionettes.[71] Fuller's witty Ombres gigantesques (1922, music by Debussy), for example, featured her troupe of young dancers clad in dark colors, moving before a large scrim (fig. 1.11). By backlighting the scrim and having her dancers run upstage and down, Fuller produced silhouettes of constantly changing proportions, which seemed to "dance" with the dancers. At the same time, one dancer remained hidden and turned her backlit hand into a demonic, giant "hand monster" who threatens to scoop up the scurrying performers.[72]

In another of these shadow dances, Soldats du Brésil (music by Darius Milhaud), all the dancers remained behind the scrim, creating an effect described in this way by a contemporary review:

> The dancers . . . are out of sight, placed behind the screen. They seem to dance two by two, one is projected in black, the other in grey, executing at the same time the same steps and the same gestures while the varied and divinely colored designs appear on the screen, changing at every moment.[73]

In other words, Fuller did not content herself with merely projecting shadow images onto a screen; she let the shadows interact with the dancers, granting

---

[70] Kermode, Loie Fuller and the Dance before Diaghilev, 36; Guy Noël, review of Loie Fuller, 18 June 1922, NYPLPA; and Jean Chantavoine, review of Loie Fuller, 25 May 1914, Collection Rondel.

[71] Lista, Danseuse, 338; Sommer, "Loie Fuller," 65.

[72] See Noël and Chantavoine reviews (n. 71 above).

[73] Marcel Fournier, qtd. in Sommer, "Loie Fuller," 65.

Figure 1.11. Program for Fuller's *Shadow Dances*, Bibliothèque Nationale de France

a kind of onstage authority to "performers" of light. As Sally Sommer explains: "Unlike [the situation of] 'The Théâtre des Ombres du Chat Noir,' the emphasis was not on seemingly autonomous movement of shadows, it was on play between live performer and shadow."[74] A 1922 review of *Sorcières gigantesques* (a dance very similar to *Ombres gigantesques*) suggests that sometimes the shadows eclipsed the human dancers in importance: "The dancers, by virtue of their dark-colored costumes, grow indistinct in the greenish light of the projectors, leaving all intensity to the 'Chinese shadows.' "[75]

In her "shadow dances," then, Fuller reveals still more of her inclination to grant pride of place to the performance of light and shadow, a facet of her work that connects her to later theorists of the modern stage such as Gordon Craig and Adolphe Appia, who saw living actors as a hindrance in the struggle for theatrical expression and sought to replace them with shadows or puppets.[76]

Cinema

Even more than shadow play, film provided Loie Fuller an arena in which to indulge her desire to dissolve all performers into mere beams of light. In the last decade of her life she therefore turned some of her attention to this medium.

Although a number of films of Fuller (and her many imitators) dancing exist, she herself only began experimenting with cinema in the 1920s, when she and her lover Gabrielle Bloch (known professionally as Gab Sorère) made three films together: *Le Lys de la vie* (1921); *Visions des rêves* (1924); and *Les Incertitudes de Coppélius* (1927), based on E.T.A. Hoffmann's *The Sandman*. While, unfortunately, only *Le Lys de la vie* survives, it provides a rich example of Fuller's extension of her work with light and shadow into the realm of cinema.[77]

As we have seen, Fuller kept most of her work nonnarrative, largely out of a wish to focus attention on the play of light—to avoid distractions. In film,

[74] Sommer, "Loie Fuller," 61.

[75] Jane Catulle Mendès, "Les Ballets fantastiques de Loie Fuller et d'Aneika Yan," 11 June 1922, Collection Rondel.

[76] "Theoreticians like Maurice Maeterlink, Gordon Craig, or Adolphe Appia sought to solve this problem [purity of expression destroyed by the mediation of the actor] by substituting for the actor a puppet or shadow that is unable to use dialogue" (Elena Cueto-Asin, "The Chat Noir's Théâtre d'Ombres," in *Montmartre and the Making of Mass Culture*, ed. Gabriel Weisberg [New Brunswick, NJ: Rutgers University Press, 2001], 237).

[77] See Lista *Danseuse*; Garafola, *Diaghilev's Ballets Russe*, Bablet, *Esthetique générale*; Current and Current, *Loie Fuller*. Only the first half of *Le Lys de la vie* has been restored for public viewing. I have seen this half, thanks to curator Nicholas Villodre of the Cinémathèque de la Danse in Paris. All information about the second half has been obtained from earlier accounts or from Mr. Villodre.

Figure 1.12. Loie Fuller with Queen Marie of Romania, Bibliothèque Nationale de France

however, she turned to storytelling, perhaps feeling that cinema, as a medium composed purely of light, afforded her more freedom to indulge her taste for the dramatic. Accordingly, *Le Lys de la vie* is based on a story written by Fuller's close friend (and, possibly, lover) Queen Marie of Romania (fig. 1.12). One year earlier, in July of 1920, Fuller had mounted a danced stage production of *Le Lys* at the Théâtre de l'Opéra, employing her magic lantern and Chinese shadow techniques. The film version, however, differed substantially from the stage show and featured almost no dancing at all (save for two brief numbers by Fuller's troupe); more precisely, it focused on the "dance" of light and shadow. Shot at Paris's famed Gaumont Studios, with exteriors filmed on the French Riviera, outside of Cannes, it was a silent film one hour and twenty minutes in length, with direction, casting, lighting, sets, costumes, and some of the camera work by Fuller.[78]

We can assume that Queen Marie was a dance aficionado, for Le Lys borrows elements from several major Romantic ballets, including *Sleeping Beauty*, *Cinderella*, *Giselle*, and *Raymonda*. The film starts out as a basic fairytale: Two sisters—Princess Corona and Princess Mora—compete for the love of a vaguely Ottoman prince (played by the young René Clair in a turban) who arrives on horseback, seeking a wife.[79] Although the rest of the story hews to standard fairytale lines, it does so with one notable twist: a reversal of gender roles which turns *Le Lys de la vie* into a kind of proto-feminist adventure story. An onscreen caption, for example, describes the prince as "handsome as a star and as delicate as a tender branch." When this fragile prince succumbs to a mysterious illness and swoons into unconsciousness, the stalwart Princess Corona sets out on a heroic search for the magical "Lily of Life," which, she has heard, can restore health and happiness. Like any brave knight, she must traverse dangerous landscapes and fend off assailants in the pursuit of her goal. Ultimately, Corona succeeds in her quest, finds the lily, and returns triumphantly to cure her prince. Her heart is broken, though, and she dies of grief when the prince ungratefully chooses to marry her sister, Mora. But the story does not end in sorrow, for the fairies then resurrect Corona and she goes to live among them in the spirit world of the forest (fig. 1.13).

This saga unfolds against a series of elaborate and visually dense backdrops that would pass as "camp" today, but which were clearly meant to convey an atmosphere of Orientalist fantasy. The palace rooms are heavily draped in animal skins and lavish, patterned fabrics; the actors' costumes consist of simi-

---

[78] The musical accompaniment (played by an in-theater orchestra) likely consisted of the music used in the stage version: *Marche de fête* by Henri Büsser, *Marche solonelle* by Tchaikovsky, *The Haunted Forest* by MacDowell, and Berlioz's *Dance of the Sylphes*. The technicians at Gaumont were apparently disgruntled at Fuller's desire to control filming. But she did manage to convince them to yield the camera to her on numerous occasions (Loie Fuller, unpublished notes on the filming of *Le Lys de la vie*, NYPLPA).

[79] Clair, known at the time as René Chomette, went on to become a major silent film star. Other actors include Marjorie Mead, Flora Hart, and members of Fuller's dance troupe (who have only one, brief circle dance number).

Figure 1.13. Corona's Death scene, Bibliothèque Nationale de France

lar drapery. The prince's male attendant wears hoop earrings, a jeweled robe, and a lot of eyeliner. The film features four black actors in unnamed roles, two men and two small children—a girl and a boy both around five years old. The men appear to be African palace guards, for they are only seen standing at attention near the throne, holding spears. But for their loincloths, they are naked. The children play together and serve as junior attendants of the royals. At one point, they comically mirror adult behavior, imitating a couple kissing (this takes place in silhouette, with both kissing "couples" behind a scrim). Like the guards, the children wear only loincloths, only theirs are sequined. All other actors remains fully dressed. Another Orientalist detail is the palace monkey who plays at sticking his head repeatedly into the gaping, fanged mouth of the dead white bear serving as throne room rug. (I shall resist any vulgar Freudian reading of this.)

The role of court jester was played by the dwarf, Jean-Paul Le Tarare, a playwright and well-known figure in the Paris art world. Le Tarare is the same height as the children, and his frizzy, uncombed hairstyle oddly resembles the little girl's. When at one point the child appears in silhouette, she is discon-

certingly easy to mistake for Le Tarare—an example perhaps of Fuller's fondness for mirror images. (Fuller herself refused to appear on camera and has no
role in the film.)[80]

Fuller was not using film to perform a fairytale so much as she was using a
fairytale to "perform" a film, to turn the stage fully over to the camera. Like a
modernist painter who draws attention to brushstroke and canvas, Fuller
sought to acknowledge her medium, rendering palpable the camera's presence.
She accomplished this in part by repeatedly using a "closing iris" motif, creating
transitions between scenes by gradually narrowing the visual field into a shrink-
ing circle and then opening out that circle again in the following scene—
reproducing what one might see while closing and opening a camera's aperture.

Fuller's most interesting effects occur though during the scenes of Corona's
mystical journey through dangerous lands, en route to find the Lily of Life.[81]
In the "Pays de l'Effroi" (or "Land of Fright"), for example, she must walk
among terrifying monsters created by projecting disembodied hands and heads
onto a black screen and having them float and fly about menacingly These
monsters, of course, echo the giant hands of Fuller's shadow dances, as well
as the "amputated" body parts visible in her "mirror room." It is in Corona's
voyage through the "Haunted Forest," though, that Fuller did her most significant experimenting, deciding to incorporate film negatives into the scene,
so that actors' bodies were rendered transparent, more spiritlike than human.
This scene likely represents the first use anywhere of "negative imaging," although Jean Cocteau would later claim credit for it after employing it in his
1930 film, Le Sang d'un poète.[82] Moreover, beyond merely projecting film negatives, Fuller chose to intersperse them with non-reversed, opaque images, creating, as Giovanni Lista has written, a "passage from negative to positive and
vice versa, allowing her to make visible the role of light."[83]

Fuller further enhanced the oneiric quality of the Haunted Forest by slowing
down the film's motion, affording a dreamy, floating motion to the witches
and fairies who populate the forest (fig. 1.14). Lynn Garafola observes that
"Fuller was one of the first filmmakers to experiment with the new technique
[of slow motion] for poetic ends, creating fleeting dreamlike images that 'freed'

[80] See Townsend, *Alchemic Visions*; also Lista, *Danseuse*, 520 ff. Additional information on this
film was gathered through personal conversation with Nicholas Villodre.

[81] For descriptions of the second half of the film, Corona's journey and the conclusion, I must
rely on written accounts, since sadly this reel is no longer available for public viewing.

[82] Silvagni, "L'Etonnante vie de la fée lumière."

[83] Lista, *Danseuse*, 535. See also Lynn Garafola, "Dance, Film, and the Ballets Russes," *Dance
Research* 16, no. 1 (Summer 1998): 3–25. Also Sommer, "Loie Fuller," in *International Encyclopedia
of Dance*.

Figure 1.14. Witches in the Haunted Forest, *Le Lys de la vie*, Bibliothèque Nationale de France

the medium from illusionism and imbued it with fantasy."[84] While *Le Lys de
la vie* met with only limited success when it appeared, Fuller's innovative
cinematography proved highly influential to many major artists, including
Fernand Léger, Man Ray, and Pavel Tchelitchev. Unfortunately, she rarely
received any acknowledgment for this influence.

Le Lys de la vie is valuable not only as evidence of Fuller's most advanced
technological experimentation, but also for its peculiar condensation and
jumble of the main aesthetic strains of her career, both those she embraced
and those she sought to leave behind. It is a film artistically at war with
itself, filled with contradictions. While unquestionably a daring and experimental foray into early modernist cinematography, it is also very much a
nineteenth-century–style, romantic fairytale, built around the Art Nouveau
motif of the lily. On the other hand, it depicts a nearly all-female universe in
which the key male figure remains unconscious through most of the story.[85]

[84] Garafola tells us that *Le Lys de la vie* had a great influence on Pavel Tchelitchev, who in
1928 produced a film for the Ballets Russes production of *Ode* in which a large hand was projected
onto a white screen, stopping over a real box appearing on stage, which is placed on the ground
by a dancer representing "la Nature" (Garafola, "Dance, Film, and the Ballets Russes," 17–18).

[85] Recent critical work on *Le Lys de la vie* finds in it a subtext of lesbian sexuality. Julie Townsend sees the film as a "mass production of queer desire insofar as it can change form at any
moment, has no heterolinear goal, and seeks to escape the constraints of narrative and the limitations of physics" (Townsend, "Alchemic Visions," 93–94). Townsend also points to how well

The film also has a complicated relationship to bodies, sex, and race. Beyond a chaste kiss, which is defused of eros by the children's mimicry of it, there is no overt display of sexual desire or passion. The enamored princess Corona not only never marries, she abandons her fleshly life for a purely spiritual one among the forest's (all female) fairies—the narrative equivalent perhaps of Fuller's constant evaporation into light and fabric onstage. Yet, at the same time, the films allows extensive glimpses of naked human flesh in those exposed bodies of the African men and children—in their virtually identical diaperlike costumes.

With this potpourri aesthetic, Le Lys de la vie may best be likened to a kind of Cubist collage of Fuller's influences and tendencies. Although we are granted no single perspective, fragments of many elements of her work are conjured by the film: the issue of balancing narrative with the performance of light and movement, the paradox of a flesh-and-blood woman who turns into a fairy (or a " fée éléctricité," perhaps), the complicated dance of real bodies and their shadow companions, a desire for wholesomeness at odds with a taste for the unsettling, uncanny power of dancing fragmented body parts, and the conventions of Orientalism.

In other words, with Le Lys de la vie Fuller's usually smooth and abstract surface gives way somewhat and offers us a more overt depiction of the issues roiling beneath Fuller's image, the persona I have named "Electric Salome." To make sense of these issues, we shall have to consider more directly the politics of Fuller's technologized veil dances within their context in the age of empire.

Fuller's work overall corresponds to Terry Castle's theory that lesbian love is often narrated through "ghostly apparitions." See Terry Castle, The Apparitional Lesbian (New York: Columbia University Press, 1993).

Chapter Two

Electric Salome: Loie Fuller at the World's Fair of 1900

A Handsome Savage

Loie Fuller's film *Le Lys de la vie* is anomalous in her oeuvre for at least two reasons: First, it features black performers—the two young children and two "African" male palace guards (whose nationalities remain unknown).[1] Second, it features performers in a state of near total undress. Of course, these unclothed performers *are* the four black actors, who all wear no more than sarong-like waist wraps. The men's bare, muscular torsos, furthermore, are repeatedly panned with delectation by the camera.

Given that she spent a career swathing herself and her dancers in hundreds of yards of fabric, what does it mean that Fuller permits a single glimpse of nakedness only in her rare use of nonwhite performers, and then only for men and children?[2] An initial answer is that Fuller was not immune to the racism of her time and saw persons of color as somehow lesser creatures, more tethered to fleshly concerns and, therefore, more appropriate to display unclothed. Another, complementary answer is that within Fuller's universe of disavowed

[1] Fuller's presentation of black people in this manner was consistent with other commercial depictions of the era. As historian Dana Hale observes, throughout the 1920s and '30s, images of blacks "in the role of the child and as soldiers" were widely used as product trademarks. Hale points, for example, to the famous wide-eyed grinning soldier whose face long adorned packages and advertisements for "Banania," a chocolate-banana–flavored breakfast drink. This figure, known as "*le tirailleur sénégalais*," actually resembles Loie Fuller's palace guards very strongly (the guards also grin conspicuously). See Dana S. Hale, "French Images of Race on Product Trademarks during the Third Republic," in *The Color of Liberty: Histories of Race in France*, ed. Sue Peabody and Tyler Stovall (Raleigh, NC: Duke University Press, 2003), 137.

[2] Fuller's only other use of a black performer seems to be in her 1907 stage production of *Salome*, in which an African slave performs the execution of John the Baptist and carries the severed head in on a charger.

eroticism, exposing a *woman's* body would be simply too charged an act, and too close to revealing her own never-to-be-seen body onstage. Consequently, she chose to unveil only those bodies that would be more erotically neutral for her: men's and children's. Or perhaps Fuller felt free to expose naked flesh only in the medium of film, which safely dissolves substance into light and shadow.

There is truth to all of these explanations, but they do little to resolve the larger issues raised by the film, for *Le Lys de la vie* makes us question more than its own limited depiction of racialized bodies. The film's very anomalous quality—its splashy Orientalism, combined with its quasi-nudity and multi-ethnic cast of characters (the apparently colonized Africans as well as the turban-wearing Middle Eastern visitors), all invite us to look back at Fuller's usually more self-contained work as a whole and investigate the assumptions about race, flesh, and empire that lay beneath its ostensibly apolitical surface.

To begin, we might turn to a curious anecdote in Fuller's autobiography which recounts an experience at the Colonial Exposition of 1907 in Marseille, where she was herself performing (in a theater that she shared with a popular all-female troupe of Cambodian dancers, underscoring Fuller's own proximity to "Oriental entertainment"). While touring the exhibition, Fuller is introduced to the king of the Djoloff tribe in Senegal: "a magnificent negro, six feet high, who looked like some prince from the *Thousand and One Nights*." "What a handsome savage," Fuller says audibly in French to friends, "I wonder if they are all built on this model in Africa."[3] To her great embarrassment, Fuller discovers that the "savage" in question has been educated in Paris and has understood her every word.

The remainder of the anecdote takes several striking turns. In her zeal to make amends for her rudeness, Fuller asks (and receives) permission to witness one of the king's religious ceremonies. She then watches as he leads a group of men in Muslim prayers:

> He gave the order to begin the ceremony. . . . The unity of the mo-
> tions of all these men was simply wonderful. All together they said
> the same brief prayer, and with mechanical precision made the same
> movement, which, from the point of view of devotion, seemed to
> have similar importance to the words of their ritual. The large
> white cloaks, spread over long blue blouses, waved round their
> bodies. The men prostrated themselves, touched the ground with

[3] Fuller, *Fifteen Years*, 171–72.

their foreheads and then raised themselves together. The rhythm and precision were most impressive.[4]

After the prayers, Fuller learns that although the king has four wives, none of them has accompanied him to France. She is surprised, she tells him, "that he traveled without them, especially in a country where there are so many pretty women." Her remark sparks the following exchange:

> *King*: From the point of view of my wives a white woman has neither charm nor beauty.
> *Fuller*: Are you so sure of that? If a white woman with long blonde hair should suddenly appear in your country, among your black women, would she not be taken for an angel?
> *King*: Oh no, she would be taken for a devil. Angels are black in our Paradise.

Fuller finds this response revelatory: "It had never before appeared so clear to me that men make their gods in their own image, rather than that the gods make men after theirs."[5]

The anecdote's circuitous trajectory is revealing. By her own account, Fuller's first view of this man is at least as racist and appraising as was her camera's gaze upon those African palace guards. Oddly, while she never permitted herself any public expression of erotic appreciation for women, Fuller was not shy when it came to her admiration for handsome (black) men.[6] At the same time, her admiration is mediated by the reference to *Thousand and One Nights*.[7] Part of her delight comes from the Orientalist fantasy of the scene, reinforced by the colonialist setting of the Marseilles Exposition. While the king of Djoloff was not a performer, he is a colonized spectacle for Fuller—a presumably uncomprehending object to gaze upon freely, in a perfect reversal of her own frequently staged scenarios of unconscious performance.

Fuller's subsequent embarrassment derives from the fact that the "savage" has understood her. She had not enjoyed the immunity of a unilateral gaze, as she had thought. Instead, the king had gazed back upon her with understanding, shattering her fantasy of his unconsciousness.

---

[4] Ibid., 174.

[5] Ibid., 174–76.

[6] Fuller's open expressions of love for women were limited to ambiguously worded paeans to "dear friends," such as Gabrielle Bloch, or Queen Marie of Romania (who was likely also one of her lovers).

[7] Fuller would later mount a rather lavish Orientalist production of *Thousand and One Nights* in 1915, with music by her friend Armande de Polignac.

Once thus "exposed," Fuller tries to evacuate some of the implied eros and
exoticism from their encounter by moving quickly from flesh to spirit—that is,
by asking to witness his evening prayers. But by granting him his piety, Fuller
also reimposes upon the king his status as spectacle, a fact confirmed by her
description of his prayers, which places them in an indisputably theatrical context. In fact, as described by Fuller, this Islamic prayer session resembles nothing
so much as one of her own mirror dances: the men pray as mirror images of
one another; they move with "mechanical" precision; they are identically
dressed; and—the most Fulleresque detail—the movement of their floating
garments rivals that of their own bodies. In other words, in her desire to disavow her frankly assessing gaze upon the king's fleshly body, Fuller repositions
him as a mirror image of herself, as a kind of magical, spiritual performer. This
tells us something about the close but uneasy relationship Fuller constructed
between the erotic on one side, and her idea of the spiritual and theatrical
worlds on the other. The latter seem to mitigate or defang the former and
provide her recourse when she is caught with her mind in the gutter. Theater
(read: Fuller's brand of theater) and spirituality are the reassuring opposites of
flesh and desire. We might recall here that in Le Lys de la vie, when Princess
Corona fails to marry her Middle Eastern prince, she dies and is resurrected as
one of the dancing fairies of the Haunted Forest, as if the consolation for the
loss of erotic union with the Orient is a bodiless, theatricalized spirituality—
the very trajectory implicit in this story of the Senegalese tribal king.

We see more of Fuller's contradictory thoughts on these matters when she
combines her sexual gaze upon the king with her new, ostensibly spiritual tack
by suggesting that his four wives ought to be sexually jealous of blond European women, whom he would surely take for "angels." Her distinction is clear
and as old as Europe's bifurcated views of the Orient and Occident: Africans
would surely assume white Europeans to be closer to God, more spiritual, even
angels. But the distinction is immediately undone by Fuller's suggestion that
these pure "angels" are also sexual sirens who could entice a man into adultery.

Fuller claims to draw from this encounter the moral lesson that both sexual
attractiveness and religious iconography are culturally determined. What she
actually recounts, though, is the inability of her religious pose to obscure erotic
expression. Fuller's exchange with the king reveals the inseparability of her
religious posturing and her private investment in her own desirability. After
all, Fuller was herself a blond, Western woman—an "angel" of presumably the
same home-wrecking attributes about which she warned the king. For Fuller,
the chaste virtue of white womanhood is apparently an easily collapsed façade—a fact we should keep in mind when studying her "bodiless" dances.
Similarly, the careful dichotomy that Fuller constructs for the Senegalese

man—handsome savage versus observant Muslim royal—collapses under the weight of her continued flirtation with him as she witnesses his prayers.[8]

The anecdote's series of uneasy dichotomies—eros versus theatrical religion; colonized savage versus pious Muslim king; Orient versus Europe—all ultimately break down. The story, furthermore, contains an odd reversal of expected gender roles (as did *Le Lys de la vie*): a man is subjected to a woman's rather macho (or butch) appraisal of his physique, through his prayer; he then performs a kind of Oriental dance for her, after which he must deflect her innuendo about provocative white women with long blond hair. And it all takes place at a French colonial fair, where Fuller herself fulfilled a double role, appearing as a Westerner, a white woman, while doing her veil dances on the same program as the colonized and very "Oriental" *cambodgiennes*.

Such uneasy dichotomies were always present in Fuller's work. Her dances enacted a struggle between eros and performance; and the subtext of her work very often treated racial and geographical difference, despite her ostensible detachment from politics. Fuller, after all, made her career performing "pseudo-Eastern veil dance[s]," as Emily Apter has remarked, as the first and arguably most famous in a long series of cabaret "Salome's."[9] Fuller had, furthermore, a special relationship with the world of colonial exhibitions, having attained a nearly mythic stature in France through her appearance at the heavily imperialist *Exposition Universelle* of 1900. To understand Loie Fuller's unique and politically charged position as the "Electric Salome" of her time, we need to begin with her status as "pseudo-Eastern veil dancer" and, accordingly, with her apotheosis at the World's Fair of 1900, where Fuller rose from the rank of cabaret performer to that of a world-renowned artist. Such a discus-

---

[8] Confirmatory evidence of Fuller's stake in "purifying" any apparent sexual impropriety appears in an anecdote recounted in her unpublished papers. In a short essay entitled "My Scotch [sic] Minister," Fuller describes making the acquaintance of a Scottish missionary at a bookstore in Edinburgh, while performing in that city. The missionary, who has never been to the theater in his life, makes an exception for Fuller and agrees to watch one of her performances from the wings. When it is all over, and she is taking her curtain call, the minister, overwhelmed by her grace and beauty, rushes onstage from his hiding place and "had me in his arms before the whole audience and this is what he said, 'It's no dance at all, it's what the angels do!' " (NYPLPA). The story encapsulates perfectly Fuller's keen interest in the proximity of religious fervor, her own art form, and the potential for unregulated physical contact or desire between men and women. The proper minister, who had always foresworn the temptations of theater, makes an exception in his moral code and winds up on the stage publicly embracing a woman. As Fuller had with the Senegalese man, the minister disavows the impropriety of his reaction by insisting she is an angel.

[9] Emily Apter, *Continental Drift: From National Characters to Virtual Subjects* (Chicago: University of Chicago Press, 1999), 142.

sion requires a brief digression into the format of this Fair, particularly its careful marriage of science and empire.

The World's Fair of 1900

"All that interests the French about the Empire is the belly dance," said Prime Minister Jules Ferry, and it was true that, despite the enormous increase in France's empire in the last quarter of the nineteenth century, the general public evinced little interest in its country's conquests.[10] Concerned by this apparent apathy, officials of the World's Fairs of 1889 and 1900 sought to promote awareness and acceptance of the Empire. Camille Guy, director of the 1900 Fair's ministry of colonies, wrote openly in his report, "The great honor of the Third Republic will be to have bestowed upon France an immense colonial empire and to have designed the practical means with which to profit from it. Our colonies do not have enough colonists, but . . . with the help of this experience [the fair] they will have more every year."[11]

Before the World's Fair of 1900 opened to the public, its commissioner general, Alfred Picard, announced his certainty that it "would inaugurate the twentieth century."[12] This insistence on the modern and on futurity, particularly on scientific advancement, was inextricable from the Fair's vast pageantry of empire. Visitors were meant to come away from the Fair with the unshakable understanding that colonialism represented one more inevitable step in France's march into the future.

Science had always been the handmaiden of imperialism, of course. Advances in technology held tremendous importance in the so-called "new imperialism" of the late nineteenth century. Steamships, railways, the telegraph, and—especially—electricity had all contributed greatly to colonial conquest. Indeed, electricity became the focal point of the whole exposition, as crowds were encouraged to marvel at countless displays of its magic, including the mechanically propelled walkways (patterned after those at Chicago's Columbia Exposition in 1893), the electrically powered panorama and stereorama displays, and the dazzling colored lights projected over the fairgrounds at night. Electricity eventually took on the allegorical weight of the whole expo-

---

[10] Qtd. in Raoul Girardet, *L'Idée coloniale en France de 1871 à 1962* (Paris: La Table Ronde, 1972), 75.

[11] Camille Guy, *Exposition Universelle de 1900, Publication de la commission* (Paris: Augustin Challamel, 1901), 28.

[12] Alfred Picard, *Le Bilan d'un siècle* (Paris: Imprimerie Nationale, 1906), 1.

sition, becoming the "fée électricité," a spirit embodying all the promise of a new century. As journalist Paul Morand wrote in his account of the Fair:

> The Electricity Fairy triumphs at the Exposition; she is born in heaven like true kings. The public laughs at the words, "danger of death," written on the pylons. It knows that electricity cures everything. It is progress, the poetry of the poor and the rich; it brings illumination. . . . At night, the spotlights sweep the Champs de Mars, the Chateau d'Eau shimmers in cyclamen tints and falls in showers of green and purple light. . . . Electricity is accumulated, condensed, transformed, bottled . . . it is the scourge and the religion of 1900.[13]

The Chateau D'Eau mentioned by Morand was an oversized waterfall illuminated at night by rotating colored lights in a style unmistakably indebted to Fuller's. This grandly lit waterfall stood at the entrance to the Fair's imperial headquarters: the Parc du Trocadéro, 50,000 square meters devoted to colonial exhibitions. The Trocadéro was divided into two main sections: French territories on one side, foreign-owned colonies on the other. On the French side, nineteen pavilions represented all the nation's colonies and protectorates. Temples, palaces, pyramids, and huts featured scenes of "native life" using live actors and electrical *trompe l'oeil* effects. At the Algerian display, for example, a moving stereorama recreated a sea voyage to Oran. Passengers boarded a realistic boat that lurched and swayed as a salty "sea breeze" wafted by and rotating panorama disks depicted the approaching Algerian coastline. Visitors "disembarked" to find a recreated Algerian café complete with music and young women performing the *danse du ventre*, because regardless of all the modern technology, alluring women of color were still hired as living advertisements for the voluptuous charms of the colonies.

This heavy marketing of exotic dancers had begun at the 1889 *Exposition*, the first to include North African and Asian dance among the attractions. At that Fair, spectators were introduced to dances from Algeria, Java, Indonesia, and—most famously—Egypt. It was the 1889 Egyptian pavilion that featured the racy "Rue du Caire" exhibition, a catchall array of Arab-influenced entertainments, but particularly devoted to the sensuous *danse du ventre* or "belly dance"; and although this was but one of dozens of different dances from myriad locales, the name stuck as a generic term for any "exotic" dance per-

[13] Paul Morand, *1900 A.D.*, trans. Rollilly Feden (New York: William Farquhar Payson, 1931), 65.

Figure 2.1. "Oriental" dancers at the 1900 World's Fair, Bibliothèque Nationale de France

formed by any woman from a colonized country (figs. 2.1, 2.2, 2.3).[14] In his memoirs, Edmond de Goncourt described visitors to the Rue du Caire as a "population in heat reminiscent of cats spraying on coals."[15] As dance historian Anne Décoret-Ahiha points out, the *danse du ventre* was "an Occidental term coined by leering colonial soldiers, implying a single choreographic essence common to the whole Orient and to all Oriental women."[16] The multi-

[14] As Anne Décoret-Ahiha writes, "Despite the multiplicity of dances presented—the Dance of Candles, The Chair Dance, The Dance of Shudders, The Handkerchief Dance, The Sword Dance—despite the plurality of cultures—Egyptian, Algerian, Moroccan, Persian, Turkish,—and of artists—the Ouled Nail of southern Algeria, the Egyptian ghawâzî, the chickhat of Morocco—in the minds of visitors an image formed of but a single dance: the 'belly dance' " (Anne Décoret-Ahiha, *Les Danses exotiques en France 1880–1940* [Paris: Centre National de la Danse, 2004], 28).

[15] Edmond de Goncourt, *Journal: Mémoires de la vie littéraire* (Monaco: Les Editions de l'Imprimerie Nationale de Monaco, 1956), 16:100, 2 July 1889. Qtd. in Zeynep Çelik and Leila Kinney, "Ethnography and Exhibitionism at the Expositions Universelles," *Assemblage* 13 Dec. 1990, 35–59.

[16] Décoret-Ahiha, *Les Danses exotiques*, 28.

Figure 2.2. World's Fair performers of "Moorish" dance, Bibliothèque Nationale de France

ple nationalities and styles of dance at the 1889 Fair coalesced into this reduc-tive stereotype of the belly dance and a concomitant stereotypical performer of said dance, "la belle Fatma," a generic, undulating, colonized woman. At the same time, another, more ancient archetypal woman melded in the popular imagination with Fatma: Salome, the biblical princess whose dance brings down a prophet. As a contemporary critic wrote of the dancing women at the 1889 Fair: "Daughters of slaves or of princesses, they all have humble souls, passive spirits, and empty heads; they know that they, *like Salome*, must en-flame men to the marrow of their bones" (emphasis added).[17] The most ac-

---

[17] Enrique Gomez-Carrillo, *Quelques petites âmes d'ici et d'ailleurs* (Paris: Sansot, 1904), qtd. in Décoret-Ahiha, *Les Danses exotiques*, 28. Sarah Graham Brown writes, "The Middle Eastern 'dancing girl' . . . the poses she adopts, and her profession itself . . . suggest lasciviousness and sensuality. Oriental dance is also associated with the biblical story of Salome, a frequent theme in Western paintings, literature and music, investing it with sinister undertones of destruction and sexual revenge" (Sarah Graham Brown, *Images of Women: The Portrayal of Women in Photog-raphy of the Middle East 1860–1950* [New York: Columbia University Press, 1988], 170).

Figure 2.3. Egyptian "almée" or dancing woman, World's Fair 1900, Bibliothèque
Nationale de France

claimed of the Fair's many belly and veil dancers were those in Algeria's all-female Ouled Nail troupe, who entertained onstage with their famous "mobile bellies" and offstage by strolling around in scanty costumes.[18]

These sensuous dances, however, did not please everyone. Some French officials, particularly a certain Senator Bérenger, found them offensive, which led not only to some censoring in 1889, but also to the imposition of "decency codes" on the subsequent World's Fair of 1900. Contemporary satirist Gaston Bergeret described the effects of these codes: "As for the belly dance . . . because of orders of the Senate, they had to remove all voluptuousness . . . these almées have been reduced to doing dislocating abdominal exercises that one could, without danger, ask twelve-year-old schoolgirls to do. Far from feeling moved to debauchery, one gets a stomach ache just looking at these controlled houris."[19]

Some of the colonized women entertaining at the Fair of 1900 did not even have to dance; they were paid simply to live their daily lives in public as part of Trocadéro's recreated "native villages," which were essentially living diorama exhibitions. Here, as at the Jardin d'Acclimatation, both men and women, imported from France's colonies, were paid to tend to their children, cook their meals, and weave cloth in full view of European passersby.[20] (They did not however, sleep at the Fair, but rather in temporary camps outside its gates, in the sixteenth arrondissement;[21] (figs. 2.4, 2.5.)

These exhibitions served a dual purpose, as Paul Greenhalgh has observed: to allow spectators "to see at a glance their empire, to take visual possession of it, and to show the backward living conditions of the colonized nations, which were being elevated by France's colonial mission civilisatrice."[22] The offi-

[18] The Ouled Nail were rare among Algerian women in that they appeared in public unveiled. They became known in France initially through Flaubert's description of them in his travel journals. Jean Lorrain described them this way: "Hairless, fragrant, cold flesh, a warm odor of spice and filth emanating from bestial nudity" (qtd. in Philippe Jullian, Jean Lorrain [Paris: Flammarion, 1950], 234). Zeynep Çelik informs us that the "Ouled Nail girls came from the poorest desert tribes" of colonial Algeria, and that the commercialization of their dance was "closely associated with prostitution under French rule, becom[ing] increasingly erotic as it changed locales from the desert . . . to urban centers, and, eventually to the stages of the Parisian universal expositions" (Çelik and Kinney, "Ethnography and Exhibition," 40).

[19] Gaston Bergeret, Journal d'un nègre à l'exposition de 1900 (Paris: Librarie L. Conque, L. Carteret et Cie, Successeur, 1901), 15.

[20] As Paul Greenhalgh observes, "The normal method of display was to create a backdrop in a more or less authentic tableau-vivant fashion and situate people in it, going about what was thought to be their daily business. . . . brought in from all French empire holdings, groups were settled in to live—night and day—for six months . . . and expected to perform religious rituals and display crafts for tourists" (Greenhalgh, Ephemeral Vistas, 83).

[21] Jullian, Art Nouveau, 165.

[22] See Greenhalgh, Ephemeral Vistas, 84.

Figure 2.4. The Congo Pavilion at the Fair, with a "native" dwelling outside, Bibliothèque Nationale de France

cial "illustrated guide" to the French colonial exhibition at the Trocadéro made this point explicitly: "The greatest desire of the Ministry of Foreign Affairs and Colonies and their collaborators, has been to develop in the eyes of visitors . . . the work of progress and humanity that France has undertaken in its overseas territories. Our country will easily see the benefits brought about by our far-off conquests, by witnessing the peoples of these countries as they once were, and as they are now. In this way, our colonial exposition will power-fully advance colonial expansion."[23] And while most of the Trocadéro's exhibi-tions were designed to be agreeable diversions, occasionally through all the entertainment, glimpses of the terrible violence inherent in colonialism would break through, as at France's Madagascar pavilion, which featured a panorama display described here by André Hallays:

[23] Commissariat de l'Exposition Coloniale, *Guide illustré de l'Exposition Coloniale Française au Trocadéro en 1900* (Paris: Cambrai, 1900), xxviii.

Figure 2.5. Daily procession of Arab "natives" in traditional dress, World's Fair 1900, Bibliothèque Nationale de France

Madagascar is exhibiting a grand panorama, the capture of Tananarivo. . . . Rarely has optical illusion been carried so far. The groups are lifelike and the view of the capital of the Hovas is picturesque. But perhaps it was not really necessary to scatter the ground with horribly blood stained Malagasy corpses. This spectacle is in rather bad taste. Unless I am mistaken, we are here in group XVII, class 113; methods of colonization.[24]

The bloody destruction inherent in colonial wars was of course the dirty little secret simmering beneath the World's Fair's pomp and circumstance, its consumable pleasures and seemingly benign ethnographic interest in the "territories overseas." As Paul Greenhalgh has written:

Empire here was transformed from military and commercial conquest, from the brutal control of other peoples for cynical economic purposes, to propagandistic entertainment, to a fair. The gaiety of the pavilions was purposely meant to hide the darker side of the gloried conquest, the

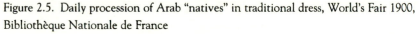

[24] André Hallays, En flânant: A Travers l'expo de 1900 (Paris: Perrin, 1901), 1.

near genocide which had at different times occurred all over the imperial world, . . . the Exposition was in every way a harlequin's mask hiding
brutish heavy features beneath.[25]

While more unsettling than most of the Trocadéro's entertainments, the
bloody corpses of Madagascar partook nonetheless of the Fair's pervasive motif
of transgressive viewing—the staged observation of objects normally hidden
from view: colonial life, foreign customs, far-off landscapes, and women. Inside
the "native villages" it was often the women being thus "enframed" as elusive,
inaccessible specimens. The colonial women, that is, appeared as the objects
of impeded vision—partly obscured to the spectator by various obstacles: a
veil, a door, a barred or covered window. The *Hachette* guide to the Fair, for
example, informs us that at the Moroccan pavilion, families observed the
Islamic custom of keeping wives and daughters hidden. Accordingly, fairgoers
could espy the women only through "little harem windows, narrow and mysterious" (fig. 2.6).[26] Women were similarly hidden in the "Algerian village," as
we learn from the *Figaro* guidebook, which also reveals how the modestly
hidden women were juxtaposed with the belly-baring ones:

> Let us cross the threshold of Babel-oued, here we are in the Rue de la
> Kasbah. The steep path snakes around . . . behind the barred doors and
> windows pass the shadows of mysterious veiled women. . . . We pass huts
> where belly dancing, sword dancing, [and] restaurants proudly displaying
> Arab cuisine all form a multicolored tableau, most animated and lively.[27]

Once again, the women are glimpsed only through doors and windows, and
to the *Figaro* correspondent, they seemed even more elusive, rendered mere
shadows in a display case. Such overt arrangement of colonized subjects in
box-like settings or vitrines—as so many scientific specimens—partook of a
very common nineteenth-century exhibitionary technique. Writing, for example, of the huge trade in photographic images of North African women
during this time, Malek Alloula has observed that the women tended to be
depicted as if unaware of the camera's gaze, as "butterflies and insects that
museums of natural history and taxidermists exhibit[ed] in their glass display
cases."[28] This kind of staged unconsciousness on the part of the photographed
subject, of course, served to intensify the viewer's experience of transgression
into a forbidden realm, heightening titillation. The World's Fair's mise-en-

[25] Greenhalgh, *Ephemeral Vistas*, 67.

[26] *Guide Hachette à l'Exposition Universelle* (Paris: Librairie Hachette 1900), 272.

[27] *Guide bleu du Figaro à L'Exposition de 1900* (Paris: Le Figaro, 1900), 88.

[28] Alloula, *The Colonial Harem*, 92.

Figure 2.6. A recreated North African street in the Trocadéro, Bibliothèque
Nationale de France

scène of indigenous colonized peoples, particularly the women, functioned precisely in this fashion.

As described in the *Figaro* guidebook, the Algerian women become mere shadows, as if the imperial gaze constructed by the Fair has deprived them of even their fleshly contours. Glimpsed through bars, they became cinematic ghosts, reminiscent of the various photographic and technological wonders displayed elsewhere at the World's Fair (including the first projection of film on giant screens, by the Lumière brothers). In this way, these exhibited women remind us of the profound connection between the colonial entertainments of the Trocadéro and the ostensibly unrelated scientific "marvels" of the Fair— most of which focused on seeing the formerly unseeable via new technologies. At the Salle Pasteur, for example, visitors could enjoy projected slide images of all of the world's known microbes, the formerly invisible causes of human pathology. In the Salles Galilée and Flammarion, stars were magnified up to 300,000 times what the naked eye could see. And at the Salle Roux, amoebae, paramecia, and other such organisms provided the entertainment, revealing their tiny, secret details thanks to the magnifying glass in an exhibition enti-tled "Living Worlds in a Drop of Salt Water."

Amid all these attractions, poised on the Right Bank between the Pont d'Iéna and the Pont des Invalides, stood Le Théâtre Loie Fuller, claiming to be neither a colonial exhibition nor a palace of scientific marvels—just the home of France's most famous adopted American woman. But every night as she performed her *danses lumineuses*, spinning her veils under the rotating lights, Fuller was also whipping up a unique amalgam of the Fair's brand of crowd-pleasing science and imperialist politics, all delivered via a scenario of trans-gressive gazing which recalled much of the implicit structure of the entire Fair.

Queen of the Fair

From this dusty and confused fair, I retain only one vibrant and flam-boyant image: Madame Loie Fuller . . . a fat, rather ugly American woman with glasses, who stood on a trap door maneuvering her veils. . . . Let us salute this dancer . . . this phantom of an era.[29]

An effigy of Loie Fuller whirling under the projectors should have crowned the [Fair's entrance], Her . . . quality of movement could be found in all the truly modern parts of the exhibition. Loie Fuller . . . seemed to epitomize the spirit of the exhibition.[30]

[29] Cocteau, 5.
[30] Jullian, *Art Nouveau*, 4.

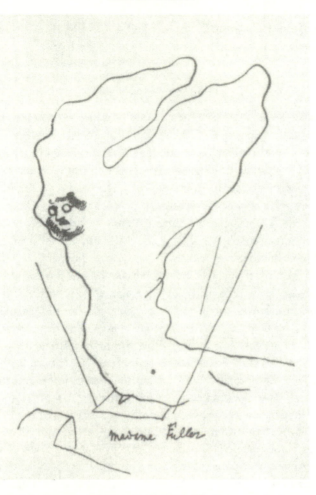

Figure 2.7. Caricature of Loie Fuller's World's Fair image by Jean
Cocteau, 1935, Bibliothèque Nationale de France

In April of 1900, when the Fair opened its gates, Loie Fuller was still known
in France by her original nickname, "la fée lumière." But by the Fair's closing
in November of that year, Fuller had become "la fée éléctricité." Having
melded metonymically with this modern allegorical sprite, she was henceforth
inextricable from the triumphal spirit of the new French century (fig. 2.7).

Fuller owed this acclaim in part to her obvious artistic alliance with electricity. But had this been her only connection to the ethos of the Exposition, she
would never have attained her apotheosis. Fuller's function at the Fair went

far beyond being "electrical." As we shall see, on many levels, her performances helped carry out the ideological work of the Fair.

Fuller and Art Nouveau

Fuller's close association with Art Nouveau was one key factor in her intense popularity at the exposition. The distinctive curvilinear elegance characteristic of Art Nouveau architecture dominated the fairgrounds, for example, in the form of two pavilions designed by architect Hector Guimard (known now largely for his ornate Métro entrances): the Grand and Petit Palais, which still stand today—the only two structures from this Fair to have been spared the wrecking ball. Throughout the Fair's galleries and boutiques, Art Nouveau *objets* of all sorts were also heavily promoted—both fine art meant for collectors and more affordable knickknacks for average shoppers.

One of the most trumpeted and popular exhibitions was the "Maison d'Art Nouveau"—a six-room model home decorated entirely with Art Nouveau art works and furnishings—prominently sitting on the Fair's Esplanade des Invalides.[31] Designed by painter Georges de Feure and commissioned by influential German-born art collector Samuel Bing, the house particularly reflected the Japanese strains within Art Nouveau style. Bing was famous for his championing of Japanese decorative arts, having traveled to Japan and subsequently published his impressions in a book—*Artistic Japan* (1885)—that would exercise profound influence over a new generation of decorative artists in Europe. As Fiona Gallagher has written, Bing "helped define the emerging key elements of the new Art Nouveau Style [which was] strongly indebted to the art of Japan."[32]

When we consider Loie Fuller's own proximity to Art Nouveau, we must, in fact, acknowledge how much her work—especially in its simple yet sinuous lines and intense colors—echoed the dominant aesthetic of Japanese decorative arts. The similarity was not accidental: "Everything that comes from Japan has always interested me intensely," she declared in her autobiography.[33] Giovanni Lista observes that Fuller was drawn to the same quality in Japanese drawing that attracted the Art Nouveau artists: the vital, expressive mobility of its lines. Lista notes especially the closeness between Fuller's mutating, ephemeral shapes and those of Japanese ornamental motifs, which "metamorphose, and continually pass from form to form . . . animal, landscape, tree, leaf

[31] See Richard D. Mandel, *Paris 1900: The Great World's Fair* (Toronto: University of Toronto Press, 1967), and Debora Silverman, *Art Nouveau in Fin-de-siècle France*.

[32] Fiona Gallagher, *Christie's Art Nouveau* (New York: Watson-Guptill Publications, 2000), 6, 121.

[33] Loie Fuller, *Fifteen Years*, 207.

... while detached from the organic whole to which the line belongs." For Lista, Japanese decorative style, Art Nouveau, and Fuller's performances all share a focus on a "repetitive and germinative power, a proliferating nature."[34]

So strong, in fact, was Fuller's fascination with Japanese art that she decided to share her own theater at the Fair with a Japanese troupe in which she had taken a serious interest after seeing them in London—Shosei Niwaka, directed by Kawakami Otojiro and featuring his wife, actress Sada Yacco, the first woman ever to appear onstage in Japanese theater history. The troupe, performing *The Geisha and the Samurai*, caused a sensation. I shall return later to the importance of this Japanese troupe to Fuller's role at the World's Fair.

More than aesthetics was at stake, though, in the World's Fair's intensive promotion of Art Nouveau, a movement which was being especially touted for its fine workmanship and rare materials, and for its status as the handiwork of old-fashioned artisans. This "spin" was deliberate, for, as Debora Silverman has pointed out, the French government sought to exploit Art Nouveau's artisanal connotations as an antidote to the damaging new image of French goods as impersonal factory creations. Art Nouveau, then, served as a corrective for the potentially dehumanizing aspects of the very same progress and technology being glorified elsewhere at the World's Fair.[35]

With her wafting veils and botanical themes, Fuller had long inspired such Art Nouveau artists as Pierre Roche, Théodore Rivière, René Lalique, and Emile Gallé, who all found in her a living embodiment of the *femme-fleur* or *femme-papillon* motif.[36] Her theater at the Fair, designed by Henri Sauvage, was an Art Nouveau masterpiece adorned with a row of marble sculptures of Fuller by Pierre Roche (fig. 2.8). Its façade consisted of a sculpted stone replica of an undulating stage curtain, recalling Fuller's own sinuous stage costumes while simultaneously giving visitors the impression of walking through a curtain and onto a stage set themselves. With its organic, mobile forms and idealized feminine sculptures, Fuller's theater announced her deep (albeit tacit) connection to Art Nouveau (fig. 2.9). But the sort of Romantic biologism that Fuller shared with Art Nouveau was somewhat undermined by its coexistence in her work with scientific wizardry and complicated stagecraft. A Loie Fuller performance was always both a mechanical production line in miniature and a virtuoso display of ephemeral floral beauty unfolding in a small interior space. Fuller then, essentially performed in microcosm the very struggle that Debora Silverman sees as central to the Fair: that between the dehumanized

[34] Lista, *Danseuse*, 374.

[35] See Silverman, *Art Nouveau in Fin-de-siècle France*, particularly her concluding chapter, 274–314.

[36] See Musée de l'Ecole de Nancy, *Loie Fuller: Danseuse de l'Art Nouveau* (Paris: Editions de la Réunion des Musées Nationaux, 2002).

Figure 2.8. Sculpture of Fuller by Pierre Roche, 1900, Bibliothèque Nationale de France

image of French commercial goods and the soothing, femininely beautiful craftsmanship of Art Nouveau.[37]

But Fuller's iconic importance at the Exposition Universelle extended far beyond the walls of her own theater; her presence made itself felt throughout the entire Fair, explicitly and implicitly as well. Astronomer Camille Flamma-

---

[37] In *The Arcades Project*, Benjamin discusses the contradictions of Art Nouveau, or *Jugendstil*, seeing in its feminine iconography a frigid woman more representative of commercial capitalism

Figure 2.9. Henri Sauvage, drawing of Le Théâtre Loie Fuller, Jerome Robbins Dance Division, New York Library for the Performing Arts, Astor, Lenox, and Tilden Foundations

rion, in his own exhibition, used glowing chemical salts to create *danses phosphorescentes*," which were modeled after Fuller's work with light-producing phosphorescent salts. And the spectacular Chateau d'Eau, for example, the waterfall that stood before the Palais d'Eléctricité, clearly owed its use of rotating colored spotlights to Loie Fuller's stagecraft. According to (a droll) Paul Morand, Fuller's influence on the Fair's lighting effects was so strong that *"The ministers of the Right Bank themselves look like so many Loie Fullers."*[38]

than of the beatified domesticity it appeared to endorse. For Benjamin, maternality and fleshliness were at odds with the Art Nouveau aesthetic: "The frigid woman," he writes, "embodies the ideal of beauty in *Jugendstil. Jugendstil* sees in every woman not Helena but Olympia" (p. 552). Fuller, of course, in her mechanomorphism and lack of maternity, falls neatly on the side of Olympia, even making a film based on Hoffmann's *Der Sandmann* later in her life. Susan Buck-Morss writes, "Women's productivity, organic in contrast to the mechanical productivity of nineteenth-century imperialism, appears threatening to capitalist society" (Susan Buck-Morss, *The Dialectics of Seeing: Walter Benjamin and the Arcades Project* [Cambridge, MA: MIT University Press, 1989], 99).

[38] Paul Morand's recollection makes Fuller's influence clear: "At night, the spotlights sweep the Champs de Mars, the Chateau d'Eau shimmers in cyclamen tints and falls in showers of green and purple light" (Morand, *1900 A.D.*, 65–66).

The Imperial Gaze

But beyond these stylistic connections, what tied Fuller most deeply to this World's Fair was her consistent reliance upon the imperialist gaze that underlay so many of the exhibitions—the nearly surgically penetrative gaze constructed to give spectators the impression of unveiling secret, hidden worlds. Just as the Trocadéro uncovered the formerly mysterious habits and appearances of the indigenous peoples of European colonies, and the Salles Roux, Pasteur, and Galilée offered magnified views of microorganisms or astral bodies, Fuller's performances, as we have seen, offered scenarios of enhanced visibility. Fuller had been making a career of her magical displays of formerly unseeable realms: the surface of the moon, the interior of a cancer cell, the skeletons of fish. In thus stripping away barriers to perception, Fuller's dances echoed the *sub rosa* themes of both the Fair's colonial and its scientific offerings. Indeed, reviewing some of the Fair's most popular attractions, one could easily mistake them for works by Fuller. Let us consider, for example, just two attractions at the popular Palais d'Optique: "*La Lune à un mètre,*"and "*Le Labyrinthe de glaces.*" The former consisted of a series of specially arranged photographic plates offering spectators a close-up view of the moon at a perceived distance of only four kilometers.[39] The latter, the "labyrinthe de glaces," consisted of a triangular room in which three entirely mirrored walls turned each visitor into an infinitely reflected crowd of identical selves.

After enjoying such optical illusions, visitors could cross the fairgrounds to Le Théâtre Loie Fuller, where its eponymous star was performing a program of four short dances: *La Danse du feu, La Danse du lys, Le Firmament,* and *Lumières et tenèbres.* Let us consider for the moment just these two last pieces. As we have seen (in chapter 1), in *Le Firmament* Fuller projected photographs of the moon onto her body as she danced before a gemstone-faceted backdrop she had patented (a device based on the "crypt of crystals" stage set of her vaudeville *Aladdin*); *Lumières et tenèbres* belonged to the highly successful "mirror dance" series, and relied upon triangular mirrors laid both on the stage floor and its sides, which created a cathedral-like setting for the infinitely reflected, brilliantly lit images of Fuller dancing.[40] In other words, these two pieces reproduced nearly exactly the visual illusions so popular at the Palais d'Optique. With *Le Firmament* and *Lumières et tenèbres* Fuller was essentially

---

[39] Rosalind Williams, *Dream Worlds: Mass Consumption in Late Nineteenth-Century France* (Berkeley: University of California Press, 1982), 210.

[40] Bergeret, *Journal d'un nègre à l'exposition de 1900,* 29.

featuring her own versions of the *"Lune à un mètre"* and the *"Labyrinthe de glaces"* attractions.

Such similarity between Fuller's program and that of the Palais d'Optique was almost certainly unintentional, but it bespeaks Fuller's profound connection not only to the Fair's promotion of optical gadgetry, but more importantly, to the underlying political message of all the optical play: that geography is mutable, that vast distances can be shrunk (the moon can seem but a meter away), and that the self can be projected beyond its physical limits (as when mirrored walls create images of multiply reproduced selves in apparently infinite space). These notions all served the imperialist goals of the World's Fair of 1900: to accustom the French public to its newly extended borders, to render the far-off colonies visible and knowable, to encourage the metropole's imaginative projection of itself into these hitherto inaccessible lands in Indochina, North Africa, the Caribbean—to help visitors "see at a glance *their* empire," to quote Greenhalgh. As Fredric Jameson has observed in his landmark article, "Modernism and Imperialism," "empire . . . stretches the road out to infinity, beyond the borders of the nation state," creating an "unrepresentable totality." For Jameson, this extension of the state results in the emergence of a concomitant new value visible in modernist style; "even if infinity and imperialism are bad, its *perception* is good, an achievement, an enlargement of our sensorium."[41] While his essay focuses on cinema and modernist novels, Jameson's remarks pertain strikingly also both to the Palais de l'Optique and to Loie Fuller's proto-cinematic legerdemain, for they both offered precisely the sort of enhanced spatial or geographical perception of which he writes.

The World's Fair of 1900, then, used entertainment and exhibition to contemplate the increasingly political concepts of nationality, spatial expansion, geography, and visibility. Indeed, the notion of the Fair as a geography lesson of sorts figured explicitly in writings by Fair officials as well as by "civilian" visitors. *The Official Illustrated Guide to the Colonial Exhibit at the Trocadéro*, for example, lamented the population's ignorance: "The French public knows little about geography," it declared, clearly positing the Trocadéro as the pedagogical remedy for this problem.[42] In his review of the closing of the World's Fair of 1900, journalist Patrick Geddes also addressed the subject of geography, proving his own absorption of Fair propaganda. For Geddes, the disjointed,

[41] Fredric Jameson, "Modernism and Imperialism," in *Nationalism, Colonialism, and Literature* (Minneapolis: University of Minnesota Press, 1990), 57–58.

[42] *Guide illustré de l'Exposition Coloniale Française au Trocadéro en 1900* (Paris: Commissariat de L'Exposition Coloniale, Cambrai, 1900), 55.

fragmented "geography" of the Trocadéro actually created for visitors its own opposite—an overarching, synthetic wholeness:

> Here, then, in this exhibition is, not indeed any completed geography, but the largest collection of elements for it which has ever been brought together. . . . The Exhibition then presents an evolution from fair and bazaar, not only to museums of arts and sciences, of discoveries and inventions, but towards the presentment of a larger and more unified conception, in which geography and history unite.[43]

But the more skeptical Paul Morand, while acknowledging French ignorance of geography, saw the Trocadéro more as an expression of that ignorance than as any kind of remedy for it:

> The French have no idea of geography. Geography comes to them. The Expo is a nameless confusion of time and space. Flemish carillons mingle with medieval bells. Muezzia chants with the tinkle of Swiss cowbells. Roumanian monasteries, Javanese palaces, the straw huts of Senegal, the castles of the Carpathians, form an astounding international medley.[44]

Mutable Geography and Adopted Nationality

Edward Said has written, "At some very basic level, imperialism means thinking about, settling on, controlling land that you do not possess, that is distant, that is lived on and owned by others."[45] And as we have seen, the World's Fair had a great stake in giving its visitors a lesson in exactly these skills, which might be grouped under the rubric of "appropriative geography"—the process of seeing, understanding, and assuming symbolic ownership of other lands, naturalizing their foreignness. And we have seen how the Fair's—and specifically Loie Fuller's—demonstrations of enhanced vision participated in these "geography lessons," helping to create that transgressive colonial gaze inherent in the Fair's propaganda. But we have yet to address the fact that Loie Fuller was herself foreign, an expatriate "born in America, but made in Paris," as she liked to say.[46] It was in this capacity as a "Paris creation" that Fuller warranted not only her own theater at the World's Fair, but a placement

---

[43] Patrick Geddes, "The Closing Exhibition—Paris 1900," *The Contemporary Review* 78 (November 1900): 662.

[44] Morand, *1900 A.D.*, 74.

[45] Edward Said, *Culture and Imperialism* (New York: Alfred A. Knopf, 1993), 7.

[46] Qtd. in Sommer, "Loie Fuller," 53.

of that theater on the Fair's famed "Rue de Paris," a strip devoted exclusively to the "most French" forms of entertainment. When Fuller brought the moon down from the sky to adorn her robes in *Le Firmament*, she offered convincing visual evidence of the manageable nearness of the heavens, promoting that theme of "mutable geography." In a sense, the World's Fair used Fuller herself to accomplish a similar goal. That is, by granting her "lone foreigner" status on the highly nationalistic Rue de Paris, the World's Fair naturalized Fuller's foreignness—her provenance in a distant, unseeable land—and used her as an adornment for their nationalistic display, as a moonscape on their own robes. To understand what made Fuller so particularly attractive to Fair organizers, we shall need to examine the sexual politics of French popular culture at the Fair, and Fuller's place within it. Especially important to this discussion will be Fuller's powerful association with the figure of Salome—the biblical dancer so bound up with colonial entertainments. The last part of this discussion will treat the role of the United States in general at this World's Fair.

Dance, Eros, and the Rue de Paris

Fuller had long known that she would have a key position in the exposition's entertainment.[47] A statue of her had been commissioned to stand above the entrance of the Palais de la Danse, whose program offered a whirlwind tour of global dance history. Beginning with *"Les Danses de la Haute Egypte,"* the Palais de la Danse moved through several countries quickly, passed through the French cancan, and finished up with the *"danses lumineuses"*—in which Fuller was intended to perform.[48] In keeping with the spirit of the Fair and its insistent worship of electricity, these electric-light dances were being marketed as the last, most modern chapter in a living history book of dance.

But for Fuller, accustomed to her solo star status, even representing the *ne plus ultra* of modernity in dance could not outweigh the indignity of being merely one in a lineup of other acts. Disgruntled, she demanded—and was granted—her own private theater, an honor granted no other Fair performer. In a turn of events typical in Fuller's career of imitation and self-replication, the statue in Fuller's likeness remained perched over the entrance of the Palais de la Danse even after Fuller had stomped off, and her *danses lumineuses* remained on the program, albeit performed by one of Fuller's many imitators, Valentine Petit.

---

[47] Hillary Bell, review of Loie Fuller, November 1896, NYPLPA. The article reveals that Fuller canceled a tour to begin preparations for her World's Fair performances nearly four years later.

[48] See Lista, *Danseuse*, 331 ff.

After some dickering with Fair officials, Fuller succeeded in having her own Art Nouveau theater built for her on the Rue de Paris.[49] Although a last-minute addition to the Fair's pavilions, the Théâtre Loie Fuller, which normally would have required six months to build, was completed in a mere six weeks—largely because of Fuller's constant goading presence on the site. (In the end, her relationship with architect Henri Sauvage turned acrimonious and she wound up suing him, following her lifelong pattern of bitter litigiousness in business dealings.[50]) The theater opened in June of 1900, with a grand celebration which proved just how "American" Fuller in fact appeared to the European public, as this contemporary review makes plain:

> Miss Loie Fuller, the American dancer, opened her theatre here last night and had the auditorium filled with her friends. Fully half of these were Americans, and the reception accorded her was largely patriotic in nature. One of the features was a display of American colors made by college boys here on their vacations.[51]

The Rue de Paris occupied a stretch of the Right Bank along the Cours la Reine, just in front of the Trocadéro, and was meant as a showcase of France's traditional popular culture. Among its exhibitions were "Le Théâtre des Tableaux Vivants," in which young women in flesh-colored tights recreated paintings by Bouguereau and Gérôme; an aquarium in which, via more tricks with mirrors, "mermaids" in green body stockings appeared to swim with live octopuses and lobsters; a burlesque house, "Le Manoir à l'Envers" or "Upside-Down House," in which visitors walked on the "ceiling" from which inverted furniture was "suspended"; a classic "Grand Guignol"; and the "Maison du Rire" (sponsored by the humor newspaper, Le Rire), featuring Chat-Noir-style shadow puppets, a marionette show, and a selection of cabaret singers. As this list makes clear, a significant number of Rue de Paris attractions relied upon bawdy or erotic appeal. Philippe Jullian has pointed out that the Rue de Paris might more accurately have been called the Rue de Montmartre, given how closely it resembled that Parisian street synonymous with racy acts.[52]

---

[49] Like all other exhibitions on the Rue de Paris, Fuller's theater operated as a concession. The Fair commission paid for the construction, and in return, Fuller paid the French government 25,000 francs for the privilege of performing in it. All box-office proceeds in excess of that amount were her profit (Ministère du Commerce et de L'Industrie, Compte des recettes et des dépenses: Exposition Universelle Internationale de 1900 à Paris [Paris: Imprimerie Nationale, 1909], 16).

[50] See Lista, Danseuse, 331 ff.

[51] Unsigned review, 26 June 1900 (NYPLPA).

[52] Jullian, Art Nouveau, 158 ff. See also Picard, Le Bilan d'un siècle, 9.

The Rue de Paris's emphasis on the erotic was deliberate. As we have seen, the new "decency codes" imposed by the Senate had restricted the level of provocation permitted in the Trocadéro's Rue du Caire, taming the many belly and veil dances, despite their earlier success in 1889. Eleven years later, Alfred Picard deprived of his colonial venue for crowd-pleasingly sexy fare, was forced to look elsewhere. The "Rue de Paris" offered an ideal legal loophole. It turned out that, since its theaters were officially designated as "French," this area of the Fair enjoyed an exemption from the decency codes and was free to feature openly erotic entertainment. The reasoning behind this exemption was simple: government officials acknowledged that French culture (as opposed, presumably, to that of the colonies) was inherently—and somehow justifiably—provocative. They therefore deemed it wrong to prohibit or impede it. As a result, the Fair Commission needed only to instruct the Rue de Paris theaters to advertise clearly their level of "gallicity," which had become the euphemism for bawdiness.

Provocative entertainment was acceptable, then, when provided by white European women within a traditional French context, but offensive when performed by women of color from North Africa and other colonial venues. Nationalism, it seemed, trumped exoticism; and titillation was less disturbing when provided by one's compatriots. Or perhaps, one suspects, "the indecency" that so scandalized le Sénateur Bérenger and his colleagues resided all along not in the sexual nature of the dances but rather in the racialized foreignness of the dancers.

Fuller, of course, had no need to advertise her level of "gallicity," no need to warn away spectators with delicate sensibilities, since her performances remained as ostensibly chaste as they had always been. But, eros apart, clearly Fuller did enjoy a considerable level of "gallicity." France had joyfully adopted her, and no one ever questioned her placement on the Rue de Paris. To understand Fuller's apparently eros-free "gallicity" in the broader sense, we must turn now to her interpretation of Salome, the biblical character associated not only with provocative colonial entertainments but also with Loie Fuller's entire career (fig. 2.10).[53]

---

[53] Elizabeth Coffman has noticed how closely Fuller represented various nationalisms: "What seems . . . disturbing . . . is the way in which Fuller's figure was appropriated to represent artistic movements that advocated nationalism. . . . The relationship between Fuller's image, her 'Americanicity,' the more abstracted icons of women in flowing gowns (e.g., the Statue of Liberty), and the visual iconography of nationalism are subjects that demand more investigation. Fuller came closest to these nationalist associations when she built her theater at the 1900 Universal Exposition in Paris and embedded an image of herself in flowing cloth over the entranceway" (Elizabeth Coffman, "Women in Motion: Loie Fuller, and the Interpenetration of Art and Science," *Camera Obscura* 17, no. 1 [2002]: 81).

Salome

"Loie Fuller is full of the idea of Salome. She talks Salome; almost thinks Salome."[54]

For Herod feared John, knowing that he was a just man and an holy. . . . Herod on his birthday made a supper to his lords, high captains, and chief estates of Galilee; And when the daughter of the said Herodias came in, and danced, and pleased Herod and them that sat with him, the king said unto the damsel, Ask of me whatsoever thou wilt, and I will give it thee. And he sware unto her, Whatsoever thou shalt ask of me, I will give it thee, unto the half of my kingdom. And she went forth, and said unto her mother, What shall I ask? And she said, The head of John the Baptist. And she came in straightway with haste unto the king, and asked, saying, I will that thou give me by and by in a charger the head of John the Baptist. And the king was exceeding sorry; yet for his oath's sake and for their sakes which sat with him, he would not reject her. And immediately the king sent an executioner, and commanded his head be brought: and he went and beheaded him in the prison. And brought his head in a charger, and gave it to the damsel: and the damsel gave it to her mother.[55]

At the Fair, Loie Fuller's program consisted of four dances. In addition to *Le Firmament* and *Lumière et ténèbres*, discussed above, she performed *La Danse du feu*, with its dramatic "walking on flames" tricks of light, set to Wagner's *Ride of the Walkyries*; and *Le Lys*, her trademark dance in which her silk "petals" reached twenty feet into the air, and her completely swathed body and uncovered face served as stamen and pistil. While no mention was made of it on the program, both of these dances were excerpted from *Salome*, Fuller's 1895 full-length dance-pantomime.

The figure of Salome, dancer of the Seven Veils, looms large in Fuller's career. As Giovanni Lista observes, "Salome was the feminine creature that

---

[54] Unidentified press clipping, NYPLPA.

[55] Mark 6: 20–28 (King James version). The only other mention of the event is found in Matthew 14: 6–12:

But when Herod's birthday was kept, the daughter of Herodias danced before them, and pleased Herod. Whereupon he promised with an oath to give her whatsoever she would ask. And she, being before instructed of her mother, said, Give me here John Baptist's head in a charger. And the king was sorry: nevertheless for the oath's sake, and them which sat with him at meat, he commanded it to be given her. And he sent, and beheaded John in the prison. And his head was brought in a charger, and given to the damsel: and she brought it to her mother. And his disciples came, and took up the body, and buried it, and went and told Jesus.

Figure 2.10. One of the many publicity photos of Fuller in Salome-inspired garb, Billy Rose Theatre Collection, New York Public Library for the Performing Arts, Astor, Lenox, and Tilden Foundations

seemed to Fuller the emblem of her destiny as a veil dancer."[56] Accordingly, Fuller would mount two different, full-length productions of the story, in 1895 and later in 1907. In 1892, when she arrived in Paris, Europe was already well in the grip of "Salomania," fueled by the vast imperialist expansions of the latter part of the nineteenth century, and the concomitant fascination with all things Oriental, particularly with those women perceived as living Salomes, the seductive, often veiled *"danseuses du ventre"* imported from the colonies.[57] Marge Garber has referred to the Salome story as the "founding fable of Orientalism."[58] And Philippe Jullian calls Salome "the little Jewish princess . . . regarded as the goddess of the Decadence."[59] Countless artists and writers were moved to depict, often with dense ornamentalism, the fatal charms of this biblical princess. Henri Regnault, Gustave Moreau, and Odilon Redon had all devoted paintings to the theme; Heinrich Heine, Gustave Flaubert, Jules Laforgue, Stéphane Mallarmé, and Joris-Karl Huysmans had all devoted texts to it.[60]

But, despite all this artistic enthusiasm, in the early 1890s the Salome story was still not the standard motif of dance that it would be in decades to come. In 1906 Maud Allen performed her version of the Dance of the Seven Veils, based on Oscar Wilde's lyrical and sexually complicated version of the story (published in 1892 but banned from the stage for years thereafter), thus

[56] Lista, *Danseuse*, 445.

[57] As Wendy Buonaventura points out, the veil dances of the Middle Eastern and North African women were not stripteases exactly, but rather overtly sensuous dances in which the hips and stomach moved provocatively (Wendy Buonaventura, *Something in the Way She Moves: Dancing Women from Salome to Madonna* [New York: Da Capo Press, 2004], 32).

[58] See Marjorie Garber, *Vested Interests: Cross-Dressing and Cultural Anxiety* (New York: Routledge, 1992), 340. In the Salome story, Garber finds a subtext about transvestism and unsettled gender identity, looking particularly at Wilde's rendition of the story and the illustrations of Aubrey Beardsley.

[59] Qtd. in Megan Becker-Leckrone, "Salome: The Fetishization of a Textual Corpus," *New Literary History* 26, no. 2 (1995): 239. See also Philippe Jullian, *Esthètes et magiciens* (Paris: Perrin et Cie., 1969), 132.

[60] See Garelick, *Rising Star*; also Rodney Shewan, "The Artist and the Dancer in Three Symbolist Salomes," *Bucknell Review* 30, no. 1 (1986): 102–30; Mario Praz, *The Romantic Agony*, trans. Angus Davidson (Oxford: Oxford University Press, 1974); Françoise Meltzer, *Salome and the Dance of Writing* (Chicago: University of Chicago Press, 1977); Jane Marcus, "Salome: The Jewish Princess Was a New Woman," *Bulletin of the New York Public Library* 78 (1974): 95–113; Frank Kermode, *Romantic Image* (London: Routledge and Kegan Paul, 1957); Elaine Showalter, *Sexual Anarchy* (New York: Viking, 1990); Richard Bizot, "The Turn of the Century Salome Era," *Choreography and Dance* 2, pt. 3 (1992): 71–87.

sparking the phenomenon of "Salomania."[61] Fuller arrived at a moment precisely ripe for Salome's transition to the dance stage. As Toni Bentley has
written, "Salome was a modern dancer waiting to happen [and] Loie Fuller
has a special place in the Salome canon for having presented one of the first
versions of the story."[62]

Fuller's two versions of *Salome* were quite different from each other (although both were critical failures). In fact, in her 1907 version, Fuller tried
to undo nearly every artistic decision she had made twelve years earlier. For
my purposes here, I shall focus on the earlier *Salome*, for it is the one that
initially established Fuller's association with the biblical story and the one
from which she excerpted her World's Fair dances.[63] Fuller's 1895 *Salome* was
performed at the Comédie Parisienne, with music by Gabriel Pierné, and sets
by the painter Georges-Antoine Rochegrosse. Fuller had particularly sought
out Rochegrosse because of his prior experience with the Salome theme,
which he had already treated at least twice—once in his erotic and Orientalist
canvas entitled *Salome dansant devant Herod* (a title borrowed from Moreau),
exhibited at the Salon of 1887, and again in 1892 when he provided sensuous
illustrations for *Hérodias*, Flaubert's 1877 novella based on the Salome story.[64]

---

[61] Fuller's own 1907 version of the tale was clearly much indebted to Wilde's interpretation.
Maud Allen also briefly toured with Loie Fuller's company and was aided by Fuller in preparing
her 1908 version of *Salome* in London.

[62] Toni Bentley, *Sisters of Salome* (New Haven, CT: Yale University Press, 2002), 44.

[63] When Fuller made her second narrative version of Salome, *La Tragédie de Salomé*, in 1907,
at 45, she was clearly intent upon not repeating the failure of the first. Accordingly, she decided
simply to do the opposite of everything she had done before. Her second *Salome* devolved into
an over-the-top extravaganza complete with 4500 feathers, 650 lamps, and 15 projectors. This
Salome was an overly voluptuous temptress who entwined herself in strings of pearls, performed
a writhing dance with a six-foot-long artificial snake covered in glittering green scales, and even
allowed a brief glimpse of herself naked silhouetted behind a screen. The production was reminiscent of Wilde's version of the story and Aubrey Beardsley's sensuous and tortuous illustrations.
For a second time, Fuller met with critical failure. Reviews were unkind toward this middle-
aged, overweight woman playing seductress. Fuller failed even to find interest in America for the
production. It was the last time she ever allowed her body to appear onstage, and the first and
last time she placed herself in an overtly sexual role onstage. (Review of Salome," *Fémina*, 15
November 1907, Collection Rondel; also Lista, *Danseuse*, 458; Jules Clarétie, "La Tragédie de
Salomé," *Le Temps*, 8 Nov. 1907; also Harris, "Loie Fuller: The Myth, the Woman and the Artist,"
27; and unidentified press clippings, NYPLPA, Robinson Locke Collection.)

[64] Rochegrosse is also noteworthy for having designed an oversized tapestry celebrating
France's colonialist mission, which was hung in the World's Fair Pavilion des Colonies. The
tapestry is unusually, nearly comically blatant in its imperialist iconography. Philippe Jullian describes it thus: "a luminous France with a laurel in her hand, but followed by soldiers, appeared

That Fuller engaged Rochegrosse for the sets proves, of course, her familiarity with and appreciation for the decadent, sensuous versions of *Salome* popular in France at the time.[65] (In 1907, her second *Salome* production relied heavily on such fin-de-siècle eroticism, although it devolved badly into an unwitting campy parody (fig. 2.11). The pantomime script for Fuller's version of the legend, however, would present a very different, far tamer Salome.[66]

In the end, as we know, Fuller's *Salome* was thoroughly disliked by critics, and salvaged only by her subsequent decision to excerpt individual dances from the production for use as cabaret acts. Thus removed from their context, the dances met with nearly universal acclaim and secured Fuller's fortune during her early years in France.[67]

But despite its box-office failure, that first, full-length *Salome* deserves our close examination. The production was judged a disappointment largely because it revealed too much of its star. In 1895, Fuller was already known for her dazzling self-transformations onstage; as Salome, though, she failed to perform her usual transubstantiation. Instead of disappearing into enormous floating lengths of fabric in every scene, as Salome, Fuller frequently permitted spectators to see her actual body dancing, without benefit of outsized veils or elaborate stagecraft and lighting. It was too close for comfort. "Seen up close by the public," wrote one review, "in a specific setting with defined action, [Fuller] loses all charm and mystery."[68] At 33, Fuller was already noticeably overweight and, apparently, perspired heavily. But these were not the only problems.

---

between the baobabs; negresses in picturesque costumes and warriors holding their spears greeted her with respectful admiration; monkeys, caymans, and pineapples decorated the border. In the shadow of the colonial palace stood the little pavilion of the Berlitz language schools" (Jullian, *Art Nouveau*, 159–60).

[65] See Lista, *Danseuse*, 223.

[66] Fuller's script was adapted by playwright Armand Sylvestre from a story entitled "La Légende dorée" by Jacques de Voragine, which featured a far more "PG" Salome, quite different from the usual femmes fatales of the era. See Lista, *Danseuse*, 221–24.

[67] "Since 1895 *Salome* had acquired a reputation that had to be lived down." wrote the *Boston Herald* ("Loie Fuller Tells Plans for Boston," *Boston Herald*, 5 April 1909). "The Salome dance of unfragrant memory must have a successor, and at the outset of another season it is comforting to be assured that the dances to which the American public will be bidden this winter are to be no worse," wrote another American paper in anticipation of Fuller's return to America (unidentified press clipping, NYPLPA, Robinson Locke Collection). "Perhaps Miss Fuller's greatest creation was that of Salome, the Judean maiden, who danced off the head of John the Baptist. It is the one over which she is most enthusiastic. But Paris would not have it" (unidentified press clipping, NYPLPA, Robinson Locke Collection).

[68] Quoted in Lista, *Danseuse*, 229.

La belle Loïe Fuller

Figure 2.11. Caricature of Loie Fuller in her 1907 *Salome* from *La Vie Parisienne*, 1907, Bibliothèque Nationale de France

Fuller's interpretation of Salome only aggravated her audience's initial discomfort at her appearance. Ignoring the usual "femme fatale" connotations surrounding Salome (such as those evident in Moreau's paintings, for example), Fuller chose to portray the dancing princess as a chaste and frightened child—"presqu'une enfant encore" according to the program. Pictures of the performance show Fuller in a virginal white gown strewn with white roses—chosen pointedly over the lotus blossom often seen in period depictions of

Salome, most notably in Moreau's paintings (fig. 2.12).[69] The lotus is an Oriental flower with erotic overtones. Known also as "the scepter of Isis," it figures in Ancient Egyptian legend, where it represents the sacrifice of that goddess's virginity. The white rose, by contrast, belongs iconographically to the Christian tradition—and is considered the flower of the Virgin Mary, "the rose without thorns." By replacing the sultry lotus with not one but a whole garland of white roses, Fuller insisted not only on Salome's sexual purity, but also on her proximity to Christianity and, implicitly, on her distance from the Orient. By virtue of both their color and their symbology, these roses connoted racial whiteness. That such subtle racial distinctions were sensed by audiences is borne out by reviews such as the following, which not only makes explicit mention of Fuller's "whitened" Salome, but openly equates that "whiteness" with moral and sexual innocence:

> [Fuller's] dancing Judean girl is not the dark-faced passionate creature the mediaeval painters have made her, but a radiant blonde, scarcely more than a child, an instrument adroitly used by a wicked mother; a girl [who loves] a dreamy-eyed apostle, who was destined to die because of that love.[70]

I shall return to the racial overtones of Fuller's Salome.

The incongruity of this overweight and visibly sweating adult woman passing herself off as a frightened, rose-bedecked child was too much for many critics. As often throughout her career, Fuller had constructed a mise-en-scène of disavowal, in this case, attempting to disavow—on a spectacular scale—her own adult womanhood and its incongruity with the "Salome" she was attempting to depict. But while her use of disavowal was often, even usually, highly successful, this time Fuller failed to get away with it.

According to Freud (who first formulated this theory in his essay on fetishism), disavowal is always, by definition, an incomplete process—a kind of failed repression:

> The disavowal is always supplemented by an acknowledgement; two contrary and independent attitudes always arise and result in the situation of there being a splitting of the ego . . . the issue depends on which of

---

[69] See Lista, *Danseuse*, 229. In 1909, Fuller revisited this *Salome* in an interview with a Boston newspaper, as follows: "This Salome," she says, "is an innocent child who dances before Herod at the instigation of her mother. She doesn't ask for the head of John the Baptist and when it is delivered to her she falls dead with fright" (unidentified press clipping, 1909, NYPLPA, Robinson Locke Collection).

[70] Unidentified press clipping, 1895, NYPLPA, Robinson Locke Collection.

LOIE FULLER, THE AMERICAN DANCER AS SALOME IN THE LYRIC PANTOMIME AT THE COMÉDIE-PARISIENNE.

Figure 2.12. Fuller as Salome, 1895, Jerome Robbins Division, New York Public Library for the Performing Arts, Astor, Lenox, and Tilden Foundations

the two can seize hold of the greater intensity . . . whatever the ego does in its efforts of defense, whether it seeks to disavow a portion of the real external world or whether it seeks to reject an instinctual demand from the internal world, its success is never complete or unqualified.[71]

In other words, disavowal leaves a trace; it acknowledges itself and "its own origin in the unspeakable," as Laura Mulvey says.[72] Seeking to deny a distressing reality, the psyche simply displaces it onto some other readable surface.[73] In Fuller's *Salome*, the failure lay not in the inadequacy of her disavowal—since disavowal can never be fully "adequate"—but rather in the *way in which* it was incomplete. Fuller had displaced the "unspeakable" (the truth of her being risibly unsuited to the role, and by extension, the truth of her sexual maturity) onto her audience. Her performance of Salome was so sorely lacking in self-awareness that it required the spectators to bear by themselves this painful "acknowledgment," the necessary complement to her disavowal. The result was horror and distaste instead of the desired suspension of disbelief.[74]

The coexistence of the disavowed truth and its acknowledgment creates a split state of simultaneous belief and denial, which has been conjured succinctly by Octave Mannoni in his now-famous phrase: "*Je sais bien, mais quand même* ("I know very well, but all the same"), which summarizes the condition of suspended disbelief.[75] The audience for Salome got as far as "*Je sais bien,*"

---

[71] Sigmund Freud, *Outline of Psychoanalysis* (New York: Norton & Co., 1949), 92–93.

[72] Laura Mulvey, "Some Thoughts on Theories of Fetishism in the Context of Contemporary Culture," *October* 65 (Summer 1993): 6.

[73] For Freud, the original distressing reality was the lack of the maternal phallus and its attendant announcement of the reality of castration. The shock of this revelation is displaced by the fetishist onto any number of possible placeholders that represent the "last impression received before the uncanny traumatic one"—hence the woman's shoe (if the boy was looking up a skirt), velvet or fur (which "reproduce the sight of pubic hair"), etc. (Sigmund Freud, "Fetishism, "in *Collected Papers* [New York: Basic Books, 1959, reprint of 1927 essay], 201).

[74] Fuller's odd disavowal of her age and size should not be likened to Sarah Bernhardt's later willingness, at the age of 58, to play Wilde's teenaged Salome, a role written expressly for her. Although Bernhardt did not get the chance, ultimately, both she and Wilde had a canny understanding of the potential for ironic play in the disparity between the actress and the role. Fuller lacked their camp sensibility.

[75] See Octave Mannoni, *Clefs pour l'imaginaire de l'autre scène* (Paris: Seuil, 1985). It is tempting simply to see Fuller's work as turning her (or failing to turn her) into a fetishized commodity. Benjamin, after all, famously saw World's Fairs as "places of pilgrimage to the fetish commodity" (Benjamin, "Paris, Capital of the Nineteenth Century" in *Charles Baudelaire, A Lyric Poet in the Era of High Capitalism*, trans. Harry Zohn (London: Verso, 1983), 17. But I want to resist falling into this label for Fuller, whose work was complex and multilayered, and therefore, irreducible to such psychoanalytic categories.

but never made it to "*mais quand même*." Ever blunt, Jean Lorrain wrote, "With the gestures of an English boxer and the physique of Oscar Wilde, this is a Salome for drunken Yankees."[76]

The Textual Subtleties of Salome

Fuller introduced one last major alteration in the story of Salome. In nearly all versions, beginning with the two descriptions in the New Testament (Mark and Matthew), the princess dances for her stepfather, Herod, and then, having been promised the reward of her choosing, horrifies him by demanding the head of John the Baptist.[77] A stricken Herod, who holds the Baptist in some awe, has no choice. Bound by his oath, he must grant his stepdaughter's wish. But Fuller reverses this scenario. In her production, it is Herod who plots John's murder, while Salome worships the Baptist, and is so virtuous and proto-Christian of spirit that she offers her own life in exchange for his, begging Herod to slay her instead. Herod refuses and proceeds with his execution. Upon seeing John's head on a platter, Fuller's Salome dies of grief and shock. Such dramatic alterations of the classic story cast significant light on both Fuller's self-presentation and her political resonances. Here, we need to look more closely at the biblical story of Salome.

As told, only sketchily, in the New Testament, the story of Salome presents many ambiguities. First, it reveals neither the name of the "daughter of Herodias" nor the slightest detail of her powerful dance. It is only through the work of Flavius Josephus that we have come to accept that the girl is called Salome, and that she performed "The Dance of the Seven Veils."[78] Several other,

---

[76] Lorrain, *Poussières*, 143–44.

[77] While the Bible does not mention the name of the princess, biblical scholars, beginning with Flavius Josephus have identified her as Salome, daughter of Herodias and Herod. For centuries, the Salome story has been connected with the power of dance and the attendant force of female sexuality. The nineteenth century's fascination with the princess arguably began in 1841 with the publication of Heinrich Heine's narrative poem *Atta Troll*, and included Flaubert's 1863 *Salammbô*, Henri Regnault's 1868 painting *Salome*, Gustave Moreau's two 1876 paintings, *Salome dansant* and *L'Apparition*, Jules Laforgue's 1885 story *Salome*, and Mallarmé's 1864 dramatic poem *Hérodiade* and his 1898 *Noces d'Hérodiade*.

[78] In 93 CE Flavius Josephus asserted that Herodias' daughter was Salome, the girl who danced for Herod. However, the Dance of the Seven Veils is probably pre-biblical in origin, especially since the number seven is most commonly associated with the seven wonders of the ancient world. A dance involving seven veils may originally have been a spectacle celebrating these cultural achievements. The dance may also have been a ritual celebrating the creation of the universe, since for a long time, only seven planets were known to exist. The story of Salome became associated with this dance during the early Renaissance (Flavius Josephus, *Antiquities of*

deeper ambiguities exist in the story as well. First among them is the question of Salome's complicity in the crime. Does she act against her will, solely to please her mother? Or does she too wish to kill the Baptist (who has accused her mother, Herodias, of incest[79])? We also never learn whether Salome is aware of Herod's interest in her and her dance. Does she dance knowing her power over him (a power proven by his oath to grant her any reward)? Or does she dance in complete innocence of her effect?

Next, there is the matter of Herod's oath, which is presented in material and geographical terms: he offers her up to half of his kingdom. But the king does not know that the terms of his promise, as he understands them, will be changed and used against him, forcing him to a heinous crime. The power of a dance performance, therefore, has pushed the scope of his promise—and of his kingdom—beyond his intellectual grasp of them. Herod must now include the head of John the Baptist within the compass of his promised "half of the kingdom." We can begin to see here the relevance of the story to nineteenth-century imperialism, for it narrates a crisis brought on by a failure to grasp the worth and power—the "reach"—of one's kingdom, and furthermore, how this failure might be connected to murder. It requires only a small leap to find in this tale an allegory for the bloody crisis that results when the body *politic* has been extended beyond the conscious intellection of its participants—as in the case of colonial acquisition. Like Herod, the nineteenth-century French public may have found itself responsible for murderous doings resulting from the extension of its kingdom beyond their sensory and intellectual grasp, by the violent acquisition of foreign territories.

For centuries, the multiple levels of epistemological doubt underlying the original Salome narrative have enticed writers and artists to fill the void with their own interpretations of the story. As a result, a wide spectrum of Salomes lives in art and literature, ranging from innocent, exploited girls to debauched sirens. One element of the story has, however, remained constant: Salome's dance is always associated with desire and always leads to John's death.

---

the Jews, 17.4). See also Rita Severi, "Oscar Wilde, La Femme Fatale and the Salome Myth," in *Proceedings of the Tenth Congress of the International Comparative Literature Association, 1982*, ed. Anna Balakian (New York: Garland Publishing, 1985): 458–63; also, Ewa Kuryluk, *Salome and Judas in the Cave of Sex* (Evanston, IL: Northwestern University Press, 1987). In a myth dating from 4500 BCE, the Middle Eastern goddess of love, Ishtar, is said to have tied a girdle around her hips, donned seven veils, and danced with them to gain entry to the seven gates of the netherworld to bring back her husband, Tammouz, who had died. While she was absent, the earth darkened and turned to winter. On her return, earth again became fertile and blossomed into spring.

[79] Herodias had broken Jewish law by leaving Salome's father and marrying his brother, Herod.

Regardless of her own motives or whether she understands the situation, Salome has always been the quintessential femme fatale.[80]

But not for Loie Fuller. Her 1895 production of this great legend abol-
ishes the *sine qua non* of Salome: the power of dance. Fuller detaches
Salome's performance from her spectator's response. Unmoved by her dance,
Herod proceeds with the murder of John *despite* Salome's efforts and not
because of them.

With this, Fuller has pushed aside any causal relationship between dance,
desire, and death. As Roger-Marx wrote (in one of the few admiring reviews
of this production): "No sooner is she approached by Loie Fuller than Salome
falls under her spell; for a miracle of faith has replaced the Salome of legend—
drunk on blood and voluptuousness—with a mystical, nearly chaste Salome."[81]
We should take special note of the fact that Roger-Marx, a World's Fair official, so completely "bought" Fuller's own saintly presentation of herself. Since
we know that Roger-Marx was, in large part, responsible for Fuller's prominent
position at the Fair, we can infer that it was this rapturous, idealized image of
a mystical and chaste Fuller that he brought to his colleagues on the Fair
Commission—the image that convinced them to grant her her own theater
on that most exclusively patriotic patch of real estate at the Expo, the Rue de
Paris. We must wonder, therefore, what political expediency was served by
Fuller and her "chastity" amid all the merry French flag-waving of the
Rue de Paris.

In Fuller's hands, *Salome*, that classic tale of dance, desire, and death, be-
came a morality tale, and one of the most famous Oriental *femmes fatales* in
history a would-be Christian martyr. Fuller, furthermore, disavowed not only
her own incongruousness for the role, but the entire bloody subtext of the
Salome story as well. The violence remained, nonetheless—the Baptist in
Fuller's version still dies brutally—but Salome's hands (or hips) are clean, for
Fuller had expunged the dangerous erotic power from both dancer and dance.
Once again, we see here Fuller's consistent juxtaposition of staged disavowal

[80] René Girard, for example, sees Salome's dance as a "mimetic crisis," in which desire sweeps
over Herod and his guest, causing "a collective trance" (René Girard, "Scandal and the Dance:
Salome in the Gospel of Mark," *New Literary History* 15, no. 2 [Winter 1984]: 116–18). Françoise
Meltzer sees her as "symbolizing . . . the pure ideal of great beauty without scruples, without
restraint, with cruel indifference" (Meltzer, *Salome and the Dance of Writing*, 16). And Frank Kermode writes that in the nineteenth century, "the beauty of a work of art, in which there is no
division of form and meaning . . . is compared with the mysterious inexpressive beauty of [the
danseuse,] and particularly with that of Salome. The femme fatale is certainly the pathological
aspect of this image" (Kermode, *Romantic Image*, 60).

[81] Roger-Marx, "Une Rénovatrice de la danse," *Le Musée* March 1907: 100.

and a complementary violence. Her interpretation of Salome's "innocence" is profoundly in keeping with the countless instances we have already seen of her reliance upon a disingenuous purity as both an artistic and a personal motif. We have seen this brand of disavowal, for example in the unacknowledged "amputation" effect of Fuller's mirror dances, in her use of disturbing images such as cancer cells or skeletons, in her consistent suppression of her own bodily presence, and in her continual insistence upon allying herself with children and angels. We have equally seen how her theatrical disavowal necessarily constructs for her spectators a transgressive gaze, an intrusive window into normally closed worlds. And finally, we have seen how this gaze partakes of the colonial gaze upon which so much imperialist propaganda was based. Clearly, Fuller's virtuous, mystical Salome not only reflects her own career tendencies, it dovetails perfectly with the World's Fair's own brand of political disavowal. Fair visitors, after all, were not encouraged to dwell on those bloody corpses at the Madagascar exhibit, but rather to delight in the whimsical fun of observing colonized subjects sing, dance, or weave cloth in staged habitats.

For these reasons, Loie Fuller's disavowed Salome was deeply consonant with the underlying ideology of France's imperialist propaganda. Fuller also helps us to see something new about the fascination with Salome in late nineteenth-century France. Beyond its Orientalist details and its obvious sex appeal, the original, biblical story of Salome is, as I have demonstrated, a tale of murder denied and disavowed. It is a tale in which many levels of desire, obligation, and causality are left to the reader's interpretation—a perfect allegory for French imperialist propaganda, particularly as seen at the World's Fair of 1900, which veiled and denied its own blood and murder—its own harsh colonial truths—with charming performances and diversions, with both the *"belles Fatmas"* and the scientific marvels. Indeed, one could say that the Fair itself served as a Salome story for the public: transmitting a tale of bloody, murderous intention dissembled prettily with amusing performance. And so, rather than dismantle or obscure the original meaning of "Salome," Fuller's alternative version may, in the end, actually unmask a quality only implied in the original text: a disingenuous refusal to explain the links among the events, an unacknowledged statement of the power of performance to undo expectations.

This brings us back to Loie Fuller's political function. What made Fuller the *"modern Salome"* may have been less her technologically revved-up version of the ancient tale than her penchant for staged disavowal. Let us recall that at the Fair, Fuller did not perform a full-length *Salome*, but rather excerpts from it—the *Fire Dance*, and the *Lily Dance*. In other words, at the Fair, Fuller did not overtly represent the character of Salome. She had stripped away the explanatory Oriental and biblical narrative of her dances, just as, five years earlier, she had pushed aside both Salome's eros and her complicity in John's murder. In Fuller's hands, Salome undergoes a progressive metamorphosis: from dangerous femme fatale to chaste child and then to a nameless vision of flame and flowers. From 1895 to 1900, Fuller's *Salome* grew ever more abstract, ever less human and dangerous. Eventually, as if adhering belatedly to the *bienséance* tradition of classical French drama, Fuller banished all gory details from the stage—leaving only the suggestion of violence in the blood-red lights of the *Fire Dance*. Her audiences were free to lose themselves in her superhuman, unearthly visions, free to suspend their disbelief in the origin of those visions. The result was a modernist spectacle that ostensibly refused the power of narrative, Orientalism, and sexuality, while being, at the same time, deeply informed by all three. Indeed, I believe that these suppressed elements of her work lie at the heart of her importance, informing her work all the more powerfully for the force with which they were denied.

Fuller's Japanese Costars at the Fair

Before moving on to further discussion of Fuller's political persona at the Fair, let us pause here to consider the performers who shared her theater: the Japanese troupe, Shosei Nikawa (already quite famous in Japan and having recently attracted notice in London, where they were championed by Ellen Terry and Henry Irving).[82] While Fuller's "modernized" and abstracted dances strongly disavowed their provenance in narrativity and Orientalism, *The Geisha and the Samurai*, starring Sada Yacco and Kawakami Otojiro, was a veritable festival of both. This melodrama, written by Kawakami, was set in sixteenth-century Japan. Its story, reminiscent of *La Dame aux camélias*, featured a vulnerable young girl, her unfaithful lover, his mistress, who performs a "seductive and profane" dance, and the innocent girl's anguished death. Done entirely in pantomime (in part to overcome the language barrier), with lighting by Fuller herself, the play borrowed the highly ritualized gestural vocabulary of traditional kabuki theater. It was a violent, emotional story to begin with, but Fuller apparently urged Sada and Kawakami to exaggerate the intensity, to make it even gorier by including a *hara-kiri* ritual suicide at the end. Although kabuki theater eschews realism and facial emotion, the Kawakamis inserted both in the geisha's death scene, following Fuller's advice.[83] The final product

[82] See Yoko Chiba, "Japonisme: East-West Renaissance in the Late Nineteenth Century," *Mosaic* 31, no. 2 (June 1998): 15.

[83] Kawakami's company was already well known in Japan, where it was considered avant-garde for its inclusion of modern political subjects onstage. By the time they appeared at the World's

was described by Camille Mauclair as "a bloody, furious, luxurious drama, presented with all the intense exactitude of the *extrême-Orient*."[84]

Although initially concerned that the Japanese troupe would puzzle French
audiences ("Paris doesn't like foreign troupes," she said), Fuller was stunned
by their success in her theater: "I turned Sada Yacco loose. I give you my word,
I never saw anything like the way those critics went wild with enthusiasm. It
was almost too good to be true. . . . Sada Yacco wasn't a success, she was a
furor. Paris was mad about her. . . . Her husband took his place by her side in
the estimation of the critics."[85] Kawakami and Sada acquired international
fame, and for two years Fuller acted as their impresario, taking their troupe
on tour with her throughout Europe, and acting as press agent.[86]

The Geisha and the Samurai was the first performance on the bill at Le Théâtre Loie Fuller. After it ended, the theater would go dark for several seconds
and Fuller would emerge to perform dances stripped bare, as we have seen, of
absolutely every element that made *The Geisha* so powerful, those elements
also inherent in the story of Salome: the Orient, love, sex, blood, death, a
seductive dance, and human storytelling in general. In his review, Camille
Mauclair made it clear that Fuller's performance provided a kind of spiritual
cleansing. For Mauclair, Fuller was an antidote for the Oriental upheaval of
Sada Yacco: "One might say that [Loie Fuller] rushes in to purify the place of
all the agonizing human fury. After the dramatic expression of passion, after
the last spasm of a desperate and convulsed humanity, she arrives, serene . . .
like a messenger from heaven. . . . Loie Fuller tears us away from the destructive conflicts of life, from ordinary life, and takes us to the purifying countries
of dreams."[87]

If Fuller was an antidote for Mauclair, Sada Yacco was an antidote for Fuller.
As Mauclair's remarks remind us, between the Japanese play and Fuller's
dances there existed no great chasm, but rather a profound complementarity.
Fuller may have disavowed her "Salome status"—her work's deep attachment

Fair of 1900, Kawakami and his actors had already met with and been influenced by such European theater mavericks as André Antoine of the pioneering Théâtre-Libre. In essence, starring
at Fuller's theater required these artists to pretend to a simplicity of performance style that was
not really their own. See Yoko Chiba, "Japonisme"; also Ann Decoret-Ahiha, *Danses exotiques*,
39–43; and J. Scott Miller, "Dispossessed Melodies: Recordings of the Kawakami Theater Troupe,"
Monumenta Nipponica 53, no. 2 (Summer 1998): 225–35.

[84] Mauclair, *Idées vivantes*, 103.

[85] Fuller, unpublished writings, NYPLPA, Robinson Locke Collection.

[86] Among the admirers in the audience at this fair were Gordon Craig, Ruth St. Denis, Sarah
Bernhardt, and a young Pablo Picasso, who was moved to do a poster of the play's dramatic death
scene, which he offered to Sada to use for subsequent theatrical engagements.

[87] Mauclair, *Idées vivantes*, 106.

Miss Loie Fuller

Figure 2.13. Publicity photo of Fuller in Madame Butterfly–inspired costume, Bibliothèque Nationale de France

to racialized otherness, violence, and eros—but as we know, disavowal is but a "half measure . . . always supplemented by an acknowledgment." A rather spectacular supplemental acknowledgment of all that Fuller disavowed exploded in the work of the Japanese actors who appeared with her, at her invitation, with her sponsorship, under lights (and some costumes) designed by her, and—crucially—acceding to her desire that they exhibit greater blood and violence onstage.

Japonisme offered Loie Fuller just the outlet she sought. Unlike the colonies of the Trocadéro, Japan was "Oriental" without being subservient, overtly sexual, or dangerous. On the contrary, Japan was associated with fine arts, Art Nouveau, delicate beauty, and in the year 1900, the much-talked-about David Belasco play that Puccini would soon turn into an opera, *Madame Butterfly* (fig. 2.13).[88] By juxtaposing her work with that of these Japanese artists, and

---

[88] Belasco's play, based on the story by John Luther Long, premiered in New York in March of 1900 and quickly traveled to London, where Puccini saw it and decided to base an opera on it. The opera premiered in 1904.

by ushering them into European culture, Fuller displaced her Orientalism onto a new Orient, exchanging Middle Eastern connotations for Far Eastern refinements, and displaced her own impulse toward narrativity onto someone else's melodramas. Indeed, she would become so enamored of Japanese theater that after her years with Sada Yacco and Kakawami, Fuller took on a new Japanese protégé, the actress Ota Hisa, known as Hanako, for whom she would actually write a number of lurid "Japanese pantomimes" further indulging her long-denied taste for melodrama. She signed these plays with the somewhat ludicrous pseudonym, "Loi-fu."[89]

A Yankee Salome on the Rue de Paris

Exploring the resonances of the Japanese artists sharing Fuller's theater, we see only more clearly her own aesthetics of displacement and disavowal. The performance style of Sada Yacco and her company provided a near-perfect complement to Fuller, a vehicle for the elements she normally spurned for herself but clearly regarded with some delectation and essentially displaced onto her chosen costars.

But we have seen such techniques of displacement before. Indeed, displacement was, in a sense, what Fuller had in common with her theatrical neighbors on the Rue de Paris. Those other attractions—the girls in body stockings, the burlesque dancers, the racy "mermaids"—functioned as receptacles for the displaced erotic charge that had been forcibly tamped down on the Rue du Caire at the Trocadéro. The Rue de Paris offered up a de-racialized, de-Orientalized sexuality to Fair visitors—a safer (or rather "whiter") series of entertainments packaged as so much robust "gallicity." Similarly, Loie Fuller—that nameless, "pseudo-Eastern," American-born Salome—portrayed a "whitened," de-racialized veil dancer for the public, in contrast to the sexy "darkfaced . . . maidens" and their ilk on the Rue du Caire. What can we learn from this?

Let us return to Jean Lorrain's bitchy dismissal of Fuller's 1895 pantomime as a "Salome for Yankee drunkards." What kind of Salome would have been appropriate for "Yankee drunkards"? The only answer is, one who mirrors her audience: "Yankees" of course are, in the French imagination, a vulgar, loud,

---

[89] *Louisville Herald*, Review of Loie Fuller, 21 February 1909, NYPLPA: "As there was no suitable play in the Japanese repertoire, the dancer obligingly wrote one herself. It was a success . . . and thus it went on. By her own account, the impresario wrote, *The Martyr*, *A Drama in the Yoshiware*, *The Political spy*, *A Japanese Ophelia*, and *A Japanese Tea House*."

and grasping lot. Drunken ones are even worse. Lorrain's point is that, in 1895, Fuller's *Salome* made her Americanness evident, failing to veil her vulgarity. But by 1900, having removed the overt Salome narrative and modestly reveiled her plump body, Fuller managed to attenuate the vulgarity of her nationality. Of her *Fire Dance* performance (now detached from its "Salome" character and disclosing no trace of Fuller's physical self) Jean Lorrain would write ecstatically: "She stood in blazing embers, and did not burn."[90]

But like all veiled things, Fuller's nationality was no less important for being covered up. Fuller never really tried to hide her nationality. She never pretended to be a Frenchwoman, and she was certainly never mistaken for one. On the contrary, her Americanness was always part of her public image. From the time of her earliest performances in France, Fuller was billed as foreign—"*la belle américaine*" on the Folies-Bergère's posters. But being American in France has always been a complicated matter. Traditionally, France has held a double perspective on the United States, regarding Americans alternately as crass and boorish or refreshingly innocent and inventive. Loie Fuller walked the fine line between these two views.[91] While she may have risked being a

---

[90] Lorrain, *Poussières*, 102.

[91] Interviews with Fuller typically used her nationality to help explain her curiously asexual, lady-scientist persona. "Fuller is a chaste dancer who lives surrounded by her family," wrote one reviewer, "and like a typical American, is of extremely practical nature" (H.C., "Loie Fuller: Educatrice de danseuses," *Revue Encyclopédique*, Feb. 1893, 109). She was variously called "sweet and gentle," "magnificently innocent," and possessed of "admirable naiveté." We know that Fuller shared the unflattering, stereotypical view of her countrymen and sought to distance herself from that image. Her autobiography contains a chapter called simply "Americans" in which she gives vent to her disapproval of American crassness. "Americans do not hesitate, if they have no receptacle within easy reach, to spit on the floor, and to throw the ends of their cigars anywhere, without even taking the trouble to extinguish them"(Fuller, *Fifteen Years*, 232). In an unpublished essay also called "Americans," Fuller includes a section about the presumptuousness of those who use the term "America" speaking only of the United States, ignoring Latin America's (and Canada's) claim to the same label: "This appropriation to themselves of something that belongs to somebody else is a good sample of the spirit of monopoly which prevails in these U.S. of America. I once in Paris made the acquaintance of a family who knew some Americans, and being one myself, they thought I might possibly have met, run across . . . these friends of theirs in America. I said, 'it's possible, where 'bouts in America do they live?' 'Buenos Ayres' was the answer. . . . That opened my mind's eye more than anything else on earth would have done to the fact that we are (as the American slang puts it) not the only pebbles on the beach" (Fuller, "Americans," unpublished essay, NYPLPA). At the same time, Fuller herself was sometimes viewed as proof of America's improved refinement, as when the *New York Times's* Paris correspondent wrote: "America is coming wonderfully forward now; grave minds are studying the Constitution, religious tolerance, the situation of the Government as regards labor associations, and so on. While the statesman, the philosopher, and the student look to the shining and humane light across the broad sea, tout Paris raves about Loie Fuller and her comparatively graceful and chaste

"Salome for Yankee drunkards," she was also, as one contemporary journalist wrote, "one of the few Americans who have ever created a sensation in Paris, and been able to hold the interest of the fickle capital for any considerable length of time."[92] Indeed, long-time admirer Claude Roger-Marx attributed Fuller's success specifically to her nationality, believing her to be possessed of "an American imagination, miraculously fertile." As we have seen, Roger-Marx agreed with Fuller's own spiritual assessment of herself, even referring to her in an interview as "*un archange*," who, like Gabriel, had flown from the New World to announce the rebirth of dance in the Old. For Roger-Marx, Fuller's work both sprang from and powerfully evoked the American landscape, the physical, geographical beauty of the United States:

> The luminous and naïve Loie Fuller is a product of American nature. Her light effects are those of the unique atmosphere of the Colorado canyons, and only the Florida butterflies in their flight can compare with her graceful movements and the chaste and diaphanous floating of her draperies.[93]

This rhapsodic account of Fuller, written—we must recall—by a World's Fair commissioner, reveals to what extent Fuller, despite her "Rue de Paris" placement, conjured the United States, or at least an oneiric, fantastical version of it. But then, Fuller had always inspired comparisons with fantastical landscapes of various sorts—paradisal, hallucinatory, or mythological. Her dances frequently brought to mind a highly abstract notion of "place" or "country." Poet Georges Rodenbach wrote that Fuller's costumes created a "land of mist"—"*un pays de brume*." Mallarmé felt that onstage Fuller "acquires the virginity of un-dreamt-of places" ("*des lieux non-rêvés*"), and that her work "institutes a place" ("*institue un lieu*"). Similarly, Paul Adam wrote that in Fuller's performances: "The divine materializes. One dreams of visions from legends, of a return to Eden." And, as we know, Camille Mauclair felt that Fuller transported audiences to other lands, "to purifying countries of dreams."

As these remarks make clear, in her dance's hypnotic play of light, color, and fabric, Fuller sparked an atavistic longing for magical "elsewheres." This phenomenon may have also resulted from the "placelike" nature of the costumes, for Fuller used her batons and veils to create a kind of casing or nest for herself, what Jean Lorrain referred to as "a seashell effect" ("*un effet de*

---

dancing. The knowing people go back to Pompeian bath ruins to seek the origin of the serpentine dance, but they find that the exquisite posing is something more original. It is funny to see the can can attraction pale before the Yankee dance" (qtd. in Current and Current, Loie Fuller, 65).

[92] Unidentified press clipping, NYPLPA, Robinson Locke Collection.

[93] Roger-Marx, "Une Rénovatrice," 101.

coquillage"). Having largely rejected such place-identifying stage markers as backdrops, narratives, and props, Fuller had, as Mallarmé wrote, "liberated the stage." Then, after thus emptying the outer stage space of reference points, Fuller was free to take the theatrical space upon her own person, becoming both occupant and place at once, enacting a microcosmic fantasy landscape.

For Felicia McCarren, who has elsewhere remarked on the physical resemblance between Fuller's onstage forms (funnel-shaped body and tubular, winged arms) and the female reproductive system (uterus and Fallopian tubes), this landscape is, ultimately, uterine: "Fuller's performances collapse the distinction between matter and the matrix space of the womb, merging the woman dancing with the womblike space in which she performs."[94] McCarren's psychoanalytic interpretation of Fuller's spatial forms is, of course, very much in keeping with the edenic and mythological visions offered by earlier critics such as Paul Adam or Camille Mauclair. In all cases, Fuller is understood to be allying herself with a nonthreatening, welcoming, and feminized home—exactly the image of the colonies most consonant with an agenda of imperialist expansion. In 1920, French historian Georges Hardy published a justification of colonialism that could not illustrate this point more clearly: "We feel the need for a sort of promised land," he wrote, "an edenic place . . . where animal and human life are embellished with all the grace of childhood. This Old Testament vision . . . is the colonial landscape."[95] (It is worth noting here that, in addition to her interest in the New Testament Salome, Fuller also felt drawn to Old Testament heroines, referring to her work as the resurrection of ancient dances: "I have been able to trace some of my dances back to four thousand years ago: to the time when Miriam and the women of Israel filled with religious fervour and rapture, celebrated their release from Egyptian captivity with . . . dances."[96] In 1911, she mounted a production based loosely on these figures (fig. 2.14).

Thus far, we have developed a theory of Loie Fuller as a whitened "Salome" who allegorically enacted several facets of France's imperialist agenda at the turn of the century. Now, taking into account her alliance in the popular imagination with paradisal landscapes—themselves so powerfully connected to the colonies—we see still more of Fuller's peculiar suitability to the cultural exigencies of imperialism. But, while she was evoking idyllic dreamscapes, Fuller was also evoking America, as Roger-Marx made clear. In fact, in his remark, America *is* the dreamscape, the only place beautiful and pure enough

[94] McCarren, "The Symptomatic Act," 758.

[95] Georges Hardy, *Les Eléments de l'histoire coloniale* (Paris: Renaissance du livre, 1920), 37.

[96] Qtd. in Griffith, "Loie Fuller: The Inventor of the Serpentine Dance," 540.

Figure 2.14. Fuller in costume as the biblical heroine Miriam, Billy Rose Theatre Collection, New York Public Library for the Performing Arts, Astor, Lenox, and Tilden Foundations

to have produced "the luminous and naïve Loie Fuller," with her "chaste and diaphanous" robes. But as one of the principal organizers of the World's Fair, Roger-Marx was likely to have had more than just an aesthetic opinion about the United States, for America had begun to pose serious political problems for Europe, which in turn took their toll on the Expo.

The New Colonial Power:
The United States at the World's Fair

In the two years leading up to the World's Fair of 1900, the United States's role in Europe had been permanently changed by the Spanish-American War of 1898. Although France had officially proclaimed neutrality as soon as hostilities had broken out between the United States and Spain, its government was concerned about the war's potentially deleterious effects on France's commerce, given the country's considerable investments in the Spanish economy (twice as much as in the United States). French Foreign Minister Gabriel Hanotaux tried on several occasions to facilitate the peace negotiations, but received a message from Assistant Secretary of State William R. Day stating, "We can under no circumstances admit European intervention in any form."[97]

The French ambassador to the United States, Jules Cambon, explicitly warned that the war marked a turning point in history. Americans, he felt, had been seduced by the notion of a "Greater America," seeking perhaps to widen the war to include the Canary Islands and the Mediterranean. They are, he wrote, "ignorant, brutal, and quite capable of carelessly destroying the complicated European structure." The "structure" in question was, of course, European imperialism, which France (and much of the rest of Europe) feared the United States would disrupt or undermine with its own. Historian Henry Blumenthal points out that even as Cambon wrote these words in the *New York Times*, the London *Daily Chronicle* was reporting that France was actually coveting the Canaries for itself, along with Ceuta in Spanish Morocco.[98]

At the end of the war, the peace treaty, brokered and signed in Paris, forced Spain to relinquish sovereignty over Cuba and to cede to the United States the islands of Puerto Rico and Guam. With this arrangement, Spain was effectively "removed from the Western hemisphere," while the United States had

[97] Qtd. in Henry Blumenthal, *American and French Culture, 1800–1900* (Baton Rouge: Louisiana State University Press, 1975), 198.

[98] *New York Times*, 2 June 1898, 1.

acquired a new colonial empire, a development that deeply alarmed the French, who began referring to the "American peril."[99]

But while the Spanish-American War effectively granted the United States a new, imperial status, it did little to temper the French disdain for American vulgarity. On the contrary, America's brand of imperialism seemed to fit perfectly into the reigning French view of the United States as a brutal, machine-driven country. America's aggressive acquisition of new territories was unfavorably compared in the French press to the more "uplifting" "civilizing" form of the French. "The irresistible force of the machine," writes Blumenthal, "which Americans had exploited to the utmost, had badly upset the normal—much slower—pace of economic development. The speed and determination with which Americans imposed their will on modern civilization did not seem to hold out much promise for moral and human values."[100] The great *mission civilisatrice* of colonialism seemed absent from the American version.

In the months before the opening of the World's Fair of 1900, the United States, emboldened perhaps by its recent conquests, began expressing disgruntlement with its allotted exhibition space. The Americans wanted twice the amount of space they had been given, and were also lobbying for space in the Trocadéro, in order to exhibit their new territories (which included the recently annexed Hawaii). Commissioner General Alfred Picard at first rejected these demands, using an ironic phrase that quickly became famous. Explaining the scarcity of exhibition space, Picard compared his commission to a young woman granting sexual favors: "Even the most beautiful girl in the world can only offer what she has," he said.[101]

As it turned out, the beautiful girl found a little more to give, and Picard eventually doubled the exhibition space given to the United States, and even allowed it a small colonial exhibition at the Trocadéro. The episode and Picard's famous remark suggest, of course, how the United States was being perceived by the French at this time. This young, newly imperialist nation was imposing enough to be cast as an insistent suitor intent on pushing for

---

[99] See Blumenthal, *American and French Culture*, 205–12, also Jacques Porter, *Une Fascination réticente: Les Etats-Unis dans l'opinion française* (Nancy: Presses Universitaires de Nancy, 1990). See also Richard H. Miller, "Introduction," in *American Imperialism in 1898: The Quest for National Fulfillment*, ed. Richard H. Miller (New York: John Wiley and Sons, 1970), 6–60. And on the Social Darwinist implications of American expansionism, see Igor Dementev, *Imperialists and Anti-Imperialists*, trans. David Skvirsky, (Moscow: Progress Publishers, 1979).

[100] Blumenthal, *American and French Culture*, 211, citing Octave Noël, "Le Péril américain," *Le Correspondent*, cxciv, 25 March 1899, 1083–1104.

[101] Qtd. in G. Moynet, "Le Pavillon national des Etats-Unis," *L'Encyclopédie du siècle* (Paris: Montgredien et Cie, 1900), 91.

more favors from a coy woman. According to historian Kristin Hoganson, such a virilized status was exactly what the United States had hoped to get out of its recent expansionist policies. For Hoganson, the Spanish-American War resulted largely from a crisis in the nation's collective sexual identity, a fear of having lost the "manly character." She cites, particularly, another famous remark, this one made by Theodore Roosevelt when he was a member of McKinley's cabinet. Frustrated that McKinley was not moving toward a war with Spain after the *Maine* was blown up in Havana harbor, Roosevelt accused the president of having "no more backbone than a chocolate éclair."[102]

Of course, éclairs are limp penises in pastry form, soft, frilly, and even worse—French, and therefore, coded culturally as female. But while they never had a problem conceiving of their *cultural* institutions as feminine (consider, for example, such allegorical females as "La "Liberté," Marianne, or "La Révolution"), when it came to colonial politics, the French wore the pants in the family.[103] Adhering to the traditional metaphors of imperialism, France had always fashioned itself as an inseminating, virile force in the edenically feminine regions of Morocco, Algeria, and Indochina. When confronted with the United States, however, it became a girl fending off a suitor—turning into a political éclair. By conceding to the Americans' demands at the Fair, Picard had essentially reversed the usual sexual metaphor implicit in France's colonialism. The struggle over territory at the Fair played out in microcosm a new, reversed story of imperialism between the Old and New Worlds. America, the former colony, elbowed its way in, guns blazing, and captured square footage from the helpless maiden, France.

The United States pavilion wound up being one of the grandest and most technologically advanced at the *Exposition Universelle*. Built with a rotunda meant to resemble that of the Capitol building in Washington, D.C., the pavilion featured advanced mechanical luxuries such as typewriters and telegraphs for use by visiting American businessmen.[104]

---

[102] Kristin Hoganson, *Fighting for American Manhood: How Gender Politics Provoked the Spanish-American and Philippine-American Wars* (New Haven: Yale University Press, 2000), 16. See also Chris Wallace, *Character: Profiles in Presidential Courage* (New York: Ruggedland Press, 2003), as well as Robert D. Schulzinger, ed., *A Companion to American Foreign Relations* (New York: Blackwell, 2003), and Frank Ninkovich, *The United States and Imperialism* (New York: Blackwell, 2000).

[103] "The French appeared to be willing and happy to recognize their culture in broad terms as being feminine . . . and stylistic traits in art and design were seen as female" (Greenhalgh, Ephemeral Vistas, 188).

[104] See Rhonda Garelick, "Electric Salome," in *Imperialism and Theatre*, ed. Ellen Gainor (New York: Routledge, 1995), 85–103.

Loie Fuller's position at the exposition takes on new meaning when considered in the context of America's new expansionism and concomitant elbow-twisting of Fair officials. Reviewing her many valences, we see that Fuller was an American whose work qualified her as "French" enough for the Rue de Paris at the Fair, and important enough to come to represent all of the Fair's implicit "progress." By virtue of her veils and well-known connection to "Salome," she was affiliated with Middle Eastern entertainments, such as those on the Rue du Caire and elsewhere on the Trocadéro. She was associated with the dazzle of machinery, of technology, and of Yankee ingenuity—the same kind of mechanical progress on display at the United States pavilion with its typewriters. Her work spoke of science, unseen marvels, and Orientalism stripped somehow of its lubricity. In other words, Fuller evoked nearly all the Fair's main themes and then removed from them their overtly troubling nature. She was faintly Oriental, but reassuringly white, a veil dancer but never unveiled, an American by birth, but French by choice. And in Fuller's work, American technology—which had engendered the United States's frightening new imperialism—was subsumed by the Gallicizing forces of Art Nouveau, cabaret, and, curiously, the implied charms of French colonial holdings. If, in its negotiations with Fair commissioners, the United States had turned France into a weak-willed maiden yielding her virtue, with Fuller France acquired a corrective symbol: a sexually impenetrable, even phallic woman who gave no quarter—an American who had implicitly changed nationality, whose Yankee ingenuity could be harnessed for and blended effortlessly with the purposes of French cultural iconography. After all, Fuller was not only an über-Gallic attraction suitable for the Rue de Paris, she was the de facto symbol for the entire World's Fair.

A Vision of America to Come

The World's Fair provides a rich context in which to examine the layered cultural politics of Loie Fuller's role in France. Such an examination sheds light on why the French government was so willing to drape its *tricolore* over Fuller, embracing her as icon of this vast pageant of nationalism.[105] Nonetheless, such an interpretation does not exhaust the political resonances of Loie Fuller's unique status at the Fair and beyond.

[105] During World War I, Fuller would resume her role as icon of French patriotism, performing at the Front for French and Belgian troops. In 1914, she even mounted a production set to Schubert's *Marche Militaire*, in which she projected the colors of the French flag onto her robes

Throughout her career Fuller was lauded precisely for having suppressed so much in her work, lauded for her sleek, abstract style, which was so often viewed as a corrective to more risqué popular dance ("debauchery marches toward its redemption," as one critic wrote of her work). But we have also seen the extent to which Fuller's apparently bodiless, ahistorical theatricality managed nonetheless to evoke and then somehow disavow or suppress a large variety of the unsettling elements traditionally associated with the performance of French colonialism—racial difference, violence, exotic eroticism, Oriental narrative. And we have seen how this process of evocation followed by suppression might have served the purposes of the French government at the World's Fair. But we have yet to acknowledge that this very process, whereby troubling details, history, and narrative specificity are all whirled away into an abstraction of "innocence" or "chastity," has something uniquely American about it, an Americanness still worth noting despite Fuller's near-conversion to French citizenship.

Fuller was, essentially, a PG version of an X-rated fantasy. "She is clear of the human mess," wrote Frank Kermode; but it might be more accurate to say that Fuller "cleared away human mess," rendering disturbing concepts palatable or assimilable to the largest possible audience.[106] This ability unquestionably made Fuller an attractive celebrity for the French government to appropriate. In other words, the World's Fair itself used Fuller as an instrument of disavowal, a silken broom with which to sweep aside such disturbances as the tensions between the United States and France. But as we have throughout this chapter, we must once more look for the "acknowledgment"—the place where the seams of disavowal show through; and we find this place of acknowledgment precisely in the stylistic difference between Fuller's veil dances and those of all the other Salomes—the difference, that is, between technological ahistoricism and recreated, "authentic" exoticism, terms which could just as easily describe the difference between American and French styles of imperialism.

In *The Empire's Old Clothes*, Ariel Dorfman has examined cultural manifestations of imperialism. In one chapter, particularly pertinent for our purposes here, Dorfman looks to French and American children's popular culture, Babar the Elephant and Disney cartoons, to illustrate the profound stylistic difference between the two countries' forms of imperialism. As Dorfman reminds us, in Jean de Brunhoff's Babar the Elephant series, an African jungle

---

as she dance, literally embodying the *tricolore* (which shares its colors, of course, with the American flag).

[106] Kermode, Loie Fuller and the Dance before Diaghilev, 47.

elephant becomes "civilized" in France via a series of stories that all feature a degree of geographical and historical specificity, despite their sugarcoating. The Babar books construct, for Dorfman, "a parallel, ideal history, [which is] none other than the fulfillment of the dominant countries' colonial dream."[107]

On the other hand, Walt Disney's cartoons make use of no such historical trappings. When Donald Duck and Mickey Mouse visit the tropics, seeking adventure in "Foola Zoola" or "San Bananador," they do so unencumbered by any history at all. Dorfman points out that, although de Brunhoff avoids mentioning individual countries' names, Babar moves from a recognizable African jungle to a recognizable Parisian household; and moments of loss and colonial violence are included in the stories. Disney's characters however, float around in caricatured parodies of Third World nations, enjoying harmless good times, avoiding any issues of colonial struggle:

> [Disney] . . . can exercise his commercial and linguistic domination in less colonial and more indirect ways than de Brunhoff could. . . . Just as Disney plunders . . . literature, reshaping it in his average North American image, so he proceeds with world geography. He feels no obligation to avoid the caricature, and rebaptizes each country as if it were a can on a shelf, an object of infinite fun.[108]

Dorfman sees the United States's image as a good-natured and innocent country as a crucial factor in the success of its economic (rather than colonial) imperialism. "America has been interpreted time and again as a domain of innocence," he writes; "[Americans] only felt comfortable if other people assented to the image they had of themselves as naïve, frolicsome, unable to harm a mouse. . . . the US managed [to become a global empire] . . . without its people losing their basic intuition that they were good, clean and wholesome. Its citizens never recognized themselves as an empire."[109]

In Disney's cartoon parodies of Third World nations Dorfman sees a desire to erase all historical and geographical detail, as well as responsibility, and a desire to replace these elements with the power and appeal of modern science. "[Disney's] response to the misfortunes of the past is a benign modernization of the untamed world, the application of . . . technology."[110] For Dorfman, the Babar books recall France's sense of responsibility, its desire to master and absorb the history and customs of its extended empire. America's empire of

---

[107] Ariel Dorfman, *The Empire's Old Clothes* (New York: Pantheon Books, 1983), 25.
[108] Ibid., 24.
[109] Ibid., 201–2.
[110] Ibid., 29.

course never really became colonial—the acquisitions of the Spanish-American War did not develop into full-fledged colonies. Instead, the United States' empire developed economically and technologically, and was, accordingly, devoid of the sense of historical specificity and cultural duty that France clearly had. In Dorfman's reading, Americans have always wanted to play Donald Duck in "Chiliburgeria," innocent adventurers in search of absurd new lands for fun and profit, always disavowing any imperialist greed.

Dorfman's vision of the United States as an imperial power obscuring its politics with insistence upon its innocence holds true even for the United States of 1900. By the turn of the twentieth century, America was well on its way to gaining its eventual place as a global power, having already demonstrated its expansionism on the North American continent, citing manifest destiny as a divinely decreed policy purified by God's word.

This kind of self-professed American purity was clearly visible in Loie Fuller's image in France. Like a good American, she also resorted quickly to professions of godliness when caught with any imperialist gleam in her eye, as we saw earlier in her account of meeting the tribal king from Senegal. Fuller was the chaste, proto-Disney Salome, the performer people could bring their children to see, an unthreatening introduction to the less pure, more disturbing veiled women on the Trocadéro. And, however politically useful this ostensible chastity may have been for the French, it must also be recognized for the way it ties Fuller symbolically to her own country, to the powerful America of the future. More than the United States's grand congressional-style pavilion on the "Rue des Nations," more than the Philippines exhibition on the Trocadéro, Fuller's pared-down, mechanical sleekness hinted at the America to come. Dematerialized under her veils, alone on a stage bare of décor, Fuller was an Electric Salome, an ideological instrument for France, certainly, but at the same time, a subtle symbol of the historically detached, technologized, and commercial imperialism that her own nation would make its trademark in the century to come.

Chapter Three
Fuller and the Romantic Ballet

*To be romantic about something is to see what you are and to wish for
something entirely different. This requires magic.*
—George Balanchine

Yankees Don't Do Ballet

Notwithstanding her four decades at the heart of the Parisian avant-garde,
Loie Fuller held fast to her chosen persona of guileless American innovator.
She routinely insisted upon the natural, instinctive originality of her dance
and teaching methods, and upon the "accidental" nature of her discoveries.
"I am like the pioneer who found the first gold nugget," she wrote of her
experiments with light, "he didn't mean it, and was probably more surprised
than any body else when he found it."[1] As this reference to the California
Gold Rush makes plain, Fuller enjoyed allying her ostensible naiveté with her
nationality. We have seen how useful such a pose of innocence could be for
Fuller as an "Electric Salome," and by extension for France's imperialist
agenda at the turn of the century; and we have seen how it also prefigured
the sleek, disavowed, "Disney-fied" imperialism of the United States in the
twentieth century.

But if Fuller had a powerful albeit disingenuous relationship with Orientalist entertainments and the concomitant figure of Salome, she had an equally
complicated one with classical European dance and *its* trademark female figure, the weightless ballerina—the sylph.

George Balanchine and Francis Mason, *Complete Stories of the Great Ballets* (Garden City:
Doubleday & Co., 1954, 1977), 281.

[1] Fuller, unpublished essay, NYPLPA, Robinson Locke Collection.

Fuller has long served as a convenient line of demarcation in dance history. "She free[d] movement from the constraining technique of ballet," according to Julia Foulkes.[2] And for Giovanni Lista, Fuller represents "le véritable clivage avec la danse classique"—a distinct turning away from European ballet and the official starting point for American modern dance.[3] But as we saw in the last chapter, Fuller was never cleanly associated with either the Old World or the New. Rather, she occupied a highly charged middle realm, absorbing, embodying, and reinterpreting traits of both the America from which she came and the Europe she made her home. As we shall see, she occupied a similarly liminal space in dance history, creating not a moment of rupture (or "*clivage*") with ballet, but a deep and lifelong dialogue with it, despite her constant protestations to the contrary.

When modern dance writes its own version of Genesis, it begins with a trio of American women—Loie Fuller, Isadora Duncan, and Ruth St. Denis—collectively turning their backs on ballet, transforming dance forever by removing constricting costumes, throwing away pointe shoes, and jettisoning character- and plot-driven narratives in favor of a "natural" style based on affective female solo performance. They are three barefoot revolutionaries who, as Elizabeth Dempster writes, "constructed images and created dances through their own unballetic bodies, producing a writing of the female body which strongly contrasted with classical inscription."[4]

The story is indisputably true in many ways—these three women did indeed change the landscape of dance; they did inaugurate a new art form. But, like all creation myths, this one splits the world improbably neatly into halves marked "before" and "after," with classical ballet firmly on the side of "before." Examining Fuller's work closely turns the creationist, "rupture" narrative of modern dance into a more nuanced story of evolution, a Darwinian tale of progress and adaptation.[5] Rather than "detonating the ballet stage," as Susan

---

[2] Julia Foulkes, *Modern Bodies: Dance and American Modernism from Martha Graham to Alvin Ailey* (Chapel Hill: University of North Carolina Press, 2002), 9.

[3] Lista, *Danseuse*, 147.

[4] Elizabeth Dempster, "Women Writing the Body, Let's Watch a Little How She Dances," in *The Routledge Dance Studies Reader*, ed. Alexandra Carter (New York: Routledge, 1998), 223–29. Dempster also includes Maud Allen in the lineup of founding figures of modern dance.

[5] Primate anthropologist Jane Goodall has written of Loie Fuller's role as a kind of visual spectacle of the theory of "transformism" in evolution:

At the turn of the century . . . the idea of a critical evolutionary transition point was compelling indeed and Fuller as the Fairy Electricity, with her Valkyrie music, was one of its definitive expressions. Such an idea was not compatible with the gradualism central to Darwin's theory of natural selection in the animal world, but it was not hard to reconcile with theories

Foster has claimed, Fuller responded to and adapted it.[6] Looking at Fuller's work from this perspective reveals, as we shall see, that she was actually the most balletic of the three founding mothers of modern dance, despite an admittedly most "unballetic body" and a total lack of formal training. She was also an important, early point of charged interaction between American modern dance and the modernist ballet revolution of Diaghilev and the Ballets Russes, a kind of hinge between these movements whose paths diverged at the beginning of the twentieth century. It is, in fact, Loie Fuller who best helps us see the important connections between ballet and modern dance, for her work offered a mise-en-scène of the transition from one to the other.

In fairness to Fuller, before studying her close relationship to ballet, we ought at least to acknowledge how much she claimed to hate it. Fuller was an ardent anti-balletist who routinely decried ballet as an inhumane art that tortured women, positing her own dance and teaching methods as healthful alternatives to it. An undated entry in her journal reads:

> The fundamental principle of dance should be health first, health afterwards, and health always. . . . Anything which deforms the body an iota should not, cannot be justifiable as an art. When a system of dance depends for its accomplishments upon torture and disfigurement . . . nothing can justify it, except the past ages which gave it birth and to which it belongs. . . . We deplore the fashion of binding the foot of the woman in China. The deformation of the foot of the ballet dancer can compare with this barbaric and inhuman custom. And we send missionaries to China![7]

While she certainly has a point, as anyone who has seen a ballerina's unshod foot can attest, Fuller reveals more here than her disgruntlement with ballet. This passage reveals ballet's rhetorical usefulness for Fuller, for her emphasis on the healthful, instinctive nature of her dancing was clearly an attempt to

---

of cultural evolution such as Spencer's or Bagehot's. The theory of natural selection, with its vision of change randomly generated and infinitely slow to take recognizable form, was difficult to interpret in performance, but evolutionary theory fused with an archaic vision of cyclic change—and all the accompanying symbolism of death, regeneration and metamorphosis—was inherently dramatic. "Transformism," the term used in the 1820s by anatomists making the first attempt to express a concept of evolutionary change in the organism, took on new meaning in Loie Fuller's personifications, which also implied that science and human agency might drive all forms toward higher levels of being. [Jane Goodall, *Performance and Evolution in the Age of Darwin: Out of the Natural Order* (New York: Routledge, 2002):218.]

[6] Susan Leigh Foster, *Choreography and Narrative* (Bloomington: Indiana University Press, 1998), 261.

[7] Fuller, unpublished essay, NYPLPA.

naturalize her own highly unconventional life. By 1909, when she founded Les Ballets Loie Fuller and established its headquarters in her own home in Neuilly, Fuller was as an unmarried, childless woman living with a cross-dressing female lover and a houseful of otherwise-unchaperoned young girls who cavorted on the lawn in flimsy "Grecian" tunics (like Isadora Duncan, Fuller favored lightweight classical garb for her disciples offstage). While such a living situation could have easily proven a career-ruining scandal, Fuller managed to use it to burnish further her image as whimsical eccentric and benevolent guardian of young ladies. "To her 'dear little darlings' Loie Fuller is a good and sweet grandmamma," wrote one interviewer, "She knows how to spoil them, rarely scolds them, and above all is beloved by them."[8] In 1910, Fuller gave an interview to *Musical America,* which made clear that her marketing of her art form was indistinguishable from her marketing of her own life and persona: "I was born to be a mother," she said, "and to spend most of my days in the kitchen. But some strange perversity of fate led me to the motherhood of natural dancing."[9] Although the intended innocence of her remarks suffered from the (probable) lapsus "strange perversity," Fuller's point was nonetheless clear: her dancing and teaching were wholesome, and she herself was a kind of Madonna of the Arts.

To shore up this chaste, maternal image, Fuller relied again on her nationality. The pose of the no-nonsense American who rejected the typical trappings of the Parisian *danseuse* offered excellent cover for her unconventional lifestyle. American women were *supposed* to be less artful in their self-presentation: "La Loie offstage is cheerful [and] blue-eyed," wrote one reporter, "frank, honest, and real, devoid of affectation . . . extremely American."[10]

Here again, ballet played a role, for Fuller could use its artificiality to offset her self-conscious naturalness; she could cite ballet's European stuffiness as the antithesis of her American ease. In other words, ballet offered a very handy foil for Fuller's carefully constructed image as a homespun, natural, *American* artist. In an interview about her newly formed dance school, Fuller made her distinctions explicit:

> I am sure that many Parisians will be surprised and say "What! You call that dance?!" Yes, it is dance, it is instinctive dance. Onstage, my girls do as they like . . . troubled by no constraints. . . . Each pupil is taught

[8] See Pierre Desclaux, "Gala de l'orphelinat des arts," 19 June 1911.
[9] Fuller, qtd. in review article, *Musical America,* 12 June 1910.
[10] "La Loie in Private Life," press clipping, NYPLPA, Robinson Locke Collection.

in a manner that suits [her] . . . by cultivation of this penchant, freedom and self-reliance are secured.[11]

The dichotomy is clear: Parisians—standing in for all of old, retrograde Europe—represent a demand for artistic and bodily constraint, while as a free-thinking, Emersonian American, Fuller upholds an ideal of self-reliance in dance instruction.[12] "Let us try to forget educational processes in so far as dance is concerned," she wrote in her autobiography, "The old ballet dancing produces a . . . rank and file from which few escape."[13]

Fuller's stance as free-spirited pioneer also worked wonders with the European cultural elite, which seemed to enjoy keeping this unusual American lady as its own noble savage—a charming Yankee upstart. Mallarmé, for example, referred to Fuller as his "barely conscious source of inspiration" (*"très peu consciente inspiratrice"*) who created "sorcery . . . by instinct."[14] Roger-Marx echoed the sentiment: "In Loie Fuller, there is nothing but the spontaneous, the supple, the easy [and] . . . the instinctive . . . no more pointe work, *jetés*, or *entre-chats*."[15] Jules Clarétie insisted that Fuller "no more learned to dance than she learned to breathe."[16] And Joris-Karl Huysmans, while acknowledging her "mediocre dancing," praised her New World–style mechanical savvy: "All the glory goes to the electrician. It's American."[17] Given how popular her Yankee naiveté and ingenuity seemed to the lions at the gates of high culture, it should not surprise us that Fuller cultivated the myth, a big part of which entailed presenting herself as the modern antidote to ballet.

Of course, while Fuller used the rigors of ballet to offset her own loudly proclaimed adherence to free-spirited and instinctive dance methods, in reality, very little in her performances was ever left to chance or to instinct. As we know, her lighting cues and choreography sequences were guarded as tightly as any state secrets; and she traveled with her own crew of up to thirty electricians, refusing to work with the in-house technical staffs of theaters where she performed. As for her revealingly named pupils, "Les Petites Loies," they were at least as regimented as any ballet students or *"petits rats"* from the Paris Opéra school, required to resemble their teacher, wear their hair as she did,

[11] Fuller, in *Musical America*, 12 June 1910.

[12] See Giovanni Lista's *Danseuse* for the influence of American transcendentalism in Fuller's work.

[13] Fuller, *Fifteen Years*, 68.

[14] Mallarmé, *Oeuvres complètes*, 308.

[15] Roger-Marx, *La Loie Fuller*, 24.

[16] Clarétie, *La Tragedie de Salomé*.

[17] Joris-Karl Huysmans, qtd. in "Loie Fuller's Glory Laid to Light," *Chicago Tribune*, 8 January 1928, Musée Rodin archives.

perform in costumes nearly identical to Fuller's (creating the uniform look of a corps de ballet), rehearse for long hours, and to obscure their identities with Fuller's choice of stage names. The troupe, furthermore, did not maintain a stable cast list; young dancers joined and quit continually, in response to the patience or finances of their parents.[18] Any dancer, moreover, such as "Orchidée" (née Vilma Banchi), who dared borrow Fuller's "free" style to launch a solo career, was swiftly served with a subpoena.[19] Even Fuller's ostensibly laudable interest in her dancers' health remains suspect, for while they may not have worn toe shoes, the girls continued to paint costumes with phosphorescent salts—at Fuller's behest—long after Thomas Edison had warned her of the chemicals' potent carcinogenic properties.[20]

And so we should file Fuller's diatribes against ballet with all her other typically disingenuous pronouncements. But whether Fuller truly disliked and intended to reject ballet is ultimately less important than the relationship—conscious or not—between her work and ballet.[21]

---

[18] "One rarely saw the same girls twice," wrote one interviewer (Yvon Novy, review article, 1947, Collection Rondel). Fuller's unpublished correspondence with Gabrielle Bloch reveals that the students' parents would grow frustrated with Fuller's disregard for their wishes, often keeping the girls traveling abroad far longer than promised, despite repeated urgent requests that they be sent home (Gabrielle Bloch to Loie Fuller, December 1915, NYPLPA).

[19] Banchi later found some success acting in silent films, starring opposite Rudolph Valentino, for example, in *The Son of the Sheik*, the 1926 sequel to the legendary 1921 *The Sheik*.

[20] There is some evidence that the continued exposure to the radioactive salts may have caused some of the young women to develop cancers later in life. In part because their names were obscured, the later lives of "Les Petites Loies" remain somewhat unknown. It is indisputable however that Fuller was apprised of the danger of these salts by Edison, who, according to her notebooks, told Fuller that he had ceased experimenting with them in order to protect his own laboratory workers from harm. Fuller notes this but never refers to it anywhere again in her published or unpublished writings. Nor does she ever acknowledge that she may have been similarly endangering her own young acolytes.

[21] Fuller had a vexed relationship to structured education of all kinds. In one journal entry, for example, she ranted violently against her notion of the arrogant, educated woman. The short piece is entitled "The Boston Bluestocking":

"She can throw statistics at you till you wish there weren't any. She can make you feel yourself the biggest fool and idiot that ever breathed on earth. She can impress you with the fact there isn't anything but learning in the world [and] that you haven't got any. . . . Why it was near Boston . . . that women were burned at the stake as witches because they knew too much. (They don't burn them now, we wish they did!) [Fuller, unpublished essay, NYPLPA]

The bitterness in this passage betrays Fuller's defensiveness about her humble background. We know that when she arrived in Paris, an uneducated vaudeville performer, Fuller's explicit goal was to ascend to the realm of high art; and for her that meant being accepted by those with

On its surface, Fuller's work differed sharply from ballet. No one ever mistook Loie Fuller for a ballerina; she had never exercised at a barre; she had never taken a dance class. She eschewed ballet's costumes as well as its notion of positions or a standard dance vocabulary. And while ballerinas in the late nineteenth century increasingly bared their bodies onstage, often in the hope of landing a wealthy gentleman patron, Fuller kept hers fully under wraps, avoiding any overt erotic enticement. While ballet grew ever more athletic and gymnastic, Fuller's bodily movements were limited and grew more so with age, consisting mainly of raising and lowering her arms and turning in small steps. She even claimed to abhor the very concept of a dance repertoire—ballet's essential practice of preserving and re-performing fixed works by a pantheon of choreographers—claiming it was merely a form of slavish imitation: "A small creation is greater than the greatest copy," she wrote dismissively of the practice.[22]

Nevertheless, Fuller was keenly aware of ballet, especially given the artistic milieu she entered in fin-de-siècle Paris.[23] One might call this era ballet's interregnum—a period marked at once by the decline of Romantic ballet in most of Europe, the migration of serious ballet choreography to Russia, and the increasing interpenetration of ballet and cabaret performance in France. The 1903 arrival in Paris of Diaghilev's Ballets Russes, which essentially marked the modernist rebirth of the art form, was still several years away.

Once Diaghilev's Ballets Russes did arrive in France however, Fuller would remain for years in a deep but unspoken dialogue with them, with the Ballets Russes often imitating Fuller or basing their own works on earlier ones by Fuller.[24] Frank Kermode has referred to Fuller as "the woman who seemed to be doing almost single-handed what Diaghilev was later to achieve only with the help of great painters, musicians, and dancers."[25] As Kermode's remark

---

formal learning. "The notion of going to Paris possessed me," she wrote; "I wanted to go to a city where, as I had been told, educated people would like my dancing and would accord it a place in the realm of art."

[22] Fuller, unpublished essay, NYPLPA.

[23] "In the United States ballet had neither evoked such shock nor carried such import. Largely a vehicle of titillation or decoration, American ballet teetered between an act in vaudeville . . . and a backdrop in Opera" (Foulkes, *Modern Bodies*, 8).

[24] The Ballets Russes, for example, performed an extravagant version of *Salome* shortly after Fuller's second production of it, and created an elaborate staging of Stravinsky's *Fireworks* directly after Fuller's interpretation of the same score. Some of the Ballets Russes' most important stage designers, notably set designer Pavel Tchelitchev, were overtly copying Fuller's lighting and stage-craft techniques, as when Tchelitchev staged a production of *Ondine*, using a "wall of water" technique identical to an earlier one of Fuller's. See chapter 4 for more on this.

[25] Kermode, "Loie Fuller and the Dance Before Diaghlev," 31

makes clear, the point of connection between Diaghilev's and Fuller's work was in their use of spectacle, their experimental work with lighting and costuming, as well as theme. Fuller's physical choreography, on which I am focusing in this chapter, did not resemble Ballets Russes choreography—in any bodily way. Lynn Garafola has done excellent scholarship on the relationship between Fuller and the Ballets Russes, as has Giovanni Lista. I shall address this relationship briefly in the next chapter.

Romantic Ballet: Sprites, Swans, and Windup Toys

Admittedly, by 1892, Romantic ballet was decades into its famous great decline. The genre that had officially begun in 1832 with the production of Filippo Taglioni's La Sylphide and reached its height nine years later with Jules Perrot's Giselle in 1841 no longer drew the same kinds of crowds or public fascination. The era of the great European ballerinas such as Marie Taglioni (daughter of Filippo), Fanny Elssler, and Emma Livry had drawn largely to its close. "[It] had become a mere industry, it was a lamentable era . . . [of] deadly ennui," writes Francis Miomandre of the state of ballet in turn-of-the-century France.[26] "By the end of the nineteenth century a measure of creative excitement had gone out of French ballet," according to Jack Anderson.[27] Nonetheless, ballet was being kept alive both at the Opéra and in venues such as music halls and cabarets, partaking of the fin de siècle's overall democratizing trend in culture. So, while Parisians still attended full-length ballets at the Opéra that starred such prominent ballerinas such as Rosita Mauri and Carlotta Zambelli, they could also pay to see some of those same ballerinas perform on more popular stages.[28] One such "crossover" dancer was the famous and beautiful Caroline Otéro (known as "la belle Otéro"), who had begun her studies at the Ecole de Danse de l'Opéra, but in 1892 was appearing onstage at the Folies-Bergère. (She later performed at two World's Fairs with the dance troupe known as "Les Cambodgiennes," essentially masquerading as an Oriental dancer.) At the Folies, she crossed paths with Loie Fuller, who would certainly have seen her performances and met her personally.[29] Fuller also regularly encountered classically trained ballerinas who sought to leave ballet and join

[26] Miomandre, Danse, 53.

[27] Jack Anderson, Ballet and Modern Dance (Princeton, NJ: Princeton University Press, 1986): 91.

[28] After closing during the Paris Commune of 1870, the Opéra had reopened in 1875.

[29] Martine Kahane and Delphine Pinasa, Le Tutu, Petit Guide (Paris: Flammarion/Opéra National de Paris, 1997), 20.

Figure 3.1. Rita Sacchetto, a classical ballerina who joined Fuller's
troupe, Billy Rose Theatre Collection, New York Public Library for
the Performing Arts, Astor, Lenox, and Tilden Foundations

her troupe. She accepted only a few (among them the well-known Italian
ballerina from La Scala, Rita Sacchetto, (fig. 3.1), finding that formal ballet
training rendered young women unfit for barefoot dance: "Out of fifty ballet
girls who came to me, not one could let their feet be seen without shoes. . . .
I was sorry, but the foot once deformed can never be made perfect again."[30]

The greatest achievements in ballet during the last decades of the nineteenth century, though, emerged not in France but in Russia, where French-
born choreographer Marius Petipa developed the style known usually as "classical ballet"—a less expressive, more technically demanding, formal, and

[30] Fuller, unpublished writings, NYPLPA.

symmetrical art form.[31] Petipa rose to fame directing St. Petersburg's Imperial Ballet at the Mariinsky Theater from 1862 to his retirement at the age of 84 in 1903. His work breathed life one last time into the great tradition of Romantic thematic ballets, reworking classic repertoire pieces by his mentors Jules Perrot and Arthur Saint Léon as well as creating new *ballets à grand spectacle*. His credits include *Le Papillon* (1874), *La Bayadère* (1877), *The Sleeping Beauty* (1890), *Cinderella* (1893), *Swan Lake* (1895), *Raymonda* (1898), and *The Magic Mirror* (1903). Petipa's work was deeply anchored in the Romantic ballet canon, which, as his titles make clear, relies heavily on narratives of magical transformation. Sometimes the transformation involves inanimate objects coming to life. We see this in the famous "White Lady sequence" in Petipa's *Raymonda*, when a statue steps off her pedestal to dance a mysterious, floating solo. Other ballets of the period, such as *Coppélia* and *The Nutcracker*, feature a similar, uncanny motif of dolls somehow coming to life through dance.

More often, the supernatural transformations of Romantic ballet result in women becoming mysterious, otherworldly creatures—ethereal, shimmering beings barely subject to the laws of gravity. The Romantic ballet heroine dazzled audiences by transforming herself into any number of floating, decorative motifs: butterflies, flowers, delicate birds, "ephemeral . . . , vaporous, [and] incomparably light," as Susan Foster writes.[32] Sometimes, the ballerina seemed to dematerialize altogether, turning into a specter or phantom beneath clouds of vaporous white or pale material—usually gauze or tulle. Echoing the themes of the era's literature and painting, Romantic ballet turned away from Enlightenment issues of earthly reason and social philosophy and toward the anguish of the individual, of the soul, and of unrequited or star-crossed love. In the so-called "*ballets blancs*" of this period, a tragic love affair leads to "the subsequent transmutation of the woman into a white-bodied natural or supernatural being, and her removal into a fantastic realm of nature; her quintessential inaccessibility, and the solitude of the man who worships but cannot possess her, who has distanced and idealized her."[33] Examples of these mystical beings include the swans of *Swan Lake*, the butterflies of *Le Papillon*, the water nymphs of *Undine*, the ghosts of dead women, such as the lapsed nuns of Louis Véron's *Robert le Diable* and the Wilis of *Giselle* (souls of brides who die before their wedding night), and the air spirit or "sylph" of *La Sylphide*, from which this

[31] See Susan Au, *Ballet and Modern Dance* (London: Thames & Hudson, 1988), 62.

[32] Susan Leigh Foster, "The Ballerina's Phallic Pointe," in *Corporealities*, ed. Susan Leigh Foster (New York; Routledge, 1996), 4.

[33] McCarren, *Dance Pathologies*, 63.

character type takes its name.[34] The sets of such ballets typically featured moonlit forests, mist-shrouded gardens, and mystical lakes shadowed by clouds—landscapes of the sort evoked in painting, for example, by J.M.W. Turner or Casper David Friedrich.

Romantic ballet did not depend entirely upon such ethereal imagery, however. Many of the stories included a counterbalancing subtext featuring far more robust, percussive or sensual "character" dances, often adapted from national or folkloric traditions. Saint-Léon's *Coppélia*, for example, ends with a rousing mazurka, a traditional Polish circle dance for couples involving much stomping and hand-waving. The plot of *Raymonda* calls also for a spirited Hungarian dance, as well as a vivid Spanish flamenco, and an "Oriental" pas de deux. *The Nutcracker* too famously presents a series of national dances during the *divertissement* section of Act II. *La Sylphide*, set in Scotland, opens with a festive performance of the Highland fling.

The female characters within these more earthbound sequences—the Gypsies, Spaniards, and other such "exotics"—represent what Susan Foster has called the "pagan counterpart" to the sylph. Some ballerinas, most notably Fanny Elssler, who was known for her Spanish "*danse tacquetée*" with castanets, achieved stardom by excelling at this other, more grounded style of choreography.[35] Occasionally, a single ballet heroine embodied this duality of the exotic and the ethereal, as in *Giselle*, whose protagonist dances as a spirited peasant girl in the first act, only to be later transformed tragically into a phantom, joining the ethereal Wilis upon her death. Felicia McCarren astutely observes that this aspect of *Giselle*, its "double subject" of "two women in one," actually hints at a deeper truth underlying all dance, particularly Romantic ballet: "Dance performance by its very nature recognizes such doubleness," she writes, "without hiding the work, or the discipline, that makes it possible, dance presents it as something else. The work that goes into the creation of danced illusion is not seen as work, but as pleasure, overlapping the work and inseparable from it."[36]

In her own way, Loie Fuller embodied a duality similar to the sylph/pagan motif of ballet, for in addition to her floating sylphlike forms, she displayed—

---

[34] See Au, *Ballet and Modern Dance*. Of the phantom nuns in *Robert le Diable*, Hans Christian Andersen wrote in 1833: "By the hundred they rise from the graveyard and drift into the cloister. They seem not to touch the earth. Like vaporous images, they glide past one another." (qtd. in Deborah Jowitt, "In Pursuit of the Sylph," in *The Routledge Dance Studies Reader*, ed. Alexandra Carter [New York: Routledge, 1998], 207). See also Erik Aschengreen, "The Beautiful Danger: Facets of Romantic Ballet," trans. Patricia N. McAndrew, *Dance Perspectives*, no. 58 (1974).

[35] See Foster, "Phallic Pointe"; also Au, *Ballet and Modern Dance*.

[36] McCarren, *Dance Pathologies*, 60, 79.

as we saw in chapter 2—a subtle, displaced Orientalism—a cabaret-style flair for exotic, biblical, and Asian themes—which would ally her somewhat with the "pagan" side of dance.[37] Nevertheless, Fuller's primary iconography, particularly in her solo pieces (and even within her minimally thematic "exotic" pieces), remained much closer to that of the sylph. I shall, therefore, focus more on her relation to this better-known side of Romantic ballet, a style often known as "*danse ballonnée*" (because of the graceful ballooning out of the tutu), for however plump or flat-footed Fuller appeared offstage, onstage she created, as we shall see, a new kind of *danse ballonnée*, the province formerly of only the sleekest ballerinas. Accordingly, it is to their art I now turn.

During ballet's nineteenth-century heyday, the most successful ballerinas were those who most closely resembled the delicate creatures they depicted onstage—those dancers who seemed effortlessly light. While often known for their offstage erotic availability and frequently working openly as prostitutes, onstage, Romantic ballerinas occupied a liminal world in which flesh seemed to dematerialize and women turned to spirits. This magical "*va-et-vient*" between embodiment and ethereality enhanced the already exciting theatricality of these women, and echoed the sylph/pagan onstage duality which we have seen. They were at once commodities available for the highest bidder and beguiling, elusive sylphs.[38] Onstage, furthermore, these dance heroines prompted comparisons to spiritual visions. The lightness of their costumes gliding over their bodies was considered a visual echo of the implied relationship between the flimsy material of the flesh and the more spiritually substantial—though invisible and weightless—soul living within. At times, the vaporous covering of the spirit was understood to be the *character* played by the ballerina. Writing of Jules Perrot's classic ballet *Eoline*, for example, dance historian Ivor Guest describes the heroine, Eoline, as "only the envelope, the transparent veil of a superior being."[39] Sometimes, the dancer herself was understood as the embodiment of a quasi-Christian spirit. Marie Taglioni particularly inspired such interpretations. In 1837, a Russian critic, rapturous over Taglioni's Bolshoi debut in *La Sylphide*, described her as "a winged, fascinating dream, elusive and undefined, [which] plays and sports before your eyes, . . .

---

[37] In addition to her two productions of *Salome*, Fuller also mounted a version of *A Thousand and One Nights*" in 1914, with music by Armande de Polignac.

[38] See Abigail Solomon Godeau, "The Legs of the Countess," *October* 39 (Winter 1986): 65–108. See also Deborah Jowitt, who writes that this obsession with "flesh made fantasy and vice versa" bespeaks the "century's uneasiness with the flesh" (Jowitt, "In Pursuit of the Sylph," 208).

[39] Qtd. in Jowitt, "In Pursuit of the Sylph," 209.

flutter[ing] like a spirit amid the transparent mists of white mousseline with which she likes to surround herself . . . pellucid and tender, like the wings of the Sylphide" (fig. 3.2).[40] Théophile Gautier (who wrote the libretto for *Giselle*) praised Taglioni in similar terms, more taken with her as a religious vision than as a human woman: "Mlle Taglioni is a Christian dancer [who] flutters like a spirit amid the transparent vapors. . . . She resembles a happy soul who, with the points of her pink feet, barely bends the tips of the celestial flowers."[41] In 1843, the *Times* of London praised prima ballerina Adele Dumilâtre for being "so ethereal . . . that she almost looked transparent."[42] And when Carlotta Grisi leapt into the arms of Lucien Petipa (brother of Marius) in *La Péri* the *Times* review described her as "supported by air alone," an impression confirmed by Gautier, who was also in the audience and who described Grisi in her leap as "a dove's feather drifting downward, rather than a human being leaping from a platform."[43]

Fuller: The Accidental Sylph

If we keep these rhapsodic descriptions in mind as we now turn our attention back to Fuller, we can see right away how deeply she subsumed the iconography of Romantic ballet, as well as its desired effect upon audiences. Her titles alone reveal Fuller's attraction to balletic motifs: *Violet, Papillon, Le Phalène noir* (*The Black Moth*), *The Lily, Clouds, La Danse blanche, Le Voile magique,* and even *Le Ballet des sylphes*—a group piece for Les Ballets Loie Fuller.[44] We have also seen, in chapter 2, how Fuller's film, *Le Lys de la vie*, replayed several classic, fairytale themes of Romantic ballet (albeit with some gender reversal). Moreover, while she displayed neither balletic technique nor ability, Fuller provoked critical reviews uncannily similar to those elicited by the greatest mid-century ballerinas, winning accolades for her apparent weightlessness, spirituality, and magicalness. One could, in fact, easily mistake some of Fuller's

[40] "La Sylphide, Debut of Mlle Taglioni at the Bolshoy Theatre," *Severynaya pchela*, 18 September 1837, 834, qtd. in Roland John Wiley, *A Century of Russian Ballet* (Oxford: Oxford University Press, 1991), 84.

[41] Qtd. in Au, *Ballet and Modern Dance*, 50.

[42] Qtd. in Jowitt, "In Pursuit of the Sylph," 209.

[43] *The Times*, 30 September 1943, qtd. In Jowitt, *Time and the Dancing Image*, 42; Théophile Gautier, *Histoire de l'art dramatique en France depuis 25 ans.*, qtd. in Jowitt, "In Pursuit of the Sylph," 209.

[44] The *Ballet des sylphes* was part of a staging by André Antoine of *Faust* (Carlo Ippolito, "Une Américaine à Paris: Loie Fuller," *Ligeia* 4, no. 7–8 [1990]: 77).

Figure 3.2. Marie Taglioni in *La Sylphide*, 1845 lithograph by Alfred E. Chalon, Jerome Robbins Dance Division, New York Public Library for the Performing Arts, Astor, Lenox, and Tilden Foundations

most glowing reviews for descriptions of Taglioni or Emma Livry. Describing
Fuller's *Papillon* dance, for example, one contemporary lauded Fuller's incarna-
tion of "a fluttering butterfly that bounds upward only to fall again, to die but
then suddenly to take wing anew in a whirl of beauty."[45] About the *Danse du
lys* another critic wrote, "One could imagine nothing more beautiful or fairy-
like, after vertiginous flights, with incomparable grace, she gives the illusion
of a gigantic lily of dazzling whiteness."[46] In 1911, a critic, describing one of
Fuller's "Ultra-violet dances" (based on her experiments with ultraviolet lighting and her work with the Curies), wrote: "In *The Blue Bird* Loie Fuller [is] a
dream, a winged poem."[47] And in 1914, a reviewer of *Le Phalène noir* was
dazzled by Fuller's portrayal of "a troubling phantom . . . [that] touches the
ground with the lightness of a dragonfly . . . barely alighting like a bird, sliding,
and then opening its trembling wings."[48]

As these and countless other reviews make plain, Fuller not only absorbed
many motifs from Romantic ballet, she infused her performances with many
of the same qualities to which the ballerina aspired. In fact, since ballet was
increasingly associated with prostitution and sexual commerce, in some ways
Fuller's ostensible sexlessness made her appear even closer to the soulful, virtuous (read: onstage) side of the ballerina ideal. It is this apparent purity that
led so many critics to view of Fuller as a chaste antidote for the morally *louche*
danseuse: "Our ballerinas try their best to undress as much as possible," wrote
Roger-Marx: "Here, on the contrary, only [Fuller's] face emerges from a long
tunic which barely outlines her waist and reaches to the floor."[49]

Fuller did far more, though, than borrow or purify the ballerina's onstage
transformation. She actually used the transformative subtext of Romantic ballet to take apart the genre, pushing it to such new, exaggerated heights that
she wound up enacting at once a kind of apotheosis of ballet's tacit ideals and
a transition into a new modernist art form. In other words, Fuller used ballet
to tell the story of ballet's own demise.

While the ballerina borrowed the delicate attributes of swans or flowers,
she remained recognizably a woman. The classical white costume for the
"sylph" roles featured "diaphanous clouds of fabric . . . [and] revealed arms,
chest, neck and head, as well as the misty outlines of thigh," as Susan Leigh

---

[45] H.C., "Loie Fuller éducatrice de danseuses," 19 June 1911, Collection Rondel.

[46] *Chronique théatrale*, review of Loie Fuller at the Folies-Bergère, 22 August 1892, Collection
Rondel.

[47] *Excelsior*, "Au Théâtre Fémina," 7 December 1911, Collection Rondel.

[48] Louis Vauxcelles, "L'Art de Loie Fuller," 10 May 1914, Collection Rondel.

[49] Roger-Marx, *La Loie Fuller*, 24.

Foster explains.[50] Fuller, on the other hand, did not so much "borrow" birdlike or floral qualities, as steal them outright, disappearing entirely within her butterflies and lilies, becoming rather than gesturing toward these iconic images. If the ballerina performed a metonymic relationship to the decorative icons of her genre, Fuller performed a metaphoric one, which literalized the transformation only hinted at by the ballerina. With her body permanently hidden, furthermore, Fuller inspired even greater comparisons with the spirit world (many of which we saw in the last chapter), since her flesh never intruded upon the disembodied shapes she described onstage.

While the narratives of Romantic ballets bore the weight of explaining the proximity of a woman to a swan or a water nymph, Fuller's dances did not usually feature stories of any kind. Within a ballet such as *Swan Lake* or *Giselle*, the plot itself—and its magical, fictional universe—explains or justifies the existence of supernatural beings. Simultaneously, though, the ballerina's alter-ego, her offstage identity as desirable, fleshly woman, was permitted to show through her onstage role. The fluttering swan or disembodied phantom coexisted easily, that is, with the erotic presence of the real human being. Indeed, these characters served partly a presentational role—offsetting the human beauty and talent of the ballerina. In Fuller's case, the absence of explanatory narrative, coupled with the far more extensive onstage transformation via costume and stagecraft, transferred the burden of explaining the "magic" entirely to the dancer, who was herself nearly completely occulted by costume and stagecraft. She was not a "real" woman performing a role within a fantastical landscape, she was a transfigured being, whose fantasy remained largely unscripted, emerging only from her own body, costuming, and stagecraft: "Without relying upon vulgar materialization, without choreographic theme, without a libretto, through only the artifice of color, [and] light," as a 1914 review explained.[51]

The result was paradoxical. Fuller's performances were, as we have seen, completely saturated with the supernatural aesthetic of Romantic ballet. But at the same time, by collapsing all the pictorial, explanatory, or "decorative" quality of ballet's scenery and stories onto the dancer's body alone, Fuller took a logical step closer to modern dance, which converts ballet's "decorativity" and externalized narrative into a deeply physical, body-centered, emotive or affective performance—one in which dancers remain fully human onstage, with swans, fairies, and flowers ceding entirely to bone, muscle, and flesh.

---

[50] Foster, *Choreography and Narrative*, 199.

[51] S. M., "Le dernier miracle de la Loïe," review of *Nuages, Fêtes, Sirènes*, 1914, Collection Rondel.

Here, we begin to see Fuller's crucial role as a bridge between ballet and modern dance. In casting aside the support provided by storytelling, and allowing her dance and stagecraft to assume the burden of theatrical transformation, Fuller focused attention on the dancer and her art in a very modern way.[52] At the same time, the highly decorative and deeply magical and transformative nature of her dance still allied her powerfully with the ballet. To understand further how Fuller occupied this transitional space between ballet and modern dance, we shall first have to examine her artistry in light of nineteenth-century balletic technique, of which I shall here offer a brief overview.

Technical Developments

Much of ballet technique as we still know it today developed during the early to mid-nineteenth century, when the physical demands upon the dancer steadily increased. "What distinguished the early nineteenth-century quest for virtuosity," writes Susan Foster, "was a new conception of bodily responsiveness evident in the training procedures for dancers . . . [who] no longer studied individually a regimen designed specifically for their physical type and inclination, but instead [learned] standardized sequences of exercises with designated shapes to which all bodies should conform."[53] As the century progressed, dancers executed more turns and higher leaps onstage, as well as acquiring ever-wider turnout, higher leg extensions, and more expansive *port de bras*.[54] The performing circumference around the dancing body widened as arms and legs reached higher and farther away from the torso. André Levinson rhapsodized thus about the spatial possibilities inherent in the increased turnout:

> [T]his turning outward of the legs permits free motion in any direction without loss of equilibrium . . . the [turnout] . . . increases this space [to move in] to an extraordinary degree, pushing back the invisible wale of the cylinder of air in the centre of which the dancer moves . . . multiplying to an infinite degree the direction of the movement as well as its various conformations. It surrounds the vertical of the body's equilibrium

---

[52] See Dempster, "Women Writing the Body," and Foulkes, "Modern Bodies," for discussions of the self-conscious nature of modern dance.

[53] Foster, "Phallic Pointe," 5.

[54] See Jowitt, *Time and the Dancing Image* (Berkeley: University of California Press, 1988), 39 on the progression of extension and port de bras, especially in the work of Taglioni.

by a vortex of curves, segments of circles, arcs; it projects the body of the dancer into magnificent parabolas, curves and into a living spiral.[55]

As ballet became more rigorous and athletic, it also became more highly gendered in its gestural vocabulary, a distinction that remains to this day. The ballerina's repertoire came to rely heavily upon complex and delicate pointe work, extended balances, and the presentational poses built on legs extending in *dévélopés* or held aloft in attitudes. Blocked toe shoes, which became standard in mid-century, visually elongated the leg, stabilizing the pointed foot and thus allowing the ballerina to hover for longer periods in an elevated position. Toe shoes also permitted the dancer to "walk" with tiny, delicate steps on pointe—in a style known as *piqué*—while imparting a distinctive, coltish quiver to the leg, all of which enhanced the impression of fragility.

Much of the art of the ballerina during this time (and even today, to a great extent) lay in concealing the effort and discipline—the raw, muscular power—of her technique. The wispy sylph onstage defied gravity, or rather belied it, with the extension of a leg in perfect arabesque, a pirouette on pointe, a supporting partner in adagio, and the filmy tutu that wafted over her muscled legs. While the outlines of her body (by the mid- to late nineteenth century as the tutu grew ever shorter) were highly visible, its relationship to the physical world was occulted, subsumed by the aesthetics of lightness, airiness, and inhuman or otherworldly grace. As Foster writes, "The tensile quality that had signified composure in performance was replaced with a ubiquitous effortlessness."[56] Helen Thomas concurs: "A central ideal of the classical technique is the masking of technique and strength, particularly so in the case of the ballerina where a display of strength would be inappropriate to the ideology that informs it."[57]

For his part, the male *danseur* began performing with more overt, visible muscularity, executing ever-higher leaps, jumps with beats, and rapid, multiple pirouettes. He also acquired new partnering responsibilities, for with the advent of Romantic ballet, the earlier tradition of side-by-side couple dance evolved into a complex new form of partner dancing, with "the male dancer supporting, guiding, and manipulating the female dancer as she balanced delicately and suspensefully in fully extended shapes." Balletic partner dancing became more sculptural, more three-dimensional, as the male dancer turned

---

[55] André Levinson, *André Levinson on Dance: Writings from Paris in the Twenties*, ed. Joan Acocella and Lynn Garafola (Middletown, CT: Wesleyan University Press, 1991): 46–47 (originally published in *Theatre Arts Monthly*, March 1925).

[56] Foster, *Choreography and Narrative*, 202.

[57] Helen Thomas, *Dance, Modernity, and Culture* (New York: Routledge, 1995), 171.

his partner, lifted her, caught her, turned, and "presented" her to the audience, allowing her various poses to be seen from multiple perspectives.[58]

But it was increasingly the ballerina alone who fascinated the public, eclipsing her male partner in importance on the Romantic stage. Ballet became, essentially, a woman's art form, turning *danseuses* into the "rock stars of the nineteenth-century bourgeoisie," as Deborah Jowitt has written.[59] Lithe female legs outlined in tights and performing demanding yet delicate choreography drew audiences and earned most of the critical acclaim. Eventually, male dancers started to disappear entirely, and male roles were taken by popular *danseuses* who were considered all the more titillating when performing *en travesti*.[60] Abigail Solomon-Godeau has commented that the "pas de deux between ballerina and travesty dancer produced its own, distinctive eroticism, subtly evoking a lesbian pairing that the libretto disavowed."[61]

As the fascination with ballet's physical virtuosity grew, reviews of performances focused increasingly on the dancers and their bodies, and less on the dramatic action of the ballet. Discussion of technique began to eclipse discussion of character. "Eighteenth-century critics," writes Susan Foster,

> had examined in detail the integrity of characters' motivations and the effectiveness of the sequence of scenes in order to rate the empathic connection of performer to character and character to audience. Now critics evidenced the same distance from characters and their situations that they maintained from the female body. It was only when they perceived the fortuitous conjunction of a well-proportioned physique ... expertise at mime and dancing, and a plausible story ... that they felt transported.[62]

Developments in ballet costumes and stage mechanics kept pace with the advances in bodily technique. While the gauzy white skirt that cinched the dancer's waist did not acquire the name of "tutu" until the late nineteenth century, its earliest version debuted in 1832 in the second act of *La Sylphide*,

---

[58] Foster, "Phallic Pointe," 4.

[59] Jowitt, "In Pursuit of the Sylph," 207.

[60] Felicia McCarren writes, "Wearing form-fitting trousers which were considered even more revealing than the bouffant skirts, the male costume seems to have reinforced the objectification of the female body onstage" (McCarren, *Dance Pathologies*, 88). Abigail Solomon-Godeau concurs: "The development of the ballet provides a particularly clear case of the imbrication of fetishism and commodification on the bodies of women" (Solomon-Godeau, "The Legs of the Countess," 84).

[61] Solomon-Godeau, "The Legs of the Countess," 91.

[62] Foster, *Choreography and Narrative*, 227.

when it added to the ethereality of the Wilis. The tutu featured a billowing muslin underskirt that lent volume and shape to the white overskirt of white silk crepe. The upper body fit snugly, revealing the dancer's neck and shoulders. Aside from a ribbon at the waist and occasionally a small bouquet of flowers adorning the bosom, the costume featured no ornamentation.[63] The tutu occupied (and continues to occupy) a crucial role in ballet choreography—a truth immediately recognized by Theophile Gautier, who attributed much of the revolutionary nature of *La Sylphide* to its costuming: "This ballet began an entirely new era in choreography, one in which Romanticism entered the realm of Terpsichore. . . . *La Sylphide* . . . brought with it a great excess of white gauze, of tulle . . . [the *Wilis*] dematerialized as a result of these transparent skirts."[64]

The tutu, then, did more than adorn the ballerina, it danced *with* her, enhancing her movement by floating above and beneath her legs, and billowing out when she turned—creating essentially a slow-motion, visual echo of individual movements. Famed nineteenth-century ballet critic Jules Janin dubbed this phenomenon the "bouffante," and explains it this way:

> When a ballerina has been in the air and shown herself off all around . . . she finishes her attack with a pirouette en pointe. This pirouette begins in a lively way and then wanes, so that the tulle dress of the goddess balloons up; intense attention is paid to this by the orchestra boxes and the front rows of the parterre; it is this swelling up that I call a bouffante. The bouffante never fails to have an effect; it is usually followed by a murmur of approval, it saves mediocrity; it protects genius, it removes years and wrinkles, it is the goal of all ballet.[65]

As Janin makes clear here, the billowing tutu served also as a device of sexual presentation, showcasing the legs as well as the erotically charged v-space between them. Nineteenth-century ballet had famously created a fetishistic cult of the ballerina's legs. "What mattered for the new enlarged [dance] public," writes Solomon-Godeau, "was legs."[66] One ballet devotee made his passion clear in this unsigned 1843 review:

---

[63] The original *La Sylphide* tutus were designed by painter Eugène Lami.

[64] Théophile Gautier, "Bénéfice de Mlle Taglioni," *La Presse*, 29 June 1844 and 1 July 1844, qtd. in Kahane, *Le Tutu*, 14.

[65] Jules Janin, *Journal des débats politiques et littéraires*, 24 Aug. 1832, qtd. in McCarren, *Dance Pathologies*, 79.

[66] Solomon-Godeau, "The Legs of the Countess," 85.

We have seen gentlemen, even old gentlemen, deeply affected by this glorious display. . . . Oh! The legs of Fanny [Elssler] displayed a vast deal of propriety and frightened sober men from their prescribed complacency. Taglioni's legs encompassed a great deal of attention; Cerrito's leg magnified excitement; Duvernay possessed a magic leg, but to dilate is useless—the Opera is a bazaar of legs.[67]

I shall return to the notion of the ballerina's magic leg.

Along with costumes, myriad tricks of lighting and machinery added to the mystery of the ballet stage. Flickering gaslights could appear to turn dancers into wispy silhouettes. Light shining upon the white muslin or tulle skirts intensified the effect.[68] Frequently, dancers were suspended from harnesses involving pulleys and wires that allowed them to "fly" across the stage, hovering above the ground. "The choreography," writes Deborah Jowitt, "could build on the optical indefiniteness afforded by the technology so as to keep viewers engrossed in deciphering shadow, image, and motion."[69]

The filmy veils, shadowy lighting, and gravity-defying choreography of Romantic ballet dematerialized the dancing bodies onstage, creating a suitably liminal zone for the ballerina, whose public status hovered between the carnal and the ethereal.[70] But Romantic ballet dissolved more than just the appearance of the female body; it frequently dissolved the solidity and individuality of character onstage as well, depending often upon stories of mistaken identity, imposters, replicated beings, or phantoms, a plot device that Deborah Jowitt has dubbed the theme of the "beguiling facsimile."[71] In Filippo Taglioni's *La Fille du Danube* (1836), for example, the hero Rodolph is nearly deceived by a veiled woman who impersonates his beloved. In Charles Didelot's *The Captive of the Caucasus*, Rostislav reaches out for his beloved, Gorslava, only to embrace empty space, for she has died and become a spirit. Gennaro, in Bournonville's *Napoli*, must discern his lover amid a throng of identical and seduc-

---

[67] Qtd. in ibid., 87. From Anon, *Illustrated London Life*, 16 April 1843.

[68] In Louis Véron's *Robert le Diable*, for example, ballerinas portraying the souls of recently deceased nuns danced under gas lights. Jack Anderson tells us that "ghosts of lapsed nuns rose from their tombs to dance by the light of the moon. The sight of flickering moonbeams . . . created by suspended gas jets—Gothic ruins, and dancing phantoms caused audiences to shiver with delight" (Anderson, *Ballet and Modern Dance*, 59).

[69] Jowitt, "In Pursuit of the Sylph," 217.

[70] Critics such as Deborah Jowitt and Abigail Solomon-Godeau read this liminality as a symptom of the nineteenth century's deep uneasiness with female sexuality and with the body in general.

[71] Jowitt, "In Pursuit of the Sylph," 205.

tive sea nymphs.[72] Prince Siegfried of *Swan Lake* is duped by Odile, the evil twin figure of his beloved Odette (the two roles generally being danced by a single dancer). He later struggles to identify Odette, who is hidden within a corps de ballet of look-alikes, identical swan-women, all bewitched by the same sorcerer's spell. And in the 1870 ballet *Coppélia* (adapted from Hoffmann's *Der Sandmann*, on which Freud based his famous essay "The Uncanny"), Franz temporarily forsakes his fiancée in favor of a convincingly human wind-up doll—the clockwork creation of the mysterious Dr. Coppelius.[73]

Fuller, Hoffmann, and the Technologized Body

These themes of confused identity, disturbing replication, and mecanomorphism were, of course, common to nineteenth-century art and literature, where they reflected anxieties produced by encroaching industrialization, alienating mechanized labor, and mass reproduction.[74] This topic has received more than enough critical attention, but it is worth noting how especially well ballet, as a deeply mechanized and fetishistic art form itself, lends expression to these themes. The ballerina, with her sleek, obedient body extended and arched into improbable, scarcely human shapes by virtue of "technique," is, after all, not very far from the robots, androids, and other supernatural creatures in the futuristic tales of Shelley, Lovecraft, Verne, or Robida. "You may ask," wrote André Levinson, "whether I am suggesting the [ballet] dancer is a machine? But most certainly! A machine for manufacturing beauty."[75] This proximity

---

[72] Ibid., 205.

[73] This uneasiness or tension surrounding the physical body appears clearly in such nineteenth-century works as Baudelaire's *La Fanfarlo*, and Villiers de l'Isle-Adam's *Future Eve*, in which a young dandy falls in love with an exquisite and elaborate female automaton, devised especially for him by a fictionalized Thomas Edison. See Rhonda Garelick, *Rising Star* (Princeton, NJ: Princeton University Press, 1998); also Michel Carrouges, *Les Machines célibataires* (Paris: Editions du Chêne, 1976), as well as Mark Seltzer, *Bodies and Machines* (New York: Routledge, 1992).

[74] Many critics, taking Benjamin's famous essay on mechanical reproduction as a starting point, have addressed this topic, among them: Mark Seltzer, Susan Buck-Morss, and Donna Haraway in her famous essay, "A Cyborg Manifesto: Science, Technology, and Socialist-Feminism in the Late Twentieth Century," in *Simians, Cyborgs and Women: The Reinvention of Nature* (New York; Routledge, 1991), 149–81.

[75] Levinson, *André Levinson on Dance*, 48. Felicia McCarren has carefully examined the evolution of the idea of mechanics and dance. She distinguishes two sides of the idea: "dancing that looks mechanical . . . and . . . dancing that works like a machine" (Felicia McCarren, *Dancing Machines* [Stanford, CA: Stanford University Press, 2003], 3).

of ballet to the mecanomorphism of science fiction, in fact, helps us understand the proximity of Loie Fuller to ballet. While Fuller's body itself remained innocent of all dance technique, her entire career was a monument to the technologized body.[76]

Coppélia is, arguably, the most "proto–sci-fi" ballet of the Romantic period; it is also often called the last of the Romantic ballets. Accordingly, it offers an apt place to begin a deeper discussion of Loie Fuller's conversation with Romantic ballet, all the more so given the fact that Fuller herself clearly felt a strong connection to the story behind *Coppélia*. At the end of her life, she and her companion Gabrielle Bloch (using the stage name "Gab Sorère") would produce two works based on Hoffmann's *The Sandman*: a 1925 dance-pantomime entitled *L'Homme au sable*, and a 1927 film, *Les Incertitudes du docteur Coppelius*. Although all footage of the film has, regrettably, been lost, we can surmise from the existence of these two projects that Fuller knew just how "Coppelian" she really was. Like Coppelius, the mysterious inventor of optical gadgets, including artificial eyes, Fuller created uncanny effects by breathing life into mechanical forms, and playing with the distinction between light and shadows, bodies and prosthetics, reality and dreams. It appears, in fact, that Fuller intended to play the role of Dr. Coppelius in her film, even though, by 1927, she had largely retired from performing.

In her sixties, after witnessing the devastation of World War I, losing some of her closest confidants,[77] and watching her own health decline, Fuller evinced a somewhat renewed interest in using structured narrative for her pieces, choosing topics from literature and theater. Although this late turn toward storytelling might have been an attempt to bring some order to her life (at least theatrically), Fuller did not altogether change her stage techniques. The plots she chose served less as strict linear narratives than as loose themes around which to group her dance tableaux. Such was the case with

[76] Toward the end of the nineteenth century, a number of ballets explicitly took on the themes of science and mechanicity, notably the 1881 *Excelsior*, by Luigi Mazzotti and Romualdo Marenco, which treated the "struggle for scientific progress," and the 1891 German ballet, *Pandora*, which dealt with the invention of various electric appliances (see Lista, *Danseuse*, 112). Conversely, there was a spate of American science fiction stories at the turn of the century whose themes of prosthetic limbs curiously resonated with Fuller's work. See Bill Brown, "Science Fiction, the World's Fair, and the Prosthetics of Empire, 1910–1915," in *Cultures of United States Imperialism*, ed. Amy Kaplan and Donald E. Pease (Raleigh, NC: Duke University Press, 1993), 129–57.

[77] In 1926, Fuller had a particularly bitter falling out with Queen Marie of Romania; see Lista, *Danseuse*, 590.

her choice of Hoffmann's *The Sandman*, which she adapted very broadly to suit her aesthetic needs.

Nevertheless, Fuller was clearly drawn to this uncanny tale, which wound up essentially capping her entire career, for her *L'Homme au sable* was the final stage piece she ever officially registered with France's Société des Auteurs et Compositeurs Dramatiques; and *Les Incertitudes* was her last film. Fuller, then, ended her career with these two doffs of her hat to *The Sandman*—a liminal text at once deeply woven into the Romantic ballet canon and yet so modern in its subject matter. And as we shall see, looking at Fuller's work in light of her stage interpretation of *The Sandman* will help us better to understand her own profoundly transitional relationship to ballet.[78]

It is not difficult to see why *The Sandman* would have appealed to Fuller; it treats many of her lifelong obsessions: the notion of doubled identities, the power of dreams, the magic of optical gadgetry, and the mechanical recreation of the body. Its dark and sinister qualities, furthermore, would have drawn Fuller all the more to the story.[79]

Unlike Saint-Léon's ballet, whose light and charming libretto played down the disturbing aspects of the story, Fuller's *Sandman* was an ominous affair. Although *Coppélia* does touch upon the unsettling implications of a man falling in love with a mechanical doll, it does not dwell long in the realm of the uncanny. The hero, Franz, learns the error of his ways, and is reunited happily with Swanilda, his (human) fiancée. As for Coppelius, the doll's magician-like creator, he turns out to be more of a grumpy old toymaker than a dangerous evil scientist. George Balanchine called *Coppélia* "ballet's great comedy."[80]

But Hoffmann's story is certainly not funny. It involves a child's terrifying nightmares, his fear of blindness, the murder of his father, and then, when he grows older, his obsessive and ultimately fatal love for the clockwork doll,

---

[78] The film was shot at Gaumont's Paris studio, and, instead of the mythic Sandman, takes as its central figure Coppelius, who is presented, as in Hoffmann's story, as a kind of satanic alter-ego of the Sandman. The film was to have featured proto-surrealist lighting designed to produce a dreamlike atmosphere; and according to Fuller's notes, it featured "a man [probably Coppelius] walking on the sky . . . a tornado that whirls across the screen . . . people . . . walking *on* not in water . . . and monocles from which drop luminous eyes."

[79] In her earlier years, this quality was visible in her use of such disturbing images as cancer cells or animal skeletons in her productions. Her depiction of the "sea of blood," or the decapitation scene in *Salome*, similarly points to Fuller's morbid side, as does her fondness for disembodied hands and heads, which float through a number of her productions. And let us recall Jean Lorrain's observation that Fuller's "Mirror Room" made her body appear to be a collection of amputated parts. Fuller's personal writings also display a curious taste for tales of torture and mutilation.

[80] Balanchine, *Complete Stories of the Great Ballets*, 140.

Olympia. Nathaniel's irrational love for this doll—the creation of Coppelius and his partner Dr. Spalanzi—drives him to madness and suicide.

Fuller's *L'Homme au sable* was faithful to the original story's dark, uncanny tone, and centered on the nightmarish figure of the Sandman, who robs children of their eyes. But Fuller left out some rather major plot points. Her version addresses only the first half of Hoffmann's tale—the half that treats *childhood* fears and obsessions. She completely ignored that part of the tale in which those early fears are translated into more adult concerns. That second half of Hoffmann's story features the now-adult Nathaniel, his encounter with the sinister "Coppola" (Coppelius in disguise), his engagement to Clara, and his dangerous erotic obsession with Olympia, the mechanical doll. But the only characters in Fuller's *L'Homme au sable* are children, save for the Sandman himself, who appears as a dream to a group of children asleep in their nursery. He throws sand in their eyes and then spirits them off to his lair on the moon. Their voyage through the stars provided an ideal context for a series of Fuller's typically fantastical tableaux, all rendered with dazzling lighting effects. The children pass through clouds, stars, a "land of fire," and a "stormy sea," while disembodied "eyes"—a reference to the Sandman's "catch"—float around them and dance in a blue light.[81]

Fuller's choices in adapting Hoffmann's story for the stage are perfectly in keeping with her usual aesthetic. As so often in her work, she opted here for an ostentatious "chastity," shunting aside concerns of adulthood, sexuality, and obsession. (We saw a similar move, for example, in her decision to turn Salome into an innocent little girl.) Most striking, though, is her omission of the clockwork doll, Olympia, who is, by any lights, the "star" of the story, and a key element in Saint-Léon's ballet (which changes her name, of course, to Coppélia).

But, as we have seen repeatedly, Fuller—as an artist of disavowal—rarely rejects anything completely; usually, the element cast aside manages to assert its presence in some indirect manner. We are now also quite familiar with the disingenuous nature of Fuller's oft-proclaimed "purity," which usually serves

---

[81] *L'Homme au sable* was directed by Fuller and her partner, Gab Sorère (the stage name of Gabrielle Bloch). The adaptation was by René Bizet and Jean Barreyre, with music by Arthur Honegger. It consisted of the following scenes: "The Sandman and his Witches," "The Nursery," "The Night," "The Sandman and the Children," "The Cloud," "The Moon," "The Land of Fire," "The Stormy Sea," "The Stars," "The Gates of Light," "The Land of Angels," "The Nursery (return)," and "The Sandman" ("Program for Les Ballets Fantastiques de Loie Fuller," 4 December 1925, Collection Rondel). See also Lista, *Danseuse*, 595, quoting a letter from Fuller to Samuel Hill. In *The Sandman*, Nathaniel's father is killed in a "chemical explosion"—something Fuller knew a lot about, having blown up her laboratory at least once.

as a cover for a more complicated affect. Such is the case with her *Sandman*, where Fuller's omission of the mechanical love object should be read less as a rejection of this element than as a displacement of it. Fuller did not depict the clockwork doll, but she hardly needed to. Olympia, or the notion of Olympia, haunted her entire life, and this production was no exception; in fact it just makes the point more overtly.

In a sense, Fuller's professional life was a thirty-year enactment of the Sandman story, which is probably why two versions of it figure among her last artistic endeavors. After all, nearly every one of Fuller's theatrical projects featured a (partially) mechanical woman (herself), a mechanical stage, special lenses, and gadgets—the mechanization of dance itself. Sometimes, like Coppelius tinkering with his doll, Fuller even played with fragmented images of human body parts, permitting hands, arms, even heads to whirl about via filmic projections, shadow trickery, or mirrored reflections. In other words, Fuller's entire *oeuvre* was devoted to the very questions addressed by Hoffmann's tale: How can we understand that the body's most human drives—its libido, its inner workings— are also its most mechanical? What is human and what is not? What is reality? How might our eyes deceive us? And can the adult female, sexually mature body be transformed or replicated as a hollow machine?

While Fuller's *Sandman* ostensibly treated only the childish fears of a mythic bogeyman, it was nonetheless a typical Fuller production replete with spellbinding stage effects; indeed it was among her most sophisticated. By virtue, therefore, of its very omission of Olympia—the seeming *sine qua non* of Hoffmann's story—Fuller's version of *The Sandman* is actually brought closer to the spirit of the original story; for while the *character* of the mechanical doll may be missing, the *concept* behind it—of a theatrically beguiling mechanical construction that replaces or improves upon human bodies—not only remains, it expands to encompass the entire stage and all the dancers. The dazzling light show, the various *trompe-l'oeil* effects of the different scenes—these constitute the Olympian aspects of the tale, as they did metaphorically in all of Fuller's work. And just as the mysterious Coppelius outfitted Olympia with her eerily lifelike prosthetic eyes, Fuller even tricked out her own production with floating eyeballs, colored lights, and other mechanical parts for the "stage-body." Here and in all her work, Fuller's mechanized stage, her costume, stagecraft, and lighting mechanisms, *are* her Olympia, her constructed techno-body. Naturally, she wished to play the role of Dr. Coppelius in her film: she had been playing a similar wizard-like role all her life.[82]

---

[82] As she grew older, furthermore, Fuller's long interest in lenses and telescopes acquired a certain poignancy, as her own eyes began to fail. Decades of close work with burning stage lights

This notion, moreover, of Fuller *qua* Coppelius, has implications in how we make sense of her role *vis-à-vis* Romantic ballet—a genre dependent upon another kind of "techno-body."

Coppélia and the Romantic Ballet Couple

Let us recall that Saint-Léon's *Coppélia* recounts the story of a beautiful mechanical doll and the man who creates her, moves her limbs, and "presents" her to his neighbors by positioning her in the window of his home. For this reason, *Coppélia* offers us an allegory of the Romantic ballet couple: the ballerina—a mechanized creature of "technique"—and the *danseur* who moves her limbs, turns her about, and "presents" her to the audience. Accordingly, *Coppélia* draws out and renders explicit the underlying mecanomorphism of all ballet, exposing the proximity of the regimented ballerina to the character of Coppélia—the perfect, seductive female automaton who is presented and controlled by a man.[83] Acknowledging *Coppélia*'s status as a kind of self-conscious, Romantic meta-ballet, we are better placed to understand how Fuller's work offered the next step in the critical rereading of ballet. We can begin to see how, through manipulation of costume and stagecraft, she quite openly dismantled and then reconstructed in modernist fashion much of Romantic ballet, operating as a latter-day Sandman for the entire genre.

We have already established how closely Fuller's themes adjoined those of Romantic ballet. We have also seen how the apparent weightlessness of her fabric sculptures prompted critical paeans similar to those of the ballerina. But a comparison of Fuller's art to ballet cannot end with these surface similarities. While Fuller's work did not exactly look like ballet, in many ways it relied heavily on balletic techniques, albeit fully externalized, nonbodily versions of them.

Despite Fuller's famous "naturalness" and reputed "rupture" with classical technique, a great many thematic and technical elements of ballet find coun-

---

had damaged Fuller's vision badly, and in her later years she was rarely seen without the dark glasses she needed for protection. If, in Hoffmann's tale, the Sandman brought blindness, perhaps Fuller's spectacularly lit stage version of the story served to counterbalance, at some level, the dreaded encroachment of darkness in her personal life. In Hoffmann's story, Nathaniel, describing the effect of Coppelius's presence, says, "I was riveted to the spot, spellbound." Fuller, as we saw in chapter 1, repeatedly describes her own effect on audiences in similar terms.

[83] Indeed, in Act II, the comparison is made explicit when the wronged fiancée, Swanilda, having discovered that her rival is a doll, masquerades as Coppelia, and performs a deliberately "mechanical" dance to convince Coppelius that his doll has come to life.

terparts within her choreography. We might begin with the question of balletic turnout and "extension." While discipline and training permitted the ballerina to extend her legs ever further into the space around her, Fuller accomplished the same effect by literally—in a sense, prosthetically—extending her arms with her famous patented bamboo and aluminum rods, which grew longer as her career progressed.[84] Ballet reviewers extolled the reach and precision of a dancer's leg turned out from the hip, extended in arabesque or limning in the air in what André Levinson called a "vortex of curves . . . whirls, parabolas, and spirals." But while Levinson had used those terms to describe the spatial possibilities afforded by the ballerina's extension and turnout, he used nearly identical words to praise the very unballetic Loie Fuller for the shapes *she* delineated in the air—not with her (hopelessly unturned-out) legs, but with her "extended" arms: "The light fabrics that she manipulates curve into spirals, swirls, and whirls (*trombes*). They animate and organize space . . . creating a volcano of forms. . . . This wand, with which Fuller elongates (*allonge*) her arms and so powerfully amplifies her movements, is the wand of a true magician."[85]

For Levinson, then, Fuller had clearly acquired much of the ballerina's virtuosic use of space. Like the ballerina whose turnout, in Levinson's words, "push[ed] back the invisible wale of the cylinder of air," Fuller widened the performing circumference around her body by virtue of her elongated arms, which reached up to twenty feet over her head. Levinson's remarks help us see that Fuller's work, in a sense, turned ballet upside down and inside out.

[84] Fuller was able to manipulate the early rods with just her thumb and forefinger. As she increased their weight and length, she needed a clenched fist to hold them. The "prosthetic" nature of the rods is in keeping with Fuller's own avowed interest in prosthetic technology. During World War I, as part of her charitable effort, Fuller championed a Parisian philanthropist, a Madame Simon, who devoted her time to helping war amputees. In a letter apparently destined for publication in the States, Fuller wrote, "There is a woman building a great factory on the lines of one in Sweden where machines take the place of lost arms and legs. And the 'unarmed' can do the work of men in their full capacity. This far-sighted and thoughtful woman is preparing now for the time, in the not far distant future, when men who are no longer men can work as they did before" (Fuller to unidentified recipient, NYPLPA). Fuller also evinced a rather morbid interest in amputation, as she displays in her "Chinese Punishment" anecdote (see chapter 1) and indirectly perhaps in the "amputation" effect—noticed by Jean Lorrain—of her mirror dances (see chapter 1, fn. 62, for a discussion of this).

[85] Levinson, "Les Ballets de Loie Fuller," 13 June 1922, unidentified press clipping, NYPLPA. Louis Vauxcelles also saw "eddies, rings, and spirals" in Fuller's work (Vauxcelles, "L'Art de Loie Fuller," 10 May 1914, Collection Rondel). And Roger-Marx described her thus: "the dancer . . . who, with her arms extended again by the batons, sways her ample sleeves and rounds them into circles, draws immense S's, twisting [the fabric] into spirals, rolling it into dome shapes" (Roger-Marx, "Loie Fuller," 270).

Her sleeve rods granted to her arms an exaggerated version of the strength and graceful length of the ballerina's legs, transferring the locus of movement from lower body to upper body (turning the body upside down) and from internal bodily technique to external stage technology (turning it inside out).[86] While the Opéra ballerina Pauline Duvernay may have "possessed a magic leg," in Loie Fuller's case, all the magic was in the arms and hands. "Since prehistoric periods dancers have danced with their feet, but Loie dances with her hands," wrote a journalist in 1896.[87] Later, Fuller would literalize this notion, choreographing her *Dance of the Hands* in which her entire body was shrouded in darkness, leaving only her hands in the light to dance— a puppet show minus the puppets.[88]

In likening Fuller's batons to a magician's wand, Levinson underscores how much her work incorporated and condensed the deep magicalness at the heart of Romantic ballet—at both narrative and technical levels. Like Coppelius, Fuller used her magic to animate the inanimate. But within this analogy, of course, Fuller must play both roles. We have already established how, in one sense, her entire stage served as an expanded version of Hoffmann's Olympia—as an arena in which to fragment and mechanize the body. But even within her own person onstage, Fuller played the complementary role of doll to doll maker. In this, she is like Saint-Léon's Coppélia, for it is Fuller who inhabits the enormous, moving silk sculptures formed by her own magician's wands. And it is Fuller whose own flesh-and-blood arms are transformed by bamboo or aluminum rods into dancing sculptures. Camille Mauclair intuited this aspect of Fuller's performances, describing her as "A passionate statue, roving, intoxicated by the shadows she has drunk."[89]

Onstage, then, enclosed in her draperies, Fuller is a dual figure: at once the ethereal, floating images of her dances—the ballerina-like birds, flowers, and butterflies—*and* the partly hidden manipulator who, *danseur*-like, uses her muscularity to present and control them.[90] In this sense, Fuller functioned

[86] Hillary Bell, review of Loie Fuller, 1896, NYPLPA.

[87] Miss Fuller is no more of a dancer than she ever was, but she appears to have a strong right arm, and a left one too," wrote a reviewer ("Review of Loie Fuller at Koster and Bial," *New York Sun*, 23 February 1896, NYPLPA).

[88] Fuller in fact evinced a strong interest in puppetry and tried to interest the United States in the "Tanagra Theater" of Léon Huret, who had popularized shadow puppetry (Lista, *Danseuse*, 338 ff).

[89] Mauclair, *Idées Vivantes*, 104.

[90] Recalling her passion for *japonisme*, we might note here how much Fuller's work resembled *bunraku*, the ancient Japanese puppet art in which the puppeteers maintain a visible yet muted presence onstage while they hold and manipulate their three-quarter life-size puppets. Of course,

much like a one-woman version of the Romantic ballet couple, assuming and literalizing the genre's motif of doubled or hidden identities, while removing entirely the already-fading presence of the male dancer. While she may not have been *en travesti* in the traditional sense (as she had been years earlier in vaudeville, and like those ballerinas who danced male roles), Fuller was taking the next step in the feminization of dance as a genre: she was playing both sexes' roles onstage.

Once we make this comparison explicit, it becomes very easy to see just how Fuller subsumed the roles of ballerina and male *danseur*. Onstage, the white tulle of the ballerina's tutu echoed and softened her movement, offering a kind of slow-motion replaying of it and creating the dramatic "bouffante" effect.[91] Fuller's robes created a strikingly similar effect: the yards of white silk whirled and billowed out around her arms like oversized, inverted tutus, inflating into "bouffantes" of exaggerated proportions and reinforcing the suggestion of an "upside-down ballet." Ballerinas often seemed to dance suspended in midair: they flew across the stage suspended in flying harnesses, or rose onto pointe and hovered, supported by their partners, stretching and turning themselves into three-dimensional shapes. Fuller too could dance as if suspended above the stage, only instead of relying upon flying harnesses or a male partner and toe shoes, she stood atop her patented glass pedestal, which, when lit properly, lent her the appearance of floating above the stage, while she stretched and turned her silks into three-dimensional shapes.[92]

Fuller's work also provided an analog for a less-discussed aspect of balletic technique: the more "masculine" side of the ballerina's technique, specifically the use of pointe. Despite the nineteenth century's increasingly sharp gender divisions in classical dance vocabulary, the ballerina's stance nevertheless harbored the potential for sexual ambiguity. Dance critics have noted that the ballerina's body was not generally admired, in fact, for its feminine, rounded or curved parts. On the contrary, it was her muscular legs and pointed feet that won raves. In blocked pointe shoes, a dancer's legs acquire a sharp and scissor-like form, and become capable of walking or gesturing with distinc-

---

I have made an elision here between the manipulator of the doll—within the libretto of *Coppelia*, Dr. Coppelius—and the male *danseur*, who manipulates the ballerina—who is played by a different, younger, dancer in Coppelia. Dr. Coppelius is a character role, and his narrative function is analogous but not identical to the *danseur noble* who plays Franz in this case.

[91] We might recall here that Fuller pioneered slow-motion techniques in her film work.

[92] "Fuller's dance responds directly to the tradition of exhibition in the ballet; the huge panels of silk that she moved around her on long sticks cover and uncover the body on a scale that belittles the alternately seductive and moralistic raising and lowering of hemlines at the Paris Opéra throughout the nineteenth century" (McCarren, "The Symptomatic Act," 757).

tively phallic thrusting or stabbing motion.[93] Susan Foster has written of this peculiarly phallic appeal of the ballerina:

> Breasts or bellies, physical features associated with motherhood, gar-
> nered no attention. . . . [The ballerina's] appeal depended upon a corpo-
> reality that verged on the phallic. [Her] legs . . . [with] their astonishing
> straightness [and] length . . . contrast with the supple, softly flowing arms
> and arching torso. . . . The legs belie the phallic identity of the ballerina.
> They signal her situatedness just in between penis and fetish. She looks
> like but isn't a penis. Her legs, her whole body become pumped up and
> hard yet always remain supple. Both the preparation, the dipping motion
> that precedes the etched shape, and the graceful fade from an extended
> pose show deflation but always on its way to re-inflation.[94]

In Fuller's upside-down version of ballet, it was her arms, extended by thin rods that pointed through her fabrics, that lent phallic rigidity, supporting her floating, feminine shapes—in near-perfect imitation of the contrast between the tutu and leg.[95] The continual rising and falling, inflation and deflation of Fuller's floating forms, moreover, reinforced the cyclically phallic nature of her choreography, in a fashion deeply similar to the ballerina's, as described by Foster above.

Beneath the rods and silk, Fuller's "natural" body did the heavy lifting, like an unobtrusive *danseur noble* who lifts his ballerina partner high in the air. In effect, like a latter-day Coppelius, Fuller had built her own doll-like replica of the fragile, ethereal ballerina, which she manipulated in puppeteer fashion. Rather than balance on the tips of her toes, Fuller's ballerina-effigy balanced her silken, fleshless body on the tips of batons. This combination of rods and fabric retained the visual pleasure and sleekness of the ballerina's tensile pointed foot. It retained also the suggestion of virtuosity, of expert technique being responsible for the forms described in the air. Fuller had simply *trans-ferred* the lightness and movement of the sylph from the flesh-and-blood fe-male body to this disembodied, floating replica of it. We can see this in a photograph that captures Fuller with batons in midair (fig. 3.3).

---

[93] Lynn Garafola has remarked on the phallic quality of the pointe work in Branislava Nijin-ska's 1924 work, *Les Biches* (See Lynn Garafola, *Diaghilev's Ballets Russes*, 126).

[94] Foster, "Phallic Pointe," 13.

[95] Were we seeking a queer or lesbian reading of Fuller here, in the tradition of Julie Townsend's work, for example, we could go further, seeing a symbolic dildo in the prosthetic, arm-extending rods that Fuller attached to her body and then thrust through the whirling, admittedly often uterine, forms of floating silk.

Figure 3.3. Fuller forming the lily for *The Lily Dance*, 1921, Bibliothèque Nationale de France

Fuller's various stagecraft inventions multiplied the ways in which she could play with conventions of the Romantic ballet. Her "mirror room," for example, recreated the "look-alike" *corps de ballet* motif by producing a sea of identical dancing reflections into which the "real" Loie disappeared. "Her image, her magical undulations repeat infinitely. One sees ten, fifteen Loie Fullers," wrote one critic of the effect.[96] Here again, Fuller had produced a strikingly literal version of a Romantic ballet motif, for while all those identically dressed ballerinas depicting phantoms or ocean sprites may have *pretended* to be weightless shadows, Fuller's techno-version of the *corps de ballet* required no such pretense; her "looking-glass dancers" actually *were* weightless shadows, mere bodiless reflections. Fuller's *Ombres gigantesques* series produced a similar effect, using a large scrim and backlighting to fashion a series of oversized and disembodied dancing shadows.

Relying upon technology in this way then, instead of the Romantic repertoire with its narrative structure, Fuller adapted many key elements of ballet for her own purposes. Pushing to a literal level the sylphic ideal of weightlessness and dematerialized flesh, Fuller had out-ballerina-ed the ballerina (fig. 3.4)—but to what end? What kind of sylph manqué was this?

Ambivalent Ballet: Fuller's Figurative and Literal Performance of Disavowal

With all its tricks for producing disembodied illusions, Fuller's work presents a paradox. It showcased many elements typical of Romantic ballet: ephemerality, whiteness, and even some of its trademark images, such as lilies, butterflies, and birds. But in her particular presentation of these elements, Fuller appeared to be thoroughly rejecting both Romanticism and ballet. She generally eschewed narrative, character, and story line. She refused to adopt the ballerina's status as erotic commodity. Fuller as a personality did not "peek out" from under her robes, nor, of course, did her body. Her diverse dancing images of light and shadow existed as aesthetic or scientific phenomena, harbingers of a deep yet inchoate modernism in dance. By stripping away or minimizing libretto and the other trappings of Romantic ballet, while retaining so many of its formal, visual, and technical desiderata, Fuller was actually uncovering the underlying modernist potential in ballet. Effectively, she pared ballet down to a deeply aestheticized meditation on the human body's relationship to gravity, physics, mechanicity, and light—the most crucial elements of twentieth-

---

[96] Review of *Lumière et ténèbres* at the Olympia, 1899, Collection Rondel.

Figure 3.4. 1903 Drawing of Fuller from *The Tatler*, emphasizing the balletic, bouffant quality of her costumes, courtesy of the Maryhill Museum of Art

century modern dance. Whirling her silk covered ballerina-creature above her head, appearing to dance in midair or amid a crowd of identical reflections, Fuller had turned herself into an extreme, literalized version of the sylphic ideal, and in so doing performed a dramatic dialogue between ballet and modern dance.

Obviously, Fuller's work bespeaks a deep ambivalence toward ballet. She at once vociferously rejected it and tacitly embraced many of its aesthetic effects—often on a spectacular, exaggerated scale. But, as we have seen, disingenuousness and deep ambivalence lie at the heart of Fuller's work, and are in keeping with what we have called her aesthetics of disavowal. Disavowal, as Freud explained it, always involves a component of splitting and displacement. The split results from "two contrary and independent attitudes" being held simultaneously; and the displacement occurs as the psyche transfers the distressing reality onto some other, more acceptable object.[97] As the philosopher Robyn Ferrell writes:

> The disavowal is a case of repression which . . . involves holding the offending idea at a distance from consciousness, from where it must make itself felt in indirect ways. The dream owes its existence to this indirectness, to the tension between distance and satisfaction.[98]

Ferrell's remarks help us see that Fuller's work entailed very clearly a disavowal of ballet, which she (Fuller) quite loudly proclaimed an "offending idea," to be "held at a distance," while simultaneously allowing that idea to make itself "felt in indirect ways" in her work. For Fuller, however, this disavowal of ballet was more than a metaphor. A closer look at her choreography reveals that Fuller actually *performed* her disavowal of ballet. That is, her work can be read as a kind of bodily translation of the disavowal process.

At its most basic level, Fuller's stage work involved a literal, physical movement of splitting and displacement very analogous to the psychical splitting and displacement of disavowal. Onstage, Fuller essentially split into two parts—her baton-and-silk creation—which powerfully evoked the Romantic ballerina—and her "natural" body beneath, which repeatedly hoisted this creation into the air, sculpted it, and then lowered it again. The ballerina-effigy then was continually "reborn" from within the silken cocoon of Fuller's dou-

[97] Sigmund Freud, *An Outline of Psychoanalysis*, trans. Alix Strachey (New York: W.W. Norton and Co., 1949, 1969), 92.

[98] Robyn Ferrell, *Passion in Theory: Conceptions of Freud and Lacan* (London: Routledge, 1996), 27.

bled self, cast away or "displaced" from Fuller's body as it took center stage as the spectacle, and then allowed to descend and wilt.

This balletic object, this "offending idea"—to borrow Ferrell's term—thus remained onstage in a perpetual state of oscillation, acting both as a part of Fuller's performing body and as a separate entity to be held aloft, at (exaggerated) arm's length. Indeed, it derived its greatest theatrical power when it attained its apogee, since it was then, when her silks towered above her and fully engulfed her, that Fuller seemed most "transformed" to her audiences. This "*fort-da*" game with a reconstructed ballerina-puppet created much of Fuller's theatrical power, for it was an enactment of transition and transformation. More than simply presenting a transfigured self to audiences as a *fait accompli*, Fuller allowed them to witness the continual process of her metamorphosis, which resulted from this repeated splitting and displacement of her body.[99]

A Balletic Dream of Modernism

Robyn Ferrell points out that, within the state of disavowal, a perpetual tension exists between "distance and satisfaction," noting that dreams exhibit just this tension. It is likely that Fuller's audiences intuited a similar tension in her performances, which emerged from the implied (as well as literal) distance between Fuller's two halves: the human being and the fantastic visions she created. This tension may in fact explain some of her famously dreamlike appeal. "She became paler and paler," wrote Camille Mauclair of a Fuller performance, "a figure like those dreamt by Rodin."[100] She created "the ambiance of a dream," wrote André Levinson; "This flower of dreams rises and rises again," exclaimed a review of the *Lily Dance*.[101]

Romantic ballet held Europe in its thrall for decades with its magical transformations and disembodied women. By the time Loie Fuller came along, the genre was not merely in decline, it was moribund. But Fuller managed to harness its appeal while appearing to offer something wholly different and revolutionary. Her creation of a mannequin-like ballerina, a sylphic doppelganger, was an idea straight out of a classic Romantic plot (indeed, straight

---

[99] Giovanni Lista has touched upon this aspect of Fuller's appeal, writing, "It is . . . the surpassing of the creator (the body) by the creature to which it gives rise (the veil-figure) that constitued without doubt the fascination of Fuller's dances" (Lista, *Danseuse*, 267).

[100] Mauclair, *Idées Vivantes*, 104.

[101] Gaston Vuillermez, quoted in Lista, *Danseuse*, 252.

out of Hoffmann), but her use of it was pure modernism. In dividing into two beings onstage, Fuller created a performance dependent not upon one or the other half of herself, but upon the relationship between the two, and the thrilling tension that resulted. This tension, between a human body and its magical creation, harkened back to the plot devices of many Romantic ballets, while also playing out the tension inherent in Fuller's relationship to ballet— a tension between an incipient modernism and the recent balletic past.

Felicia McCarren has observed correctly that "doubleness" lies at the heart of all dance performances. Dance, McCarren tells us, occupies perpetually a liminal realm in which "the dancer moves back and forth between labor and illusion."[102] The Romantic ballerina embodied that division subtly, obscuring her physical effort, her athleticism, and often her erotic self with the decorative trappings of her genre. Romantic libretti, as we have seen, often recapitulated that division by recounting stories of doubled selves and "beguiling facsimiles," as Deborah Jowitt has shown—*Coppélia* being perhaps the most explicit of these stories.

But Fuller—in her person—literalized the doubleness and the back-and-forth movement of which McCarren writes. She astounded audiences by allowing them to watch her *as* she split and doubled herself over and over again, mutating into a series of dramatic and ever-changing shapes. Despite her love of fairytale magic and her careful safeguarding of her stage secrets, Fuller did not hide her transformation from her audience. Her "technique" was not contained *inside* her body but displayed on the *outside*, in the form of machinery, costume, and the three-dimensional shapes she created into the air. She staged, in other words, a process of exposing the secrets hidden within Romantic ballet—its internalized form and discipline, and its obsession with metamorphosis. Fuller turned ballet inside out, as I have said, allowing audiences to witness technique and transformation as a process unfolding on her body and on her stage.

Paradoxically, then, it is in acknowledging Fuller's obviously heavy debt to Romantic ballet that we can best see how she enacted its transition to modern dance. Fuller effectively transferred both the technical and the narrative magic of Romantic ballet onto her arsenal of batons, lights, costumes, and stagecraft. She externalized and rendered visible much that had remained below the surface in ballet.[103] This is a crucial first step toward modern dance's

---

[102] McCarren, *Dance Pathologies*, 103.

[103] In this, she also resembles modernists of other media, including painters such as Pissarro or, much later, Rothko who showcased brushstroke and canvas; or architects who uncovered the supporting structures of buildings, such as Walter Gropius of the Bauhaus, or later, Renzo Piano and Richard Rogers, whose Pompidou Center featured a famously exoskeletal structure.

open embracing of both the physical body and the natural forces upon it. Later modern dancers, such as Martha Graham, would cast aside the notion of obscuring gravity's effect on a dancer, the force of a dancer's breathing, or the solidity of her flesh. Fuller did not achieve such a level of "reality" in her work. Hers was still a world of theatrical legerdemain. But Graham is impossible without Fuller and her balletic dream of disavowal—a dream that ushered ballet into the twentieth century and, as we shall see, wove it into the American modern dance tradition waiting in the wings.

Chapter Four

Scarring the Air:
Loie Fuller's Bodily Modernism

Fuller's Invisibility: Modernist Physicality,
Sex, and Cultural Legacy

Historians of modern dance differ little in their opinions of Loie Fuller. They readily credit her as one of the first of the so-called "aesthetic" dancers—female solo artists whose apparently free style opened a new realm in which recital dance could earn the respect denied it on the music-hall stage, while being liberated from the artistic and physical constraints of ballet. But among these artists, Fuller has always remained the odd woman out, eclipsed by the "real" modern dancers who followed her—the more "high-art" serious, such as Martha Graham, or the slightly earlier, more glamorous artists such as Isadora Duncan or Ruth St. Denis. "Dancers such as Fuller . . . seem of secondary importance in comparison with Isadora Duncan," writes Jack Anderson.[1] Even in death Fuller was not spared this kind of unflattering comparison. Noting the proximity of Fuller's passing (in January of 1928) to that of the much younger Duncan (in September of 1927), an American obituary declared: "In the last . . . months, two of the most noted women in the world of dance have passed away. Loie Fuller has followed Isadora Duncan. There is scarcely any just comparison between them, because Miss Duncan was in reality an artist while Loie Fuller . . . gained no greater credit than attaches to a clever mechanicien."[2]

This last word, the oddly Gallic "mechanicien," brings us to the crucial issue surrounding Fuller's diminished role in modern dance: her apparent refusal of the body and her preference for mechanics over the ostensible *sine qua non* of

[1] Anderson, *Ballet and Modern Dance*, 114
[2] Unsigned obituary article, 4 January 1928, NYPLPA, Robinson Locke.

the American moderns: naturalness. While as a nation, early-twentieth-century America may have been associated with mechanicity and science, "American modern dance" (particularly *early* modern dance) showcased just the opposite: the human body moving in accordance with natural forces, allowing gravity, breath, and the dancer's own physical weight to play a visible role onstage, "freeing movement from the constraining technique of ballet . . . liberat[ing] the body in reverence to the freedom of the individual spirit," as Julia Foulkes has written.[3] Personal feeling is expected to triumph over soulless mechanicity. "The governing logic of modern dance is . . . affective," explains Elizabeth Dempster.[4]

In their encyclopedic study of twentieth-century dance, *No Fixed Points*, Nancy Reynolds and Malcolm McCormick acknowledge Fuller's loss of status in modern dance history, and touch precisely on this question of self-expression and naturalness:

> Loie's performances markedly broadened prevailing concepts of dance and helped lay a foundation for the moderns who came later. She was among the first of a long line of dancers who have been called "modern" to make an intensely personal form of expression widely accepted as art. But she left no viable school or followers to carry on her methods, and mention of her influence or inspiration is almost wholly absent in the annals of modern movement of the 1920s and afterward, when such pioneers as Mary Wigman, Martha Graham, and Doris Humphrey focused so intensely on personal kinetics and expressed themselves with little attention to elaborate production values.[5]

Reynolds and McCormick make the distinction very clear: to be "called 'modern'" in the dance world has traditionally required a performance based on "personal kinetics," not on "production values." Here is where Loie Fuller loses ground among her contemporaries, for while critics grant that Fuller broke ground for American modern dance, her rejection of both the natural body and overt emotion has impeded any deeper consideration of her work in relation to that of the great, more "natural" moderns. Women such as Duncan or Graham are lauded for their fluid or intricate physicality on stage; but since Fuller's artistry expressed itself largely through technology, she seems to re-

---

[3] Foulkes, *Modern Bodies*, 9.

[4] Dempster "Women Writing the Body," 224–26.

[5] Nancy Reynolds and Malcolm McCormick, *No Fixed Points: Dance in the Twentieth Century* (New Haven: Yale University Press, 2003), 9–10.

move herself from the ranks of her more famous colleagues.[6] This reliance on technology, furthermore, coupled with Fuller's own curiously ambivalent (and even litigious) feelings about being "copied," made for a style of dance very difficult to turn into a reproducible "movement," as Reynolds and McCormick point out.

Not only did Fuller totally obscure her body onstage, she also obscured the fact that she was dancing at all. Critics tend to overlook Fuller's choreographic contributions in large part because she was considered, simply, a bad or rather a "non-"dancer. "*Danseuse? Non*," opined one early review; "Fuller hardly danced at all," concurs Marcia Siegel. Of course, it is true that Fuller did not allow audiences to see her body creating movement onstage.[7] It is also true that Fuller was not a technically trained or especially supple or adept dancer, which the few extant films of her confirm. And in obscuring her physical self and relying on her external instruments, her "elaborate production values," to create movement, Fuller convinced the world that her art form was somehow separate from "normal" dancing—dancing, that is, done by visible bodies. An early review described neatly this dual absence of both body and dance in Fuller's work: "In her infinitely long veils, she was invisible. Was she dancing? No."[8] And Mallarmé, whose essay on Fuller famously used her as a symbol of disembodied art, wrote: "The *danseuse* is not a woman who dances, for these juxtaposed reasons that *she is not a woman* . . . and that *she does not dance*."[9]

Another reason why Fuller's contemporaries have enjoyed greater renown is that their bodily performances extended beyond the stage. In addition, that is, to dancing in a more natural or recognizable fashion onstage, Fuller's more famous colleagues were more "bodily" in private life as well, producing the kind of social narrative expected of women, which confirmed and reinforced their onstage personae. More conventionally beautiful (as well as heterosexual) dancers such as Duncan and St. Denis learned early how to work the machine of modern stardom.[10] Capitalizing on their photogenic looks and

---

[6] It is too simple, however, to rank Graham among the "natural" dancers, for her dances and stylized lexicon of movement were really highly constructed, even mechanical. Mark Franko has written of the mechanicity and inorganic nature of Graham's work. See Franko, *Dancing Modernism/Performing Politics* (Bloomington: Indiana University Press, 1995), 51 ff. I will discuss this aspect of Graham's work later in this chapter.

[7] Siegel, *The Shapes of Change: Images of Americas Modern Dance*, 7.

[8] Etienne Brion, "La Fée des flammes," *Argus de la Presse*, 9 January 1929, Musée Rodin Archives.

[9] Mallarmé, *Oeuvres complètes*, 304.

[10] As Richard Dyer writes: "The star phenomenon consists of everything that is publicly available about stars . . . a star's image is also what people say or write about him or her." Richard Dyer, *Heavenly Bodies: Film Stars and Society* (New York: St. Martin's Press, 1986), 3–4.

Figure 4.1. Isadora Duncan in 1916, Jerome Robbins Dance Division, New York Public Library for the Performing Arts, Astor, Lenox, and Tilden Foundations

well-known love affairs, they were able to fuse their offstage and onstage images fully enough to acquire and sustain the most lasting kind of fame (figs. 4.1, 4.2). Duncan was, in fact, the first of the modern dancers to see how effective it would be to meld her high-profile, adventurous (and ultimately tragic) personal life with her onstage persona as a free-spirited beauty, whose costumes often "accidentally" exposed her breasts.[11] As Mark Franko observes:

[11] Duncan was introduced to the European public when Loie Fuller took her on tour with her company to Austria and Germany. During her first solo performance in Vienna, Duncan horrified Fuller, as well as the audience—which included Princess Metternich of Vienna—by dancing in a dress of completely transparent gauze. Fuller later made excuses to the princess, claiming that Duncan's luggage had been delayed and that the see-through outfit was her "practicing costume." Fuller, *Fifteen Years*, 227. See also Peter Kurth, *Isadora: A Sensational Life* (New York: Little Brown and Co., 2001), 84–88. "Why should I care what part of my body I reveal," Duncan later wrote in response to critics of her partial nudity onstage, "Why is one part more evil than another?" (Isadora Duncan, "The Freedom of Woman" [1922], in *Isadora Speaks* [Chicago: Charles Kerr Publishing, 1994], 48).

Figure 4.2. Ruth St. Denis in *Egypta*, 1910, Jerome Robbins Dance Division, New York Public Library for the Performing Arts, Astor, Lenox, and Tilden Foundations

Duncan was known for her multiple lovers, for baring her breasts onstage, and for bearing children out of wedlock. Her famous affair with the dashing E. Gordon Craig also brought her publicity. Her life brought multiple tragedies as well; she suffered a stillbirth, the freakish accidental drowning of two of her children, and finally, of course, the ghastly accident that killed her. See Kurth, *Isadora*; Duncan, *Isadora speaks*. Ruth St. Denis used her showgirl's figure to advantage in the revealing Orientalist costumes of her early career. Her famous marriage to Ted Shawn (with whom she founded the Denishawn school) also kept her in the headlines.

"[Duncan's] career as a self-producing female soloist effectively challenged the separation of public and private spheres . . . she took performance where she found it as a public act for a private self. . . . [D]ance history has monumentalized Duncan's personal presence—her charisma, the Duncan myth"[12] . . . Of Ruth St. Denis's appeal, Marcia Siegel succinctly observes, "[She] was a very beautiful woman and she put on a good show."[13]

While more queenly and severe than either Duncan or St. Denis, Martha Graham achieved stardom via no less cultivated a persona. As Eric Bentley has written, "She can stand or sit doing nothing and keep our attention, not by 'personality' in the ruined, everyday sense, not by her private ego, . . . not wholly by her beauty either, but by a personality that she achieves . . . by sheer concentration of purpose. She is a priestess. A present-day priestess of an ancient cult."[14] With time, furthermore, Graham became a compellingly erotic figure as her stage work dealt ever more openly with womanhood and sexuality.

Fuller, though, is the woman who famously said, "My personality counts for nothing"; and, true to her word, she did not produce a memorable public personality.[15] She recounted no social narrative with her body, and so never managed to become a full-fledged media star. Her sexual self—a crucial part of the early modern dancers' stardom—was subdued if not completely obscured. She was unadorned, matronly, and guarded about her personal life, described by journalists as "a chaste dancer," "a hundred times less pretty than . . . this or that other dancer."[16] And onstage, her appeal, while potent, seemed wholly separate from her physical, sexual body, "transcend[ing] entirely femininity and eroticism . . . she created the negation of all sensuality . . . refusing everything [in dance] related to the amorous encounter," as Patrizia Veroli has written.[17]

But this is not the end of the story. To accept Fuller's work as "a negation of sensuality" is to fail to see the powerful albeit subtle physicality of her performances. In the last chapter we examined Fuller's unacknowledged relationship to Romantic ballet, her borrowing of its aesthetic effects. We saw how, through stagecraft, she performed an externalization of bodily tech-

[12] Franko, *Dancing Modernism*, 4.

[13] Siegel, *The Shapes of Change*, 8

[14] Eric Bentley, *In Search of Theatre* (New York: Applause Theater Book Publishers, 1947), 183.

[15] Fuller, *Fifteen Years*, 148.

[16] H.C., "Loie Fuller Educatrice de danseuses" 1893; Rastignac (pseudonym), "L'Illustration," *Courrier de Paris*, 14 January 1893, 26, Collection Rondel.

[17] Patrizia Veroli, *Baccanti et dive dell'aria: Donne danza et società in Italia*, 1900–1945 (Perugia: Edimond, 2001), 100.

nique—turning ballet "inside out." We saw, finally, how this process of externalization could be read as an enactment of a transition from ballet to modern
dance, from an art form that conceals technique and the physical forces at
work in and on the body, to one that exposes these elements, incorporating
them into the choreography. In this chapter, we shall again examine Fuller's
work in dialogue with an art form with which she has been denied any mean-
ingful comparison: American modern dance. Our goal will be to understand
Fuller more as a true, practicing artist of the movement and less as a mere
precursor to it. Toward that end, we shall look at how, rather than reject bodily
or physical movement outright, Fuller in fact created a fusion of "personal
kinetics" and her trademark "elaborate production values. " And we shall look
at the relationship of her choreography to such modernist elements as breath,
gravity, and bodily interiority, using the work of Martha Graham as our point
of comparison.[18]

A key to seeing these aspects of her work will be first to look at Fuller as a
sexual being, to understand how her erotic presence—however much she may
have pushed it aside—made itself felt. Indeed, as I have suggested earlier, the
sheer force with which Fuller pushed back her physical, sexual self may have
actually resulted in a kind of *subrosa*, displaced performance of both eros and
violence—which likely explains the extremely passionate responses she
evoked. We shall then look at Fuller's choreography in her group works, which
were more openly physical than her solo pieces and partook more clearly of
the vocabulary of modern dance. The group pieces, in fact, reveal Fuller's
startling proximity to Graham's work, as we shall see at the end of the chapter,
which looks particularly at Graham's landmark piece, the 1930 solo *Lamentation*, while touching briefly as well on some pieces from her more narrative
series based on Greek drama, from the 1940s and '50s.

Fleur du Sang: Fuller's Violent and Erotic Physicality

In May of 1896, Belgian symbolist poet Georges Rodenbach attended a performance of Fuller's famous *Fire Dance*, set to Wagner's *Ride of the Valkyries*. Enraptured, he returned home and composed a 58-line poem (later published in *Le*

---

[18] One of the very few critics to take seriously Fuller's relationship to later modern dancers is
Sally Sommer, who has observed that artists such as "Mary Wigman, Ruth St. Denis . . . and
Martha Graham" all experiment with aspects of dance pioneered by Fuller, including "theories
about idiosyncratic movement, the use of the untrained dancer as performer, the task orientation
of her dances, the choreographic structure which allowed for freedom of choice, [and] the use of
outside space" (see Sommer, "Loie Fuller," 66).

Figaro) that challenges his colleague Mallarmé's vision of Fuller, conjuring her in dramatically modernist terms as an erotic, deeply physical performer:

> *Brusquely ripping through the shadows, she is there. And it is dawn!*
> *From a mauve prelude that swells to lilac,*
> *Having tailored her flounces out of the clouds,*
> *She fades to paleness only to regain her colors.*
> *This is a miracle disguised as play.*
> *Her robe becomes suddenly a land of mist;*
> *She is flaming spirits and incense burning;*
> *Her robe is a pyre of lilies . . .*
>
> *Then, as the volcano is filled up with lava,*
> *It seems as if she had created the rivers of fire that surround her, her slaves,*
> *Writhing over her, like serpents.*
> *O Tree of Temptation! Oh temptress!*
> *The Tree of Paradise, where she has entwined our creeping desires that twist*
> *together like colored serpents.*
>
> *A pause.*
> *She comes, her hair a green red, tinted by these delirious clouds;*
> *One might think a great wind returned from afar;*
> *For already, amid the swirling fabric, her body loses its foamy wake;*
> *disappearing into wisps.*
> *Oh darkness, what do you do to turn her robe thus into an ocean of flame,*
> *Glittering with gemstones?*
> *Brunehilde, it is you, queen of Valkryies*
> *Every man dreams of becoming a god, in order to be your chosen one.*
>
> *It is over;*
> *Brusquely, the air is scarred*
> *By this flower-shaped wound from which it has bled.*[19]

For Rodenbach, clearly, Fuller's *Fire Dance* transforms her into a seductress, reminiscent at once of mythic warrior women, the Valkyries conjured by Wagner's music, and the ultimate temptress, Eve. At the same time, the serpents writhing about her suggest the petrifying power of a Medusa. All, of course, are iconic women associated with death and the downfall of men. The most telling parts of this (admittedly melodramatic) poem are its first and last

---

[19] Georges Rodenbach, *Le Figaro*, 5 May 1896, qtd. in Kermode, "Loie Fuller and the Dance before Diaghilev," 40. The translation of this excerpt is a combination of my own and that of Philippe Rein, which appears in Kermode's article.

stanzas. Rodenbach imagines Fuller both beginning and ending her performance with a deeply female, birth-like violence with which she tears open the space around her. It is easy to understand the first metaphor: bursting onto the darkened, black-velvet draped stage, Fuller seems to open the surrounding space with her forceful explosion of color, "ripping through the shadows" ("*déchirant l'ombre*"). In his closing image, though, Rodenbach complicates his metaphors. He waxes Baudelairean with the conceit of the bleeding, floral wound left by Fuller, which now scars over. As she whirls around in a spiral of blood-red light, Fuller seems to have set the air itself on fire, violently opening up a distinctly feminine, even vaginal rupture—a bleeding flower— in the planar space around her. In Rodenbach's vision, Fuller's performance forces the spectator to acknowledge the three-dimensionality of space, not only by creating the ephemeral shapes with her robes but by doing it so violently that the surrounding air suffers permanent damage. The air has lost its transparency and its two-dimensionality and, in their place, acquired a skin-like thickness—a phenomenon akin to what Stephen Kern has called the "materialization of space" in the paintings of Braque and Cézanne. The modernist paintings of those artists command attention for the materiality of their media as well as for their figurative content. Brushstroke, paint, the thickness of the canvas—all were consciously displayed, lending thickness or "thingness" to the space depicted, while pure pictoriality or figuration was resisted.[20] For Rodenbach, clearly, Fuller's dance achieved a similar modernist self-consciousness. Her performance drew attention to *its* own physicality: its existence as bodily motion cutting through surrounding space, carving out a negative, woundlike space around itself in the "thickness," the materiality of the air. As early as 1896, Rodenbach had perceived Fuller's deep and modernist physicality, understanding its power, its violence, and its beauty—all of which are usually ignored by critics in favor of her technological modernism. But as this poem so powerfully suggests, in Fuller's work, the technological and the biological are deeply intertwined.

Rodenbach's reaction tells us that such a performance could force spectators to acknowledge not only the colorful, mechanical, or even supernatural aspects of Fuller's dance, but also its powerful use of space and its creation of physical depth. The air, no longer a transparent or unacknowledged window through which to view the performance, has taken on a human, specifically female vulnerability: it can be penetrated; it can bleed and form scars. Fuller has extended her body so forcefully into space that that space itself is granted, as if by contagion, physical depth and human blood. This is how we must

[20] Kern, *The Culture of Time and Space 1880–1918*, 162.

begin to think of Fuller's bodily modernism, as a process of transference—of force, of motion, of physicality—from a body onto its surroundings, be they mechanical trappings or even the simple air around her.

Rodenbach makes clear that Fuller, however chaste her dance or covered her body, created nonetheless a kind of spectacular femaleness onstage. His metaphors of rupture, blood, scars, and flowers lead us unmistakably to a whole series of associations, all of which evoke uniquely female reproductive or sexual events: menstruation, childbirth, and perhaps even rape or a violent "deflowering." While the *Fire Dance* is highly abstract, with Fuller clearly depicting no one woman or character, but rather flame itself, for Rodenbach, its effect is powerfully physically, eliciting a conjoined violence and female sexuality.

Let us note however that in Rodenbach's vision, Fuller herself is the perpetrator, not the victim, of the violence. In this poem, the narrator-spectator figures himself as a supplicant to this overwhelming seductress, dreaming of being chosen by her. She is not the bleeding flower, rather she rips it into existence and then emerges from it autochthonously, giving birth to herself and leaving the audience with the resultant gore. The *Fire Dance*, that is, testifies to Fuller's self-contained, somewhat hermaphroditic sexuality: her forms are strikingly female, but the action that shapes them is penetrative, masculine, and violent. Her effect on the audience is hypnotic, but when she leaves the stage, she has separated herself from the attendant images of sex and birth. She sweeps off with her robes still pristine; it's the air that is bloody. Once again, we see an example of Fuller's work as a splitting of the self into two parts. In the last chapter we noted how Fuller's body seemed to separate into two: a baton-and-fabric, ballerina-like effigy and the cocooned lower half below, manipulating the creature. Here, Rodenbach suggests a more radical image still, in which Fuller uses her techno-body to forge a bloody, even vulval shape and then separates from it.[21]

If it were only Rodenbach's poem that conjured Fuller with such powerful and complex sexual imagery, we would not be justified in using it as "proof" of anything more than one man's idiosyncratic view of her. But the poem's view of Fuller is anomalous neither in its portrayal of violence nor in its suggestion of a strong sexual presence. We have already seen the peculiar underside of violence in Fuller's work, and how it fit subtly into the performance of French imperialism, for example.[22] We recall Jean Lorrain's dismay over her

---

[21] Rodenbach's image reminds us of Felicia McCarren's likening of Fuller's fabric forms to the uterus and fallopian tubes. For Rodenbach, though, Fuller creates female reproductive shapes that linger even after her silk sculptures have disappeared. See McCarren, *Dance Pathologies*, 169.

[22] See chapter 1.

apparent display of "self-amputation" in the mirror dances. Fuller's violence lies, of course, beneath her polished and wholesome surface. The same is true for her erotic side. The fact is that, despite all her ostentatious sexlessness and chastity, Fuller was often viewed—by artists, critics, journalists, even members of her own family—as quite a sexual, even scandalous performer. Exploring this curious tendency to "sex up" Fuller will help us situate her more effectively in the realm of modern dance, for while erotic movement and the "personal kinetics" of a Graham or a Duncan are not identical, they are deeply related as expressions of the human, biological body. Unveiling the effects of Fuller's erotic presence is, therefore, crucial.

The Erotic Fuller

As we know, by the time she arrived in Paris, Fuller was noticeably plump, covered up from head to toe both onstage and off, and openly passionate on only two subjects: art and her love for her mother. Despite this, there exist hundreds of paintings, sculptures, figurines, and posters—created from 1893 through the 1920s—that portray Fuller as a svelte, beguiling girl of the sort she had, frankly, never been. One of the most famous of these images is Jules Chéret's 1893 poster of Fuller for the Folies-Bergère, in which a twirling, semi-clad dancer looks over her shoulder at the spectator, twisting her body to permit a view of bare breasts, nipples erect (fig. 4.3). The poster bears not the slightest resemblance to Fuller; Chéret did not even attempt to render the face accurately, replacing Fuller's features with a generic, conventionally pretty cartoon of a girl. To complete his transformation, Chéret depicts Fuller raising her stage costume to reveal improbably slim, dainty legs, one lifted upward in a modified ballet *attitude*, the other poised lightly on demi-pointe. As Joseph Mazo writes, "Fuller . . . is obviously not the sylph of Chéret's poster."[23]

There are a number of similar Folies posters, also done in the late 1890s, by various artists, in which Fuller is again rendered as a smiling (and very slim) showgirl whose robes fall open to reveal fetching expanses of neck, shoulder, back, or bosom (fig. 4.4). We might assume that the Folies management simply didn't know how to advertise Fuller, and so resorted to the usual devices for marketing their traditional, racier fare. But these altered or standardized depictions of Fuller persisted throughout her career, even long after

---

[23] Joseph Mazo, *Prime Movers: The Makers of Modern Dance in America* (New York: Morrow, 1977), 26.

Figure 4.3. Jules Chéret's poster for Fuller's appearance at the Folies-Bergère

Figure 4.4. Poster for Fuller's Folies performance, by Ferdinand Bac, courtesy of Maryhill Museum of Art

Figure 4.5. Bronze sculpture of Fuller in the Lily Dance by Thomas Rivière, 1896 courtesy of the Maryhill Museum of Art

she had become famous as a kind of anti-showgirl. The Art Nouveau artists, in particular, displayed a penchant for recasting Fuller's body and face, preferring her redrawn as something of a Greek goddess with perfect proportions. We can find a bare-breasted and very slim Fuller in the swirling bronzes of Raoul-François Larche, Bernhard Hoetger, and Thomas Rivière (fig. 4.5). Pierre Roche designed exquisite—and equally "airbrushed"—figurines of Fuller in porcelain, in bronze, and even in plaster medallions and paper *estampes*.

From 1897 through 1902 (when Fuller was between 35 and 40 years old and quite stout) François-Rupert Carabin produced a series of sculptures depicting her as a young girl bending elastically from the waist, her torso nude, with rib cage visible and, once again, breasts bared. Countless other examples exist in glass, terra-cotta, and crystal, by some of the finest artists and craftsmen of Europe.[24]

Why did these artists return again and again to a model whose own figure differed so much from the proportions they clearly preferred? Why did they label these nubile (and often nude) creatures "Loie Fuller"? Certainly, they did not intend them as faithful reproductions. Instead, these artworks result from the similar impetus that led Rodenbach to imagine he saw a bleeding flower in the air once Fuller left the stage. While she did not offer her audience an overtly corporeal sexuality, Fuller clearly did something onstage that elicited visions of the most deeply feminine and erotically available shapes: uncovered breasts, arched backs, supple waists, even genital openings. For all her butch mastery of stagecraft and technology, and despite her heavy, flat-footed body that barely danced, Fuller managed, with her movement and her floating draperies, to conjure these sexualized images, which ranged from raunchy to idealized.[25]

The process by which Fuller communicated this intense female appeal was the very process that Rodenbach intuited when he imagined the floral wound left hanging in the air by Fuller: a process of redirection and transference. Those artists who chose to render her as a bare-breasted beauty or sexy show-girl were responding to and taking part in that process. Fuller enacted the redirection or transferring of bodiliness and physical force—a displacement of erotic kineticism—onto her costumes, onto her technology, onto the air, and ultimately onto members of her public—including the artists who created with marble and bronze the very image being denied by all the fabric. They expressed, in other words, what Fuller disavowed. They also expressed, to be sure, their own desires—for which Fuller's performances made space via her own deflection of personal eros. In this way did she become an apparent tabula rasa, a living projection screen, as I said in the introduction to this book, for a kind of ideal (and surprisingly conventional) view of womanhood.

---

[24] While some of these idealized depictions of Fuller may have been commissioned by her and among those "souvenirs" sold during her performances, the majority were not vanity projects of this sort.

[25] This sexual view of Fuller is confirmed by her great-grandnephew, Donald Fuller, of Hinsdale, Illinois, who remembers older relatives speaking in whispers about their scandalous Aunt Loie who had led, somehow, an inappropriate life in Europe; "she was risqué," he says, "they knew she was a burlesque queen" (Donald Fuller, in discussion with the author, 25 October 2005).

The Scandalous Ballets Loie Fuller

When she performed alone, this process of deflection or redirection was restricted to the play between Fuller's body and her costume, or between Fuller and the surrounding stage space. Once she began working with her many young pupils, however, Fuller had another medium onto which to displace her sexual energy: the girls themselves. During her early, solo career, despite the many eroticized "Loie Fuller's" that appeared as artworks, few reviewers directly suggested that Fuller's performances were openly erotic; and no one *ever* found her morally objectionable. The same cannot be said of reviews of Les Ballets Loie Fuller, in which we can find acknowledgment of a more overt brand of erotic "spillover" or redirection.

It is unsurprising that Fuller's work seemed more erotic once she began working with other dancers. Upon gathering the first version of her troupe in 1909, Fuller was forced, at least in part, to humanize her productions, to work with bodies as well as batons, robes, and lights. These bodies, moreover, ranged in age from five or six all the way up to twenty-five. Regardless of their age, all the girls wore the same costumes, generally the light, Grecian-inspired tunics also popularized by Isadora Duncan and her own troupe of acolytes.

While Fuller's costumes were always voluminous and opaque, the girls' versions were distinctly less so and worn with the most minimal of undergarments—a fact frequently noted by critics (fig. 4.6). Some were guardedly appreciative: "Her students dance in the manner of Isadora Duncan," wrote a Parisian reviewer in 1911, "schoolgirls nude beneath their transparent tunics, some are no more than ten years old and show their skinny little bodies; others though have a distinctly more feminine appearance; Miss Karina has a fragile silhouette, but Orchidée is in full bloom."[26] Other critics, particularly some in the United States, were more direct. The *Washington Post* declared: "As for the costuming of the dancers . . . to [some] they will seem entirely too daring to be countenanced even in the magic name of art."[27] A New York review disapproved even more openly: "Is it necessary for art's sake to make young girls appear without fleshings [leotards] and in bare feet? With naught to shield their form save a few folds of filmy gauze?"[28]

---

[26] Philippe Nozière, "L'Ecole de Loie Fuller," *Matinale*, 22 June 1911, Collection Rondel.

[27] "La Loie Fuller and Her Company," *Washington Post*, 12 October 1909, NYPLPA, Robinson Locke Collection.

[28] Review from *New York Dramatic Mirror*, qtd. in de Morinni, "Loie Fuller: The Fairy of Light," 206.

Figure 4.6. Fuller's barefoot pupils perform *The Diana Dance*, 1910, Billy Rose
Theatre Collection, New York Public Library for the Performing Arts, Astor, Lenox,
and Tilden Foundations

This last remark confirms Fuller's own complaints about the moralizing re-
strictions placed on her troupe in North America. Fuller insisted that the
diaphanous costumes were an innocent and necessary part of her productions,
telling a journalist: "There is something about the thinnest covering that
spoils the lines under the drapery and really makes the effect more common-
place and suggestive than the beautiful simplicity of the nude limbs. But
America! America! You never know what to expect."[29] One of Fuller's dancers
echoed this sentiment in an interview about the company's running afoul of
an ordinance prohibiting bare feet on a New York stage, "I see by the papers
that according to the new law we girls will not be allowed to appear without
fleshings—bare feet and legs are prohibited in Puritanic America."[30]

At another point in their North American tour, a Canadian church tried
to stop a performance in which Fuller presented the girls—all in various states
of half-dress—as individual representatives of the dance of different regions
and historical eras. The beautiful Orchidée, for example, embodied the "An-

[29] Fuller qtd. in an interview, 24 August, no year, unidentified press clipping, NYPLPA, Robinson Locke Collection.

[30] Unidentified press clipping, NYPLPA, Robinson Locke Collection.

cient Middle East," while ballerina Gertrude Van Axen reproduced Greek vase dancing. Fuller successfully opposed the church and the show went on, but the aura of titillation remained with the company.[31]

At times, the aristocratic background of the girls made their naked limbs seem that much more striking:

> Loie Fuller brings to America fifty young girls, all of whom are daughters of members of the nobility or of excellent society abroad, or are proté-gées of distinguished Parisians. And when these girls go dancing about on their bare toes ... the occupants of the boxes will feel almost as much at home as they did at charity teas last winter, when certain society leaders cast clothes and conservatism to the winds.[32]

As for Fuller, she never openly acknowledged any desire to arouse the public or any awareness that her girls might seem anything but pure. We should keep in mind, though, Fuller's requirement that her pupils resemble her physically and maintain hair styles like her own. As we have seen, these young girls were chosen expressly to represent an extension or replication of Fuller's own person onstage. That she then allowed them to provoke the public in this way, presenting them seminude at times, only confirms these young girls' status as representatives or receptacles of Fuller's own pushed-back erotic physicality. By including many prepubescent girls in her troupe, however, Fuller was able better to justify her claims about the groups' total innocence and her own purity of intention. Maintaining her typical disingenuousness when asked about the obvious physical charms of her young charges, Fuller answered: "When people see [my students'] healthy and delicious svelteness, I want them to think of little wildflowers bathing in the sun. . . . [The dancing] will reveal their strange and natural charm."[33]

But Fuller's troupe of half-naked young ladies provoked thoughts of more than wildflowers (as she hinted at perhaps with the curious phrase "strange and natural charm"). When the troupe returned to the States in 1911, another journalist, John Corbin, confirmed that Loie Fuller's girls seemed daringly to challenge America's conventional mores and sexual timidity:

> We Americans who have been so long a laughing stock for our prudery are at last discovering that we have bodies. The world and the flesh are no longer, to our thinking, co-partners with the devil. That is the

---

[31] See Lista, *Danseuse*, 479 ff.

[32] Unidentified press clipping, NYPLPA, Robinson Locke Collection.

[33] Pierre Desclaux, "Gala de l'orphelinat des arts," unidentified publication, 19 June 1911, Collection Rondel.

significant fact behind the interest which the public has lately shown in the art of dancing. . . . In the grace of the highly trained human body we have discovered a fresh, new vehicle and powerful expression. Loie Fuller, Isadora Duncan, Ruth St. Denis . . . —where can one find so much of vital, classic beauty as in their limbs and outward flourishes?[34]

Corbin's remarks make plain that, when presented by her group of young girls, Fuller's work seemed erotically alive enough to storm the gates of American "prudery." His review tells us not only that Fuller's troupe had the potential to titillate the public, but that this very fact placed Les Ballets Loie Fuller among the new stars of American modern dance, alongside Duncan and St. Denis. Corbin thereby helps us see the connection between the bodily charisma of Fuller's troupe and the "personal kinetics" of American modern dance—that side of dance from which Fuller has been so often excluded.

Fuller had, of course, often been compared to Duncan, largely for the apparent "freedom" both women exhibited—their rejection of ballet, their use of solo performance, and their preference for flowing, classical garb onstage.[35] Both seemed to be returning to the ancient roots of dance.[36] While the two women were rarely compared personally, their teaching methods and resultant group pieces looked extremely similar to many critics: "It's curious," wrote a review in 1911, "[Fuller's] students all dance like Isadora Duncan."[37] Another

[34] John Corbin, "Dancing," July 1911, NYPLPA.

[35] And indeed, Fuller was, in part, responsible for Duncan's European debut, having taken the younger dancer on tour with her troupe to Vienna, where Duncan proceeded to scandalize everyone by making her debut virtually naked, clad only in transparent gauze. The collaboration ended quickly and bitterly with Duncan accusing Fuller's troupe of sapphic aggressions toward her, and Fuller feeling betrayed and exploited by a dancer she deeply admired and perhaps had even loved a little. See Kurth, *Isadora*; Fuller, *Fifteen Years*; Lista, *Danseuse*.

[36] Anatole France extolled Fuller as a reincarnation of Greece's ancient theatrical arts: "Loie Fuller . . . reanimates within herself and restores to us the lost wonders of Greek mimicry, the art of those motions, at once voluptuous and mystical, which interpret the phenomena of nature and the life history of living beings" (Anatole France, "Introduction" to Loie Fuller's *Fifteen Years of a Dancer's Life*, ix). Roger-Marx hailed her for "having reincarnated the soul of antiquity . . . reconnecting . . . with the sublime dancing women who inspired Paeonios to sculpt his Victory . . . having returned to the very springtime of humanity (Roger-Marx, *La Loie Fuller*, 8–9). "She sits at the head of her school in her Greek robes, with all her pupils in their Greek robes, and instructs them how to find truth and beauty and self-expression in dancing" (unidentified press clipping, NYPLPA, Robinson Locke Collection).
As for Duncan, as biographer Peter Kurth writes, "Isadora's girlhood dream of Greece . . . became her active study. In her dances, she no longer sought to 'copy' the poses and postures of the ancient world, but to live them" (Kurth, *Isadora*, 58).

[37] Nozière, "L'Ecole de la Loie Fuller," *Matinale* 22 June 1911.

critic reported in 1922: "I was thinking of Isadora Duncan as I watched Loie Fuller's company evolve. It's the same steps, the same movements, the same abandonment to the winds of nature. What does Isadora Duncan owe to Loie Fuller? What does Loie Fuller owe to Duncan?"[38]

Fuller was extremely aware of these comparisons and, as time passed, began to feel threatened by the younger Duncan (whose career she had helped launch, only to be later bitterly rejected her protégé).[39] Often, when trying to distance herself from Duncan and the "Isadorables," Fuller would proclaim her own methods superior for their greater "naturalness." Her teaching, she insisted, was less forced than Duncan's (whose name she would only imply, never mention), and somehow more instinctive: "My children reproduce, without being aware of it, the Greek dances, and yet, I assure you that I have never uttered this word 'Greece' to them, nor have I shown them friezes or vases illustrating beautiful poses."[40] (We might wonder how then she rehearsed Gertrude in her "Grecian vase" dance.) A similar sentiment appears in Fuller's personal journal, where she wrote:

> I do not think that natural dancing should be confounded with those dances of today which are confined to the copying of the Greek art as seen in vases and friezes and which consists of certain set morsels but which are all more or less familiar and which have to be (or are) learned in the old fashioned way, like steps which are practiced mechanically and strung together to fit a certain number of bars in music.[41]

Beyond the irony of Fuller, queen of technology, accusing Duncan of being too "mechanical," a larger, more important point lies in these quotations. Fuller, in her teaching, strove greatly to tap into some kind of instinctual movement and expression. Her goal, she insisted, was to ferret out and develop each girl's individual style of expression, allowing a pigeon-toed youngster, for example, to dance with feet turned inward. "The teacher discusses . . . the dancing that suits the pupil. . . . The so-called 'faults' [of movement or posture,] when understood, are frequently just the things most worthy of develop-

---

[38] Review of Loie Fuller, *Avenir* 1922, NYPLPA.

[39] A 1914 letter from Gabrielle Bloch to Fuller reveals the open competitiveness between the two dancers. Bloch urged Fuller to return from touring in order better to compete with Duncan in attracting profitable dance students: "speaking of school and what we must do and where is lot of money is to make your school at once when you return. You have all the advantage on Isadora now but after it *will be too late*. Everybody wants to send children to you not her. You must have a house like hers" (Gabrielle Bloch to Loie Fuller, 14 August 1914, NYPLPA).

[40] Desclaux, "Gala de l'orphelinat des arts."

[41] Fuller, unpublished essay, NYPLPA.

ment," Fuller told a journalist.[42] But while the students may have gamboled about freely while at Fuller's home in Neuilly and in some productions, most of the time they enjoyed somewhat less freedom onstage. Fuller's claims of pedagogical permissiveness were disingenuous, as we have already noted. In performance, the troupe did not so much dance about as individual free spirits as enact large-scale versions of Fuller's own aesthetic. Nevertheless, the notion of dance driven by instinct and inwardness has an important, albeit subtler place in Fuller's group work.

Instinct, Nature, and Versions of Interiority

An inroad into understanding Fuller's group modernism lies in her claim, cited above, that her students "reproduce [ancient Greek dances] without being aware of it." She claimed, that is, to be able to direct her students to a kind of collective memory of dance history, which led back to ancient Greece—exhibiting a typically modernist Hellenism. Working with "her girls," Fuller often employed techniques unmistakably indebted to modernist principles of instinctive, "internally driven" movement. Isadora Duncan would espouse a very similar teaching philosophy, claiming that she never imposed choreography, preferring simply to liberate her students' natural abilities. "I never taught my pupils any steps," she wrote. "I never taught myself technique. I told them to appeal to their spirit, as I did to mine. Art is nothing else."[43]

But Fuller's notion that she could lead her girls back to ancient Greek dance simply by guiding their instincts also demonstrates the proto-Jungian cast that her thinking took on later in her career. In this, Fuller strikingly anticipates the interests of Martha Graham, who as of the 1940s turned to Jung, drawn by his notion of a mythic, collective unconscious composed of archetypal figures.[44] Graham's quest to "define the archetypal images of woman in herself

---

[42] Fuller, qtd. in Sommer, "Loie Fuller," 65. Fuller also seemed to feel there was a kind of equally instinctive ethical or moral component to her teaching. "My children," she said, "do good because that is beautiful and an interior voice tells them to do so." Visited by a journalist in 1912, Fuller had her students put on a little display of their dance exercises. One girl performed as "Saint Francis of Assisi preaching to little birds. One girl evoked . . . before us the movement of water and wind, another showed us the anguish of plucking one by one the petals of a rose, the sadness of 'killing a flower' . . . such a pure and delicately classic art." (Louis Sabarin, "La Loie Fuller présente ses petites éleves," 4 October 1912, Collection Rondel).

[43] Duncan, *Isadora Speaks*, 58.

[44] Deborah Jowitt explains Graham's interest in Jung as an attempt to "objectify her emotional life and forge a dancing persona" at a particularly difficult time in her personal and artistic life (Jowitt, *Time and the Dancing Image*, 206).

and in relation to her world" inspired her interpretations of such biblical and Christian heroines as Herodias, Joan of Arc, Eve, Mary Magdalene and the Virgin Mary, and Greek figures such as Medea, Jocasta, Clytemnestra, and Phaedra. Graham used these mythic women as figures through which to explore universal truths about female sexuality and desire.[45]

Graham's search for archetypal femininity led her to more narrative, psychological choreography, based on religious and literary texts. She also invented and codified an entirely new lexicon of dance movements and positions. Duncan's passion to "discover the roots of that impulse toward movement" was less formulaic, more free-form.[46] But these dancers—and virtually all of the moderns who left their mark on the first half of the twentieth century—shared a desire to make an interior truth visible. Modern dance, as Elizabeth Dempster has explained, "is an expression of interiority: interior feeling guiding the movement of the body into external forms."[47]

As a dancer who refused to cultivate a stage persona, exhibit overt sexuality, or show any part of her body, Fuller may seem to be completely at odds with the modernist insistence on revealing interiors. Yet, in her own way, Fuller cared deeply about peering beneath the surfaces of things and presenting the hidden truths discovered. While not overtly psychological, and only occasionally narrative, Fuller's work, as we shall see, presented a physical and visual predecessor for the kind of emotional interiority later explored by Graham.

Understanding the proto-Graham in Fuller requires an investigation into her use of interiority, which played a role in her work on several levels. To begin with, Fuller's fundamental solo technique enacted a very basic game of hide-and-seek with her body—hiding it, reshaping it, scientifically altering its visibility through lights and stagecraft. By virtue of being nearly always invisible, her literal, biological self acquired a kind of powerful, negative stage presence, which forced audiences to wonder where her body was and what it was doing. Fuller's body was always "inside," within the veils, the secret source of movement of all the floating forms she created. Since those forms, furthermore, were always container-shaped—tubular, funnel- or balloon-like—they presented volume and three-dimensionality, creating what Jean Lorrain called

---

[45] Graham's mentor, composer Louis Horst, wrote in 1961, "Martha Graham's typical dramatic scene is laid within the mind or heart of a woman faced with an urgency of decision or action, and with the dramatis personae of the group performing as symbols of her complex emotional reactions"(qtd. in Lynn Garafola, *Legacies of Twentieth Century Dance* [Middletown, CT: Wesleyan University Press, 2005], 235).

[46] See John Martin, "Isadora Duncan and Basic Dance," in *Nijinsky, Pavlova, Duncan: Three Lives*, ed. Paul Magriel (New York: Da Capo Press, 1978), 1–17.

[47] Dempster, "Women Writing the Body," 224.

the "*effet de coquillage*" and what Felicia McCarren has compared to the female reproductive system. By masking her body with these evocative forms, Fuller continually *performed* a kind of bodily, even sexual interiority—an effect that accounts for Georges Rodenbach's suggestive vaginal imagery.

Fuller performed interiority in metaphorical as well as visual fashion. As we have seen repeatedly, she had a scientist's interest in penetrating beneath the surface of appearance to learn what lies beneath. Her fascination with all manner of optical gadgets—telescopes, microscopes, X-ray machines—testified to her love of the "interior" world.[48] She brought this fascination to the stage, treating her public to astronomical visions, the sights hidden within a drop of water, or the mutated cells hidden in a cancer patient's body.[49] These visual, scientific "interiors" uncovered by Fuller's work functioned as figurative extensions of the literal, physical interiors that continually reformed themselves with the rising and falling of her silks—all of which served as replacements for (or improvements upon) the never-to-appear naked body beneath the costumes.

When Fuller expanded her work to include group choreography, her mise-en-scène of interiority took on larger as well as more human dimensions. Working with a troupe enabled Fuller to multiply her sculptural floating forms

---

[48] In the early twentieth century, a certain feminism attached itself to the possibilities of science, which seemed allied with the potential freedom attendant upon greater knowledge of the body's secrets. As historian Bettyann Kevles has pointed out, modern dance felt an explicit connection to these new scientific tools: "For women, the new ability to see through their bodies was a path to freedom. Those who needed evidence found that the x-ray images supported their demands to free themselves from the unhealthy constraints of corsets: ardent feminists saw the rays as dissolving the barriers of all obstructive clothing. The American dancers Isadora Duncan and Loie Fuller were convinced that new technologies like x-rays would interact with the arts. . . . Fuller designed colored lights so that as she whirled on her own axis, countless yards of veil-like materials gave the impression that she appeared and disappeared as she spun, a body seen through a fluoroscope" (Bettyann Kevles, *Naked to the Bone: Medical Imaging in the Twentieth Century* [New York: Perseus Books, 1998], 119).

[49] Perhaps the interior that most fascinated Fuller belonged to light itself, which she claimed to be able to see "as if in a kaleidoscope"—fragmented, broken open to reveal its constitutive colors, separated as if by a prism. In an unpublished lecture on color and light, Fuller wrote: "There are over 13,000 colours all with names . . . but under the microscope . . . the colours are countless. They shift, ever changing, till the brain grows dizzy with only looking at them . . . we are beginning to see that we can direct to great use and beauty the decomposition of rays of light. We know that colour is in fact, a condition of light rays, but to play upon it for orchestrations of harmony to the eye as music is to the ear seems far far away into the unknown world, and so it is, but since science has produced powerful lenses that can magnify and bring to our imperfect sight a perfect sight, we are enabled to see and learn the wonders of decaying light, in the microscopic world, a world not yet made use of for beauty's sake" (Fuller, "Prelude to Light," unpublished essay, NYPLPA).

and send them spinning across the stage, using the girls to animate them. In other words, Fuller would cover the young dancers with varying expanses of drapery and then send them—singly or in groups—moving about the stage as lights and images were projected upon them. In this way, Fuller used her students much as she had used her patented sleeve batons. By "filling" her forms with living young girls, Fuller was offering spectators a new inducement to "look inside," for now there were visible (and often nubile) bodies hiding beneath the veils. Dressed in transparent tunics without "fleshings" underneath, the girls' bodies lent another level of "visual interiority" to the group productions. And so, in this most obvious way, the group pieces enhanced the sexual element of Fuller's "performance of interiority": underneath all the idealized shapes and lights lurked glimpses of actual naked flesh.[50]

Let us look now at some explicit examples of how Fuller's troupe performed, specifically at how Fuller used the girls to develop her staged meditations on physical, natural, and sexual interiority.

The Mechanics of the Group

Fuller did not so much change her aesthetic when choreographing with her troupe as use her students to portray, shape, and animate those images and shapes she had once created using only inorganic materials—fabric, lights, or projected designs and photographs. The inclusion of moving human beings, however, inevitably altered the tenor of the performances.

In 1913, for example, Fuller created a production around *Nocturnes* by Debussy, consisting of three movements: "Nuages," "Fêtes," and "Sirènes." Here, the clouds of the first segment appeared not only as filmic projections, but also as groups of veiled dancers who "wafted" across the stage. Contemporary critic Louis Schneider described it thus:

Two porticos framed a terrace that dominated a deep blue night sky. While this atmosphere was evoked by the exquisite [music], the clouds pass before our eyes, not clouds made of cardboard or painted canvas, but made by the . . . tight groupings of the little girls of Loie Fuller's school, hidden under silver veils. A cloud glides by, slow and mysterious,

[50] It is possible that some of the sculptors who produced those perfectly—and inaccurately— proportioned figurines of Fuller might have been responding more to the youthful and alluring bodies of her troupe members.

then another, then a third, each more supple . . . than the next . . . the
veils slightly ballooning, as if blown up by wind.[51]

We see here Fuller using the young dancers as fragmented extensions of her
own techno-body. The veils ballooning around the small groups of hidden
dancers mimic the air-filled forms created by Fuller's batons and veils, only
this time entire bodies dance beneath. The ballooning of the veils furthermore
would have been created by the movement of the girls' bodies, which now
replaces Fuller's rotating batons. Schneider's description tells us that Fuller
made no effort to conceal the reality of her dancers' bodies beneath the veils.
While hidden, they were perfectly distinguishable as the "little girls." While
Fuller's own body was a mysterious absence in her solo pieces, the girls' bodies
functioned differently onstage. Younger, smaller, and more overt, they human-
ized the work and "filled up" the ballooning shapes of the veils over them with
recognizable human shapes, much like actors wearing body mask costumes.
Thus did Fuller create a new kind of "bodily interior" onstage—using whole
bodies (or groups of bodies) as the "fillings" of fantastical forms, such as these
clouds. She would use a very similar technique in 1914 for *Fireworks*, and in
1915 for her *Night on Bald Mountain*.[52]

Sometimes, instead of veiling individual groupings of girls, Fuller placed
the entire troupe behind a scrim, as she did in her 1909 *Ballet de lumière*. For
this piece, Fuller positioned thirty girls behind a vast gauze curtain at New
York's Metropolitan Opera House. The girls then danced as projectors played
colored lights and scenes of natural landscapes upon the gauze, including the
ocean, erupting volcanoes, the snows of the polar region, and the aurora borealis. The troupe's movements coordinated with the screened images, so that
the volcano's tongues of flame, for example, seemed animated by waving
movements of the dancers behind the scrim.[53] Here again, Fuller had invited
audiences to peer through her images at living bodies. During her solo performances, while her filmic projections were naturally translucent, to peer
through them meant only to look upon the whirling veils, since no portion
of Fuller's physical self was ever visible or really even delineated. With the
girls, however, multiple young bodies doubled as film screens, and provided a

---

[51] Louis Schneider qtd. in Lista, *Danseuse*, 492.

[52] For *Fireworks*, which deeply influenced the Ballets Russes, Fuller hid her dancers completely
beneath black cloaks, having them run in and out of projected beams of changing jewel-toned
lights, which they "caught" on sheer fabrics that they twirled overhead. The dancers' bodies,
while unseen, became the animating force of the "fireworks" display.

[53] Lista, *Danseuse*, 477.

Figure 4.7. Loie Fuller and her troupe in an unidentified group piece using large veils, Bibliothèque Nationale de France

living, breathing core for Fuller's weightless projections, a visual "discovery" for spectators gazing past or through the outer shells of silk or tulle.

In her group choreography, Fuller also began to employ what we might call "the giant veil" technique. We have seen that Fuller routinely used her troupe to extend and enlarge her trademark visions onstage. In the "giant veil" dances, it was her already-voluminous veil costume that grew substantially. Instead of veiling the girls individually or in groups, in these works Fuller used veils big enough to envelop the entire lot of them (fig. 4.7).

At times, the gigantic veil served as a stage prop, as in the 1915 *Night on Bald Mountain*, set to the famous Mussorgsky piece. Here, Fuller used a gigantic blue veil that she had rolled into an enormous cone shape to symbolize the "vault of heaven." The towering blue cone remained center stage, as if one of her whirling forms had somehow flown off her body and frozen into place. In 1920, *Le Voile magique*, performed at Paris's Olympia Theater, made more ac- tive use of the giant veil. For this, twelve girls stood in a circle holding on to an enormous round veil. Again serving as extensions of Fuller's batons, the girls agitated the veil—as one might a sheet when making a bed—so that it rose and fell in various artful ways, filling with air and then deflating while colored lights and designs were projected upon it.[54] A journalist described it as "a vault . . . that breathes currents of air *like a living being*."[55]

The Triumph of *La Mer*

An Historic and Influential Performance

Fuller's giant veil technique reached it apotheosis on June 16, 1925, with her dance interpretation of Debussy's 1905 "tone poem" *La Mer*, produced by the renowned theater impresario Gabriel Astruc as part of the Fête du Théâtre et de la Parure at Paris's 1925 Exposition des Arts Décoratifs et Industriels.[56] Indisputably the largest, most ambitious live production of Fuller's career, *La Mer* was a reworking of Fuller's earlier piece, *Sirènes*, here performed with 75 dancers on the steps of Paris's Grand Palais, the Art Nouveau masterpiece designed by Hector Guimard for the 1900 *Exposition Universelle* (and one of only two buildings remaining from that fair).[57] It was especially fitting that Fuller—the unofficial Queen of that Exposition twenty-five years earlier—

[54] (Empasis added.)"It's the dance of the great veil," wrote a critic, "a little girl strikes poses, stands up, lies down, all under a transparent veil that the others agitate and make fly. There are colors of every tone, it is dark, sad, troubling, pure, magnificent. [The veil] evokes all the sentiments of the little soul turning beneath it" (Nozière, review of Loie Fuller, Collection Rondel).

[55] Qtd. in Lista, *Danseuse*, 517. Giovanni Lista sees Fuller's use of the large veils in her later group pieces as an attempt to create a kind of visual signifier of wide-open country: "The veil had become the equivalent for her of nature. . . . As she matured, the veil would be used across the entire stage until it became something grandiose, the equivalent of the immense American landscape" (Lista, *Danseuse*, 463). In the 1921 film *Le Lys de la vie*, when Corona meets with the King of the Mountains, Fuller's dancers performed the *Dance of the Great Opal*, in which a large white veil was agitated collectively until it formed a great hemisphere, which was then lit from within with opalescent light.

[56] Also known as "Night of the Grand Palais," the event was organized by Astruc, with the collaboration of the couturier Paul Poiret and several theater directors. It consisted of fashion shows interspersed with scenes done by actors and dancers from the Comédie Française, the Paris Opéra, the Opéra Comique, dancers and clowns from several music halls, and haute couture models. Even the famous Tiller Girls performed, a number called *Dance of the Flowers* (Legrand-Chabrier, "Les Fêtes," in *Exposition des Arts Décoratifs et Industriels*, edited by L'Art Vivant, special issue of *L'Art Vivant*, vol. 1 (July–September, 1925): 136–38).

[57] Fuller had performed this piece, called varyingly *Sirènes*, *La Mer*, and *Sur la mer immense*, numerous times over the years. But the 1925 performance was the grandest and most developed by far.

Figure 4.8. A lone dancer walks over the waves in Loie Fuller's *La Mer*, 1925, Bancroft Library, University of California, Berkeley

should return to this World's Fair site to mount the most spectacular production of her career, at the age of 63 (fig. 4.8).

For this production, Fuller—in striking anticipation of the "wrappings" of husband-and-wife team Christo and Jeanne-Claude—draped 4000 square meters of iridescent silk taffeta over the staircase of the Grand Palais, covering it entirely. The silk, which she had had specially made for her by the Indian textile company Kahn and Kahn of Bombay, was shot through with tones of violet, red, green, and orange.[58] Fuller's army of 75 dancers stood on the staircase, their bodies fully covered by the fabric, their forms discernible only as so many silk-covered moving sculptures.

While Debussy's music played, the dancers under the silk simulated the rhythmic undulations of the ocean, creating waves through a combination of their own bodily movement and the rushing currents of air that they sent circulating under the fabric. As always, Fuller employed rotating light projectors, which here cast a series of changing "sea" tones of green and blue over the fabric, heightening the gradations of its own iridescence. The "waves" of

[58] Lista, *Danseuse*, 563.

the fabric were so large that at times they nearly touched the spectators seated in the first row.

Any discussion of La Mer must include mention of one particular spectator in the crowd that June night. Pavel Tchelitchev, a twenty-seven-year-old Russian painter and set designer, attended the performance, and its profound effect upon him wound up, indirectly, changing the course of modern ballet history. Drawn to technology and deeply sensitive to color, Tchelitchev was most impressed with Fuller's electric-light recreation of a shimmering seascape. Indeed the production so affected him that three years later (in 1928, the year of Fuller's death), when Sergei Diaghilev hired him as a set designer for the Ballets Russes, Tchelitchev set about incorporating many recognizably Fuller-esque techniques into his work.[59] A number of his designs bore the stamp of Fuller's influence, but his 1933 production of L'Errante, based on Schubert's "Wanderer" Fantasy, would prove the most influential.[60] For this piece, Tchelitchev channeled Fuller by outfitting the leading lady in a vast costume of diaphanous trailing scarves, "her great train of lacquered green silk rippl[ing] behind her like the waves of the sea."[61] The decor consisted of white muslin strips, lit from behind with lights of mutating colors. At the end, "a great wet cloud of white Chinese silk cascades from heaven and obliterates the woman, leaving the [muslin] crystal, white, and empty."[62]

Lincoln Kirstein, the great American patron of the arts and balletomane, particularly loved L'Errante, and praised Tchelitchev for his "phosphorescent kinetics"—a term that Fuller herself might have invented.[63] So pleased was Kirstein with this production, in fact, that it convinced him to invite its young choreographer, George Balanchine, to New York City. The famous result of

---

[59] See Garafola, "Dance, Film and the Ballets Russes," for a discussion on Diaghilev's initial (unhappy) response to Tchelitchev's ideas. Tchelitchev used Fuller's techniques in other Ballets Russes productions as well, including Ode, St. Francis, and Ondine.

[60] In his sets for the Ballets Russes production of Ode, for example, Tchelitchev incorporated an onstage film highly reminiscent of Fuller's late-career "shadow dances." "A different sombre blue light is interrupted by the projection of a great hand on the white screen. . . . It halts and . . . a real box materializes from the screen. The illusive hand continues to descend, and La Nature, stepping forward, receives the box and places it on the ground as the hand fades." (Garafola, "Dance, Film, and the Ballets Russes," 17).

[61] In a burst of science-fiction whimsy, likely also inspired by Fuller, Tchelitchev also studded the dancer's hairpiece with working light bulbs. See Donald Wyndham, "The Stage and Ballet Design of Pavel Tchelitchev," Dance Index 3 (1944): 4–32. See also Lincoln Kirstein, Tchelitchev (New York: Twelvetrees, 1994).

[62] See Baird Hastings, "Hide and Seek: Illusion and Fantasy in the Scenic Design of Pavel Tchelitchev," Ballet Review 23, no. 5 (Fall 1995): 91–96.

[63] Qtd. in Garafola, "Dance, Film and the Ballets Russes," 17.

this invitation was the establishment of the company that would eventually become the New York City Ballet, the first world-class, permanent ballet company in the United States—a country where ballet had been virtually unknown.[64] Ironically then, via this group of expatriate Russians, Fuller's famously "elaborate production values"—the very aspect of her work that deprived her of lasting fame in American modern dance—actually led to her having a role in the birth of American modern ballet.[65]

The Emotional Power of "La Mer"

Tchelitchev was hardly alone in his powerful reaction to Fuller's La Mer. By all accounts, it was a staggering performance. Spectators described feeling overwhelmed by the experience; many became deeply emotional. Producer Gabriel Astruc (hardly a naïve critic of the arts) pronounced it "An unforgettable vision. One of the most moving things my eyes have ever seen."[66] "Loie Fuller has created a miracle!" exclaimed one reviewer.[67] "The ocean . . . in all its immense mystery, poetry, and its legends," wrote another.[68] Theatrical lighting designer, Daniel Garric, who was 14 when he attended La Mer, said of the evening: "I was so dazzled by what I saw that I decided then and there to devote my life to this, to this magic I was watching. I swore to my mother that one day I would work for this woman." Two years later he was apprenticed to Fuller's company as a stagehand, beginning his career in the theater.[69]

What accounted for this powerful effect on audiences? In part, it was a matter of sheer size. With La Mer Fuller had increased the scale of her performance to its vastest proportions. In place of one body, or even many bodies, she was now filling her veils with the front half of one of Paris's grandest buildings. The 75 dancers, furthermore, were able to augment the natural force of the night air in moving the enormous silk taffeta covering. The great power of this piece then emerged from this unusual combination of factors:

---

[64] See Richard Buckle, Diaghilev (New York: Atheneum, 1984). See also Baird Hastings, "Hide and Seek: Illusion and Fantasy in the Scenic Design of Pavel Tchelitchev," pp. 91–96. Tchelitchev would also live in New York for many years, where he pursued a highly successful career in painting and set design, enjoying the patronage of Edith Sitwell. Tchelitchev would do more designs for Balanchine, including the 1942 sets for Apollon Musagète in Buenos Aires.

[65] For discussion of the state of knowledge about ballet in the United States at the turn of the century, and a comparison with the long dance history of Russia, see Elizabeth Kendall, "1900: A Doorway to Revolution," Dance Magazine January 1999, 80–83.

[66] Qtd. in Lista, Danseuse, 568.

[67] René Bizet, "Les Conquêtes de Loie Fuller," L'Intransigeant, 2 July 1925, Collection Rondel.

[68] Gustave de Fréjaville, "Loie Fuller," Comoedia, 10 December 1925, Collection Rondel.

[69] Daniel Garric, in discussion with the author, June 1994.

Fuller had harnessed the usual dazzle of her stagecraft to two kinds of natural force—the girls and the element of wind—as well as to the monumentality of the Grand Palais.

The unspoken bodiliness of Fuller's work provided the driving force behind *La Mer*, provided by the vast army of girls hidden beneath the silk taffeta, propelling its movements, but also by the extended metaphoric significance of these girls and their fabric covering. Keeping in mind Rodenbach's early vision of Fuller's deeply female, birthlike imagery, we can see that *La Mer* represents the fullest flowering of this aspect of her work. What the audience saw that night in June was a vast array of young bodies completely covered by a thin silk dome, all moving rhythmically in waves. Fuller had taken her *"effet de coquillage"* and blown it up to monumental proportions. These silk covered forms in the night must have conjured a sort of gigantic, fertile womb, pregnant, teeming with living creatures, whose scale would have been dwarfed—fetus-like—by the enormous size of the Grand Palais. Fuller, who called herself "the mother of natural dancing," had placed "her girls" in an enormous tableau of primeval birth. The Grand Palais staircase became the sea, the mother of all life, figured as a kind of outsized uterine container—the ultimate magnification of the whirling, silk-covered forms that Fuller had spun around herself during her earlier, solo career. We have seen the extent to which Fuller's basic techniques mimed a kind of repetitive birth, with her "ballerina-effigy" rising out of her seashell-like lower form. The 4000 meters of silk in *La Mer* represented an ambitious, outsized version of that seashell shape, a surreal blowup of the sylph's tutu, with the young dancers repeatedly miming the effort to rise up out of it.[70] The metaphoric reference to pregnancy and the effort of birth might account, in part, for the emotional response of the audience. Peggy Phelan has written compellingly of the metaphoric relationship between images of motherhood and pregnancy and the essential work of theater: "The theatricality of motherhood, the 'double' body . . . can 'work' in the theatre because the body of the actor is similarly doubled (by the character the actor portrays). Excluding women from the stage, as many theatrical traditions did . . . is a way of limiting the double and quadruple effect of the woman-mother's acting body."[71] Here, Fuller had transformed the majestic marble staircase of the Grand Palais into just such a theatrical body, a female space of multiple identities.

---

[70] It is worth noting that the last performance to take place in the Fête du Théâtre et de la Parure was a large-scale, traditional *"ballet blanc,"* with dozens of ballerinas in white tutus arrayed on the stairs, "a symphony in white," according to the journal *L'Art Vivant*. (Legrand-Chabrier, "Les Fêtes," 136–38.)

[71] Peggy Phelan, *Unmarked: The Politics of Performance* (New York: Routledge, 1993), 128.

La Mer, *Interiority, and Modern Dance*

In discerning the 75 living dancers beneath the silk of La Mer, audience members had essentially been invited to turn their gaze into a kind of x-ray vision, seeing the silken dancing forms but also intuiting the human bodies beneath the membrane-like covering of the staircase.[72] We saw in the last chapter how Fuller's "ballerina-effigy" itself suggested a kind of birth process. We also saw that process as one that reached ultimately away from ballet and toward modern dance. Here, the near-separation of Fuller's two bodily halves—her upper and lower forms—expands to encompass 75 bodies, all straining beneath fabric, straining, I would contend, all the more powerfully toward the vocabulary of American modern dance.

In La Mer, we can again see the crucial role of modernist "interiority" in Fuller's late work, her insistent creation of inside-ness, here figured by the continual ballooning and descent of the fabric, and by the many spaces created between the individual dancers' limbs and the fabric. While not a characterological or overtly psychological interiority, it is its closest predecessor—a physical analogue for emotional interiority, a breaking up of the planarity of the dance space to showcase the three-dimensionality of the body. Such a mise-en-scène of physiological interiority also figured in modern dance, particularly in its display of such internal bodily processes as breathing. If we imagine the silken covering of the stairs in La Mer and the girls beneath it all as one, giant body (the kind of "living being" a journalist saw in the earlier Le Voile magique), then—by analogy—the propelling force of this body, the air, is analogous to the breath of one individual. With this in mind, we begin to see how Fuller's giant veil technique presages the breath-centered work of modern dancers, especially Martha Graham, who harnessed breath to create her signa-

---

[72] We know that Fuller was particularly entranced by the X-ray machine, having encountered it at Thomas Edison's laboratory. In her unpublished 1911 lecture on radium, Fuller recounts her first experience with the miraculous machine. Her description of her own X-rayed hand strikingly prefigures the vision she created on a massive scale with La Mer: "It was a little box just like those in which we see stereoscopic views. . . . You held your hand at the back. . . . As soon as the light was turned on I saw all the bones of my hand and the flesh about them looked like a veil in the shape of fingers. . . . the bones . . . were outlined against a light because they were thick and solid and the flesh around the bones resembles matter like a veil. This curious stuff all aglow held me spellbound" (Fuller, "Radium," unpublished essay, NYPLPA). The vast silk taffeta covering of La Mer might be seen as the analogue for the veil-like flesh under the X-ray machine, the moving dancers are like the bones. The gaze of audience members who know of but cannot fully discern the live dancers moving beneath the fabric become party to a kind of spectatorial X-ray experience.

ture motions of "contraction" and "release."[73] As Deborah Jowitt explains, "To Graham, breath was also crucial—not so much everyday, even-rhythmed breathing, but the gasp, the sob, the slow sigh of relief, and the ways in which these—heightened and abstracted—could affect the dancer's muscles and skeleton. Her theory of 'contraction and release' was built on the act of inhaling and exhaling."[74] Graham's contraction gathered and stored up bodily energy, only to perform its expulsion, in the release. The result was a body that, rather than suppress nature or overcome it, performed its most basic function—breathing—on a spectacular, grand scale. The corporeal rhythms of breathing were stylized and exaggerated, used by Graham to emphasize the inner workings of the body, turning interior functioning outward. Reynolds and McCormick write, "[Graham] discovered that forceful exhalation of breath produced a percussive flexion of the torso and that this 'contraction' could initiate a sequence of wavelike impulses flowing from the center of the body outward. The opposite action—the intake of air in which the body seemed to renew itself—she called 'release.' "[75]

In La Mer, Fuller's fabric performed much like a Graham dancer, pulsing and waving as the "breath" of the night wind was manipulated internally by the 75 dancers, together functioning like the interior of one outsized and deeply female body. In fact, La Mer helps us see, retroactively, that even Fuller's solo work employed the power of air in a fashion much like that used by Graham to work with breath. Fuller inflated and deflated her fabric forms via manipulation of air currents. The shapes, which substituted for Fuller's own body, "breathed" in and out, took flight and fell, with the air currents Fuller whipped up with her batons. In La Mer, she simply extended the phenomenon to include a virtual army of dancers and the evening wind of Paris.

The best way to appreciate the startling modernism of La Mer, and its profound connection to Martha Graham's work, is to examine it in light of a specific piece by Graham. Although La Mer employed 75 dancers, we can compare it most productively to a solo by Martha Graham, her landmark early work, Lamentation, which was produced only five years after La Mer, in 1930 (fig. 4.9).

---

[73] Doris Humphrey was another pioneer in the use of breath. As Deborah Jowitt explains: "Breath played a major role in the dynamic of fall and recovery and other aspects of Humphrey's style. It was the source of many vital, nonmetrical rhythms, of fluid successional movements" (Jowitt, Time and the Dancing Image, 166).

[74] Jowitt, Time and the Dancing Image, 166.

[75] Reynolds and McCormick, No Fixed Points, 146.

Figure 4.9. Martha Graham in *Lamentation*, 1935, © Barbara Morgan, the Barbara Morgan Archives

Martha Graham's *Lamentation*

On the simplest level, *Lamentation* resembles much of Fuller's work in that it depends so heavily on an unusual costume. In this famous piece, Graham encased her entire body in a tube of lavender elastic jersey, leaving only her face, hands, and feet exposed. She performed the entire piece, furthermore, while seated on a wooden bench. For Marcia Siegel, *Lamentation* represents a radical rethinking of dance itself:

> Perhaps no dance up to 1930 . . . so thoroughly destroyed the conventional image of the dancer as did *Lamentation* . . . everywhere in the Western world, right up to the present time, our idea of dancing includes some picture of a person on his feet. Dancing is running, jumping, leaping, skipping, bourréeing, bowing, . . . even walking or standing still. *Lamentation* is dancing sitting down . . . encased in a tube . . . with only her feet, hands, and part of her face and neck showing . . . [Graham] deprived the audience of one of the sights it expected to see, the dancer's body—limbs, waist, arms, torso, all of the suggestive apparatus upon which the ballet depended so heavily.[76]

Lamentation is unmistakably a dance of grief, albeit one with no narrative explanation for this sadness. Instead, *Lamentation* presents the stark, physical reality of grief, expressed purely through the body, with no overt facial expression.[77] Graham found inspiration for this dance in the Old Testament book of *Lamentations*, which begins "How doth the city sit solitary, that was full of people! How is she become as a widow."[78] The city, Jerusalem, here personified as a woman, is in mourning for its now-enslaved citizens.

In *Lamentation*, the solo dancer evokes a kind of universal female mourning. Grief is expressed through bodily writhing dramatized by the second-skin-like layer that reveals the articulation of the limbs. Encased in her elasticized tube, Graham stretches her limbs underneath the material, creating both a series of planar shapes and three-dimensional hollows and undulations. At times, she moves with robotic rigidity, bent over from the waist: she swivels right and left as if on a hinge, hands stiffly extended, elbows bent into tense right angles.

---

[76] Siegel, *The Shapes of Change*, 39. We might note here that, years before Graham's experiments, Fuller had of course been dancing while obscuring her own body parts, and while making use of elaborate costume possibilities.

[77] In Graham's original version of *Lamentation*, no facial emotion is expressed. Later versions of the dance included some facial emotion.

[78] Lamentations, 1:1.

Throughout the piece, the stretched expanse of fabric enables the spectator to appreciate the entire range of each motion, since the limbs are slowed down by the medium of the fabric—almost as though the dancer's body were moving through water. Emphasizing this aquatic quality, Graham at times inserts her hands into the fabric covering, which lends them a curious "webbed" look, turning the dancer into a kind of hybrid, amphibious creature—a human being but somehow also a paddling, web-winged bird.

Since the dancer in *Lamentation* remains seated, her body cannot "progress" in any way, cannot delineate its motion by crossing over floor space. All movement here is contained within the range permitted a person seated in a small space. With feet planted, Graham sways side to side, forward and back. By so drastically curtailing her physical range, Graham has turned her dance movement *inward*. That is, she has effectively transferred the spectator's attention to the fine gradations of movements accomplished between the dancer's body and its jersey covering, to the motion occurring inside a circumscribed interior space. There are no arms raised gracefully overhead here, no legs extended in arabesque. *Lamentation* therefore offers a very pure example of Graham's intense focus on motifs based on twisting, her "spiral," and on contracting. By creating, moreover, an elasticized second skin for the body, the costume insists upon Graham's trademark motions, since as the fabric stretches over a limb and then retracts, *it essentially turns all movement into a version of the contract/release cycle*. The fabric, that is, performs its own continual contraction and release.

For Graham, the contractions offered a way to render visible the confrontation between the body's internal existence and its outer environment. As Susan Foster explains, "Graham's choreography focuses on the connection between a person's interior and exterior."[79] With each contraction and release, the Graham dancer harnesses the power of her breath; the body's interior air flow is rendered visible, meeting the external world.

The Graham contraction also gestures visually toward the body's interior. It shapes the outer body into a curving container-like space that alludes to or echoes the caverns within the body. In the contraction, the dancer exhales and simultaneously draws her ribcage toward her spine while tilting her pelvis up and forward; at the same time, she will often raise inward-curving arms to delineate and contain the space created by the contracted torso. This space, this now-visible void, reinforces the three-dimensionality of the body; it "hollows out" the body visually, thereby creating a visible analogue for the secret,

[79] Foster, *Choreography and Narrative*, 28.

invisible hollows within. Deborah Jowitt describes the Graham contraction
this way:

> The dancer, whether sitting, standing, kneeling or lying down, caves in
> as if suddenly hit with a blow to the center of her body. But "caves in"
> is the wrong term if that implies any relaxation of tension. This impulse
> may be a small one or a series of small ones that affect the body only
> slightly and momentarily, but it may also be huge, causing her arms to
> swing sharply forward, her head to bow over, completing the curve in
> her back. . . . As Graham developed her technique, a contraction might
> hit the dancer sideways, make her twist, spiral, or be spun to the floor.
> It might attack her percussively, then deepen slowly, resonating
> throughout her body. But always, no matter how drastic the fall, there
> is a release, a rise, an advance, an inhalation.[80]

Lamentation spectacularly stages Graham's interest in interiority because the
costume echoes and duplicates the bodily hollow created by the contraction.
As it creates membrane-like partitions, the elasticized fabric also forms a series
of new bodily crevices and caverns: between the arm and the rib cage; between
the legs; between the head and an arm; and generally, between the whole
body and its elasticized covering. While this is unquestionably a somber and
dignified dance, these many bodily pockets and hollows—delineated by purple
elastic fabric—unmistakably suggest intimate, even genital female spaces,
thereby lending *Lamentation* a strikingly erotic quality.

Lamentation's female quality seems, furthermore, *maternal*. Watching Graham's elasticized fabric covering strain and expand to accommodate the reach-
ing movements of the limbs beneath, one thinks necessarily of pregnant bellies
pulsing and reacting to the fetal movements within. This dance enacts a woman's grief; but it also seems to suggest the struggle of birth. This birth scene,
furthermore, manages curiously to suggest both halves of the process: the physical struggles of both mother and baby. The dancer suggests the bodily motions
of a woman giving birth: she sits knees apart, writhing and struggling. But she
is also the child being born: her limbs are encased in an elastic sheath; they
push and stretch outward, straining toward release, with only the head visible.[81] That Graham constructed a dance so starkly alluding to reproduction is
unsurprising, given the primacy she would grant to the female pelvis and lower

[80] Jowitt, *Time and the Dancing Image*, 166.

[81] Lincoln Kirstein once characterized Graham's face in performance as having an "expression
half between pain and foetal blindness" (Lincoln Kirstein, *Ballet: Bias and Belief: Three Pamphlets
Collected and Other Dance Writings of Lincoln Kirstein* [New York: Dance Horizons, 1983], 39; qtd.
in Franko, *Dancing Modernism*, 158.)

abdomen in her choreography. Indeed the Graham body finds its center in the very site of conception and birth. In later works, such as *Night Journey*, *Cave of the Heart*, and *Clytemnestra*, Graham would expressly study the tragic and violent struggles of maternal figures in Greek mythology.[82]

Graham herself never offered any one particular explanation of *Lamentation*; but she did often recount an anecdote about the dance according to which a female audience member had emotionally thanked her for the piece, claiming that it had enabled her better to feel and express her own grief about the recent death of her son.[83]

That Graham was fond of retelling that story, connecting *Lamentation* to a woman's grief over the death of her son, suggests that the piece may have roots in the New Testament as well as the Old. Although she never acknowledged any reference to the Virgin Mary, icon of maternal grief, Graham may well have meant to evoke her with this dance. Indeed, the arrangement of the jersey fabric around the dancer's face is highly reminiscent of Mary's wimple in traditional Christian iconography.[84]

Lamentation is also an excellent example of Graham's fascination with pure form, with physics and geometry. The body rocks and tilts—the arms, extended and locked together by tightly clasped hands, move up and the knee rises with them, as if on a pulley. This long, thin triangle described by the arms with the chest rises up again, and again the bent knee rises, itself triangulating the fabric stretched over it, mirroring the triangle of the arms. The

---

[82] In these narrative pieces, Graham's conception of female sexuality made itself felt at the choreographic as well as the thematic level, for Graham invented physical movements that, while wholly unseductive, were meant to evoke starkly bodily and sexual female truths. In *Night Journey*, for example, Jocasta performs a series of walking steps, taking each with a high, lock-kneed kick— in a style reminiscent of Soviet military processions. Graham referred to that step as Jocasta's "vaginal cry"; she imagined it, that is, as a bodily scream from the hollow to which each high kick drew attention, the space through which Jocasta became both mother and wife to Oedipus: "Now Jocasta kneels on the floor at the foot of the bed and then she rises with her leg close to her breast and to her head, her foot way beyond her head, her body open in a deep contraction. I call this the vaginal cry; it is the cry from her vagina. It is either the cry for her lover, her husband, or the cry for her children" (Martha Graham, *Blood Memory* [New York: Macmillan, 1991], 214).

[83] People who saw Martha Graham perform this dance would never forget it. After one performance a woman in the audience asked to see Graham backstage. Weeping bitterly, she explained that her nine-year-old son had been struck and killed by a car several months earlier. She had been unable to express her grief and surrender to tears until the evening she saw *Lamentation*. "You will never know what you have done for me tonight," she said (Graham, *Blood Memory*, 117–18; see also Russell Freedman, *Martha Graham: A Dancer's Life* [New York: Clarion Books 1998], 61).

[84] Ten years later, furthermore, Graham's 1940 *El Penitente* would explicitly stage Jesus on the cross, being mourned by Mary. And of course in 1947, she imagined another mother's horrific grief when she created *Night Journey*, her reworking of *Oedipus Rex* from Jocasta's point of view.

dancer sinks down on bent knees over and over again, giving into gravity only to fight against it again, the weight and mass of the body are not denied—they are the basic matter of the dance. Graham's body in this dance is a Euclidean marvel.

This intense visual geometry should not, however, be considered separately from the more emotional resonances of the piece. On the contrary, the shapes described by the dancer's body and costume all suggest the physical manifestation of an inner, emotional pain. As Deborah Jowitt has pointed out:

> The pull of one part of her body against another, away from her heart, creates diagonal folds of tension in the fabric, until it seems the embodiment of her grief, and that grief becomes a palpable thing that constricts her movements and against which she must fight. It is this presentation of mourning in formal terms—as active struggle and shifting design, rather than as the self-preoccupied emoting of a single woman—that gives *Lamentation* its essential and universal power.[85]

Throughout her career, Graham would continually make obvious, visual use of gravity. We can see this in her use of momentum in such techniques as the pitch-forward fall (used in *Night Journey* and in *Appalachian Spring*, for example), in which dancers appear to fall freely face down to the floor, their legs spreading into parallel second position until they look like so many sprawling dolls.[86] Sometimes, Graham would play with momentum by creating a kind of two-person human seesaw. In *Appalachian Spring*, for example, pairs of standing dancers lean against each other, hip to hip, and then take turns rocking sideways onto bent outer legs, using momentum to swing each other alternately into the air and then down again.

Fuller in a New Light

Returning to consider Fuller's *La Mer* in light of Graham's *Lamentation*, we are struck by the many compelling connections between the works: the near-

---

[85] Jowitt, *Time and the Dancing Image*, 169. I would also point out that the 1947 *Night Journey* makes distinctly narrative and emotional use of geometry. Graham begins the piece with Jocasta contemplating a rope stretched tautly into a triangle shape—an almost Jungian female symbol. Tiresias enters the scene and immediately thrusts his walking stick through the triangle's opening, indicating both the sexual and the destructive nature of the terrible truth to be revealed.

[86] "Graham developed a system of movement that was unmistakably her own. It incorporated weight made visible in suspensions and falls, using the thighs and knees as a hinge," write Reynolds and McCormick, *No Fixed Points*, 146.

total obscuring of the bodies by fabric; the references to the sea or water (obvious in Fuller, implicit in Graham); the suggestion in each of parturition, of birth struggles and female container-like shapes, and the overt harnessing of physical forces: the wind and moving silk in Fuller's case; gravity, breath, and momentum in Graham's.

These works also reveal Graham's and Fuller's shared insistence upon the sculptural beauty of dance. Fuller's mobile silk sculptures—on the epic scale of *La Mer* or even when emanating from just her own body onstage—lent a dramatic three-dimensionality to her movement. As Rodenbach's poem so starkly made clear, Fuller's performances burst open the planar space around her, creating constantly changing images of bodily depth. When Fuller's silks billowed into flowers and flames over her head, or into gigantic expanses of ocean over the heads (and bodies) of 75 young women, the air itself shared center stage with her. Whether Fuller was circling her batons to inflate her vast silk robes, or using the evening wind to fill up the silk taffeta of *La Mer*, she was choreographing with natural forces—with air currents, with centrifugal force, with momentum.

Martha Graham did the same thing, only instead of relying on external, substitutive bodily shapes (such as Fuller created with fabric) and external air currents, she grounded her dance in the body's own shapes and in its own, internal air current—human respiration. Since the elastic fabric in *Lamentation* so closely follows and outlines the dancer's body, this piece offers an especially stark illustration of Graham's trademark use of contraction and release—both powered by breath and muscular elasticity. Stripped of overt narrative and character, *Lamentation* permits us to concentrate on the intricate geometry of the dancer's body as it contorts itself into a series of changing, three-dimensional shapes, showcasing the body's interiority, and indeed intensifying this interiority by echoing it visually with the costume's peculiar hollows.[87] Graham's use of momentum in her rocking or "swinging-hinge" motions in the piece similarly expose the physics of bodily movement.

Looking at *La Mer* alongside *Lamentation*, we can see Fuller passing the torch to Graham. With *Lamentation*, Graham takes the next step in the modernist investigation of the body begun by Fuller. As we have seen, Fuller's work repeatedly figured a kind of "interiority"—the many secret "insides" of her sculptural shapes, the secrets revealed by her staging of a penetrative, scientificized gaze, the vast interior spaces created in her "giant veil" pieces.

---

[87] In her later work, Graham would more overtly showcase her interest in sculptural form by collaborating with Isamu Noguchi, who created sculptural sets and costumes for twenty-three pieces, including *Letter to the World*, *Night Journey*, and *Clytemnestra*.

All these are the forerunners of Graham's more personal, bodily interiority. While Fuller conjured her myriad "interiors" via costume and technology—her "elaborate production values"—these internal spaces prefigure the more biological, bodily hollows and spaces that would become the focus of Graham's work, just as the air granting form and fullness to Fuller's veils prefigures the dancer's breath that will later become an overt part not only of Graham's work but of much modern dance to come.

In *La Mer*, Fuller exaggerated to nearly mythic proportion the elements that had comprised her long career: veils, lights, classical music, totally obscured dancers, and a highly abstract, nonnarrative subject—the sea. Curiously, though, this gigantic production, the apotheosis of her career as an artist of the machine, resembles nothing so much as it does the inward-turned, body-centered work of Martha Graham. Fuller's monumental recreation of the "sea" must be read as a kind of technological augur of the modern-dance body, a body that openly performed, even celebrated its relationship to gravity, to air, to breath, to momentum, and to its own internal workings. With its heaving membrane-like covering and the pulsing bodies hidden within, *La Mer* conjured a sexual, even reproductive female body, devoid of frills or prettiness—a vision very close to Graham's in *Lamentation*, as well as in the many woman-centered, more narrative pieces she created in subsequent decades.

The Physical Analogue of the Psychological

Although devoid of facial expression, characters, and story, *Lamentation* was dance on a grand, emotional scale. Former Graham dancer Jean Erdman explained this effect very well: "*Lamentation* is a mythic dance. Martha's own stylized body was already in the . . . mode that created the connection between the aesthetic element and the mythic element."[88] Similarly, with *La Mer*, Fuller had created a dance of mythic stature that deeply moved its audience, while relying solely on abstract form and color.

Erdman's observation casts light on an important truth, relevant to both Fuller's and Graham's work, as well as to modernist performance in general: profound psychological and emotional drama can emerge without benefit of narrative of any kind. *Lamentation* achieves its mythic, emotional power using no myth at all, drawing its force entirely from physical movement

---

[88] Jean Erdman, "The Dance Theater Pieces of the 1940s: A Conversation with Jean Erdman and Erich Hawkins," *Choreography and Dance* (special issue on Martha Graham, ed. Alice Helpern) 5, pt. 2 (1999): 39.

performed by a nameless entity, an expressionless solo dancer. Fuller's work conjured emotion much the same way: indirectly, via abstract form. She moved audiences by effacing herself. By replacing personality with movement and technology, Fuller could inspire spectators, as we have seen, to erotic and spiritual paroxysms.

Looking at *La Mer* alongside *Lamentation*, we are easily able to see this similarity between Fuller and Graham. Yet, *Lamentation* may appear to be anomalous in Graham's oeuvre, its condensed, and unadorned style seemingly at odds with her subsequent decades of large-scale, narrative-driven work. Is it fair then to look to *Lamentation* as evidence of any sort of deep connection between Graham and the highly abstract, body- and psychology-denying Loie Fuller?

The answer is yes, but requires further explanation. In truth, *Lamentation* is not the anomaly it appears to be within Graham's canon. On the contrary, it is like an X-ray of her later work, an unusually clear, uncluttered example of qualities that underlie all of her later choreography, even when it grew to encompass dozens of dancers and complicated plots and characters. In its geometric spareness, in its freedom from plot line and character, *Lamentation* simply offers us a particularly "clean" example of what we might call Graham's "emotional mechanicity," her ability to depict and provoke feeling via physical, mechanical movement.

Although Graham eschewed obvious technology of the sort Fuller used, and although she seemed to focus only on bodily, human movement, she was, in the end, every bit as mechanical as Loie Fuller. Like Fuller, she suppressed her personal psychology onstage in favor of showcasing more universal, biomechanical processes, which in her work—as in Fuller's—take on psychological depth. As Mark Franko has written, "Graham's materialist approach . . . is prior to and beyond personality; emotion is presented dispassionately in its very 'mechanism.' . . . Graham's modern dance reconfigures emotional depth as primal energy manifested in the abstract design qualities imposed on human form and movement by machines."[89]

Graham's only machine was the body itself, of course, presented and performed as a complex system of internal and external parts and forces—an "unorganic" body, as Edwin Denby has written.[90] Yet, this mechanicity that

---

[89] Franko, *Dancing Modernism*, 51. Franko goes on to point out that Graham's unfluid manner, her "elimination of flow," caused her dance to resemble a series of "cinematic stills" (pp. 57–59). Graham's emotional use of abstract form makes her also an important forerunner of Abstract Expressionism. See Stephen Polcari, "Martha Graham and Abstract Expressionism," *Smithsonian Studies in American Art* 4, no. 1, (Winter 1990): 2–27.

[90] Qtd. in Franko, *Dancing Modernism*, 51.

Fuller and Graham shared existed in complex relation to human emotion, psychology, and even physiology. Both artists, as we have now seen, used the visible, physical, and mechanical realms as analogues for or pathways into the unseeable realms of the human psyche and spirit. Graham's father, a neurologist who studied psychological disorders, had taught his daughter that she could never succeed in lying to him, for the simple reason that "you will always reveal what is in your heart with your movement." Martha learned this lesson well. "The dancer's world," she wrote, "is the heart of man, with its joys, its hopes, its fears, and its loves." And the goal of dance, she would claim, "is to make visible the interior landscape."[91]

As her choreography developed to include large group pieces based on themes borrowed from myth, religion, and literature, Graham did not use those themes to replace or obviate her body-based quest for emotional truth. On the contrary, for her, myth and religion were conduits to deep, universalizing human truths, truths that resided deep within the cultural collective unconscious—almost as additional levels of physical or bodily truths. As Deborah Jowitt writes, "the deliberate search for an emotional center produced a correlative physical principle: 'moving from the inside out' [which] also means initiating movement from the center of the body."[92] Fuller relied on a highly similar process, privileging abstract form over story, and thereby evoking powerful (if often contradictory) emotions in her audience.

This process that connects Fuller and Graham, their shared ability to perform and stimulate emotional power through mechanical and bodily techne, reminds us also of both women's ties to modernist theater, particularly to the work of designers and theorists such as Tsevelod Meyerhold, Max Reinhardt, Adolphe Appia, Enrico Prampolini, Giacomo Balla, and Gordon Craig. All of these artists believed in creating drama through means other than psychological realism, some seeking at times even to obviate human beings entirely.[93] We have long known of Fuller's influence on these proponents of mechanomorphism and disembodied theater, all of whom were familiar with her work and freely adapted aspects of it for their own productions.[94] Indeed, Fuller's

---

[91] Qtd. in Foster, *Choreography and Narrative*, 25.

[92] Jowitt, *Time and the Dancing Image*, 164. As Mark Franko has observed, Graham's early work is marked by its "refusal of psychological depth," in favor of more "formal physical geometry" (Franko, *Dancing Modernism*, 41).

[93] Meyerhold developed his famous theory of "biomechanics" in acting; Prampolini and Appia both imagined light beams replacing actors; and Gordon Craig famously wrote of "übermarionnettes" replacing living actors on stage.

[94] After attending a performance of Fuller's, Meyerhold borrowed heavily from her techniques in his subsequent staging of *L'Inconnue*, in which a starry sky was evoked by live actors agitating

status in the realm of mechanical modernism has never been questioned—Marinetti himself mentions her in his *Futurist Manifesto of Dance*.[95]

But this aspect of Fuller's work, her "elaborate production values," has always seemed somehow incommensurable with her role as "modern dance pioneer," the first of the barefoot, free-form, "natural" dancers. These two sides have remained critically separate, never noticed together. In reconsidering Fuller as a corporeal, even sexual artist, and in viewing her work in light of Martha Graham's, however, we reunite these two apparently antithetical sides of her (Fuller's) work, while placing her more firmly in dialogue with the most important artist of early American modern dance. As a result, we are able to see that Fuller's mecanomorphism did not distance her from early modern dance, but served, rather, as an expressive vehicle for many of the movement's key tenets: organic bodiliness, eros, and psychological depth. A side effect, furthermore, of revealing Fuller's more complex connection to Graham is that we are able to appreciate more fully the counterintuitive connection between the organic, gravity-bound style of the early American modern dance movement (its "personal kinetics") and the pyrotechnic, machine-based modernism ("the elaborate production values") of Europe's avant-garde stage theorists. In our next (and concluding) chapter, we shall consider Fuller's relationship to modernist European drama, looking particularly at issues of character, realism, and experimentalism.

---

large, azure-colored veils. Gordon Craig, who also knew Fuller's work, relied on her lighting techniques for his production of Ibsen's *Romersholm* with Eleanora Duse, in 1902 (See Lista, *Danseuse*, 497 ff). Also see Lista on Prampolini's heavy debt to Loie Fuller in his use of light and space (Giovanni Lista, "Prampolini scenografia," in *Prampolini: Dal futurismo all'informale* [Rome: Edizioni Carte Segrete, 1992], 108–44).

[95] After attending Fuller's production of *Peer Gynt*, Marinetti patterned his own *Tambour de feu* according to Fuller's use of light (Lista, *Danseuse*, 497). Stephen Kern has called Fuller a "futurist painting come to life" (Kern, *The Culture of Time and Space*, 199).

Chapter Five

Of Veils and Onion Skins: Fuller and Modern European Drama

Radical Mechanicity

The goal of this book has been to reweave Loie Fuller back into the fabric of performance history, to demonstrate how her work, beyond merely heralding a litany of "modernist" cues, actually participated in and reinterpreted several key theatrical modes of her era, from vaudeville to Orientalist cabaret, from shadow puppets to cinema, from burlesque to high modern dance. My goal has not been to deprive Fuller of her usual rank as "pioneer" or "precursor" but to demonstrate the limitations of such labels, for Loie Fuller was far more than the "point of departure" for later, greater artists. Rather, she managed to create a lifetime's worth of unusually charged, responsive art—art with an uncanny power to illuminate not the disjunctions between genres, but the fluid connections between them. We have already seen how Fuller's work both embodied and transmuted Romantic ballet, how it served as a bridge between music-hall and American modern dance, as well as between American modern dance and the modernist ballet revolution of the Ballets Russes. Similarly, we have seen how the political valences of Fuller's work cast light on Franco-American relations at a crucial historic moment.

Here, in this final chapter, we shall once more consider Fuller's relationship to a performance genre in which her influence has been acknowledged, but only insufficiently: European modern drama. Fuller's role in modern drama has seemed fixed and obvious: she was an inspiring proponent of mechanics. That is, critics cite Fuller for her technical contributions to the field, which are in line with the depersonalizing, abstract stage concepts of artists such as Adolphe Appia, Ernst Stern, Pavel Tchelitchev, and Gordon Craig, and Futurists such as Filippo Marinetti, Giacomo Balla, and Enrico Prampolini.[1]

---

[1] Theater historian Jacques Baril is typical in his praise of Fuller: "Loie Fuller's contribution to the evolution of theatrical presentation is as important and influential as the theories espoused

Fuller's influence on these "radical mechanists" (to borrow Joseph Roach's term) is indisputable; nearly all of them were familiar with her work.[2] Gordon Craig, who would espouse a theater of inanimate beings or "übermarionnet-tes," borrowed Fuller's colored lighting techniques for his 1906 production of Ibsen's *Romersholm*, starring Eleanora Duse. He also devoted an essay in his journal *Mask* to the techniques of Fuller's early protégé Sada Yacco, in whom he found an avatar of his preferred anti-psychological, abstract acting.[3] Adolphe Appia, Swiss-born pioneer of stage lighting, was even more clearly a disciple of Fuller's, dreaming of a theater in which light would become "an aesthetic medium," an independent, central entity. "Light," he wrote, "once liberated for the most part from the task of simply illuminating painted flats, will recover its proper independent role. . . . The sovereign power of light cannot be proven to one who has not experienced it."[4]

Fuller's influence on the presentation of modern drama also made itself felt in the color and light designs of Ernst Stern, Max Reinhardt's stage designer, although Stern insisted on his own radical originality. For Reinhardt's productions of Hugo von Hofmannsthal's *The Green Flute* and George Büchner's *Danton's Death*, for example, Stern relied on typically "Fullerian" backdrops of black velvet, rotating colored lights, and a filmy veil curtain hung in front of the stage.[5]

Fuller held a powerful appeal for the Futurists, with whom she openly shared an aesthetic of technologized bodies, as well as a penchant for violent, even bloody images (although in Fuller's case, as we have seen, this less-pretty element remains somewhat implicit). Indeed, Fuller's early and long-standing

---

and applied for example by Gordon Craig or Adolphe Appia" (Jacques Baril, *La Danse Moderne* [Paris: Editions Vigot, 1977], 36). While Baril is respectful of her importance, he fails to look beyond the context of mechanicity.

[2] I borrow the term "radical mechanists" from Joseph Roach, *The Player's Passion: Studies in the Science of Acting* (Newark: University of Delaware Press, 1985), 202.

[3] Although Craig strongly disapproved of women onstage, he found Sada Yacco's company inspirational. See Sang-Kyong Lee, "Edward Gordon Craig and Japanese Theatre," *Asian Theatre Journal* 17, no. 2 (Fall 2000): 215–35.

[4] Adolphe Appia, "Music and the Art of the Theatre," in Appia, *Texts on Theatre*, ed. Richard Beacham (New York and London: Routledge, 1993; repr. 2002), 35, 52. Appia designed lighting for many operas, including Wagner's and Glück's. In his 1912 production of Glück's *Orfeo ed Eurydice*, he shone lights onto the bodies of black-clad pantomimists who stood before a wall. The resultant giant, dancing silhouettes created a dramatic effect for the scene in which Orfeo descends into the frightening underworld of Hades. The production clearly owed a lot to Fuller's earlier series, *Ombres gigantesques*. (For more on this, see Hastings, "Hide and Seek: Illusion and Fantasy in the Scenic Design of Pavel Tchelitchev"; Léon, "Art du théâtre"; also Richard Beacham, *Adolphe Appia, Theatre Artist* [Cambridge: Cambridge University Press, 1987].)

[5] Lista, *Danseuse*, 487 ff. See also Martin Esslin, "Max Reinhardt High Priest of Theatricality," *Drama Review* 21, no. 2 (June 1977): 3–27.

visionary notion of creating a "theater of light"—in which light and colors would entirely replace human performance—might easily be mistaken for an idea of Marinetti's.[6] "I consider my work," she told an interviewer, "to be the point of departure of the great light symphony which will transform the theatre of the future."[7] In his *Manifesto of Futurist Dance*, Marinetti acknowledged his admiration for Fuller, praising her superiority to other modern dancers and grouping her work with another American form of dance he found similarly sleek and impersonal: "We Futurists prefer Loie Fuller and the negro cakewalk ([for their] utilization of light and mechanics."[8]

Futurists such as painter Giacomo Balla and lighting designer Enrico Prampolini were similarly drawn to Fuller; and both borrowed from her openly. Balla's sets for the 1915 Ballets Russes production of Stravinsky's *Fireworks* were clearly inspired by Fuller's own production of the same piece one year earlier, and featured colored lights moving over a series of geometrical solids. Similarly, Balla's 1916 *Dance of Geometric Splendor* (a sequence in his and Marinetti's film, *La Vita futurista*) was based on Fuller's *Danse de l'acier*.[9] As for Prampolini, his 1915 essay, "Scenografia e coreografia," displays his deep affinity for Fuller's project, proposing a theater of color and space, in which "electromechanical architecture [is] given powerful life by chromatic emanations from a luminous source provided by electric reflections of multicolored panes of glass."[10]

We see then that Prampolini—this obvious disciple of Fuller's—in turn exerted great influence on Diaghilev. Thus are we again reminded of the many strands of connection, both direct and indirect, between Loie Fuller's work and that of the Ballets Russes. We have already touched on set designer Pavel Tchelitchev's great admiration for Fuller; he overtly borrowed from and developed many of her techniques for a series of Ballets Russes productions, including *Ode*, *L'Errante*, and *Ondine*. This creative dialogue (and rivalry) between Fuller and Diaghilev continued for two decades and represents perhaps the most significant aspect of Fuller's influence in the realm of stage design. "The

[6] "There is a direct rapport," writes Leonetta Bentivoglio, "between the Futurists' experiments in the 1910s and the work of American dancer Loie Fuller." Leonetta Bentivoglio, "Danza e futurismo in Italia," *La Danza Italiana* 1 (Autumn 1984): 64.

[7] Qtd. in James Roose-Evans, *Experimental Theatre: From Stanislavksy to Peter Brook* (London: Routledge, 1970), 50.

[8] Filippo Marinetti, *Manifesto of the Futurist Dance*, 8 July 1917, http://www.futurism.org.uk/manifestoes.

[9] See Lista, *Danseuse*, 358, also Garafola, *Diaghilev's Ballets Russes*, 79–80.

[10] Enrico Prampolini, "Futurist Scenography," trans. V. N. Kirby, in Michael Kirby. *Futurist Performance* (New York: E. P. Dutton, 1971), 204.

exchange between the Russian impresario [Diaghilev] and the American dancer was one of the most powerful moments of theatrical creation during this era," writes Giovanni Lista.[11] And Diaghilev's long-time collaborator, Boris Kochno, wrote of Fuller: "She was a woman of the theater more than a dancer, but . . . through her discoveries, she made possible the revolution of the Ballets Russes."[12]

It is, of course, no small achievement to have helped shape the modernist stage revolution of Diaghilev and company, as well as countless other European set designers. Yet, Fuller's relationship to the modern theater was not purely about her "discoveries," nor did it exist only in the realm of stage design. While her lights, colors, and machines were undoubtedly both gorgeous and in nearly perfect step with the aesthetic of her time, Fuller's work contains other theatrical elements that reach more deeply into dramatic composition and technique, into the realms of character, realism, emotional depth or psychology, acting, and identity—all areas she is presumed to have rejected entirely, in favor of her abstract mechanics. This relationship to these more "traditional" aspects of the theater is analogous in some ways to Fuller's relationship to the more bodily side of dance—a relationship we have examined over the last two chapters. Just as dance history has tended to remove Fuller's bodily reality from consideration of her work, theater history has overlooked her "dramatic" self. Yet, as we shall see, Fuller's work reflects and responds to many of the key elements of nonmechanical modern drama being investigated by some of the most important playwrights and directors of her time.

Character and Identity

While Loie Fuller's cabaret spectacles may seem light-years away from the talk-centered stage plays of Ibsen or Strindberg, in fact these two realms were deeply connected. Harold Segel writes of the relationship between dance and drama of the late nineteenth and early twentieth centuries, noting what he calls a "modernist preoccupation with physicality," and a concomitant view of the "body as language."[13] Segel looks to such pivotal stage moments as Nora's tarantella in *A Doll's House* and the peasant folk dance in *Miss Julie* as evidence of this turn away from language and toward a theater based more on

[11] Lista, *Danseuse*, 500.

[12] Kochno, *Diaghilev and the Ballets Russes*, 127.

[13] Harold B. Segel, *Body Ascendant: Modernism and the Physical Imperative* (Baltimore: Johns Hopkins University Press, 1998), 1.

the figurative possibilities of movement. He cites specifically the influence on playwrights of dancers such as Fuller:

> The incorporation of dance scenes in modernist drama, the appropria-
> tion . . . of dance by the drama . . . [is] evidence both of the movement
> away from the verbal to the gestural and of the cohering modernist cult
> of physicality. There is also the overwhelming impact of the modern
> dance phenomenon and the celebrity of such dancers as Fuller, Duncan,
> St. Denis, Wigman . . . and others. . . . It would hardly be an exaggera-
> tion to regard modernism as the great age of the dancer.[14]

Segel rightly acknowledges the strong bonds in modernist performance between dance and drama, but his model for their connection remains unilateral.
Segel looks mainly at how drama borrowed from dance in a literal way, at
where drama stopped for dance. He does not explore the ways in which early
modern dance was itself always-already dramatic, addressing issues such as
psychology, character presentation, or verisimilitude.

Despite its abstractness and its rejection of the most recognizable of drama's
features—overt narrative—Fuller's work actually offers a curiously apt illustration of some of the characterological and staging investigations of modern
playwrights, sometimes even appearing to be performing a literalized version
of questions raised in realist and naturalist plays. This should not surprise
us. Fuller's work always exceeded the bounds of pure dance, fitting more
comfortably under the rubric of dramatic performance. As Roger-Marx
wrote of her in 1905, "To those unaware of her past as an actress, Loie Fuller
revealed herself to be a mime without peer . . . with a truly sovereign power
of expression."[15]

As we have already seen, Fuller did care about storytelling; and, as Roger-
Marx reminds us, she got her start as an actress. Long after her official transformation into a French cultural icon, Fuller continued to draw on her long years
in American vaudeville for inspiration; and even some of her most abstract
productions were based on well-known literary and dramatic texts. That, in
essence, was always Fuller's theatrical trajectory: from narrative to abstraction.
We saw this process in her adaptations of *Salome*, which failed when presented
as full-length dramas, but succeeded when boiled down into a series of abstract
dances. We saw it as well in Fuller's production of Hoffmann's *The Sandman*,
which suppressed the story's main plot and retained only its more fantastical
adventures—those parts more easily depicted nonverbally.

---

[14] Ibid., 91.
[15] Roger-Marx, "Loie Fuller," 272.

At times, Fuller looked specifically to dramatic literature for her ideas, although she did not present entire plays in dance. Her choices, furthermore, came consistently from more fantastical plots. In 1911 in London, for example, she collaborated with British stage actor and director Herbert Beerbohm Tree on a "divertissement borrowed from *A Midsummer Night's Dream*," with music by Felix Mendelssohn, which did not attempt to cover the plot of Shakespeare's play but tried instead to capture some of its spirit of abandonment and frolic.[16] A review of a 1914 French reprise of this production explains well how Fuller adapted the play for her usual purposes: "The decor represents a forest . . . but it is idealized by jewel-toned lights, and if the characters do pantomime and dance as they normally do, they are doing so in a delicate, mutable atmosphere that somehow dematerializes them. This is a dream. . . . We see the air sprites just as we might imagine them fluttering around the [sleeping shepherd]."[17]

In 1914, Fuller borrowed again from the genre of theatrical fantasy, mounting a series of dances based on Ibsen's 1867 dramatic poem, *Peer Gynt*, to which she was introduced visually, via Jean-Francis Aubertin's Symbolist painting based on the text, *The Dance of Anitra*.[18] Using the Edvard Grieg score, Fuller presented four dances: "La Mort d'Ase," "Le Matin," "La Danse d'Anitra," and "Dans le hall du roi des montagnes."

Peer Gynt was an obvious choice for Fuller. A phantasmagoric tale based on Norwegian folklore, it predates Ibsen's turn to the social realism of later plays such as *The League of Youth, Pillars of Society, A Doll's House,* and *Hedda Gabler*. It recounts the life journey of its peasant hero, Peer, over the course of fifty years. Peer passes through a series of symbolic, dreamlike adventures and landscapes, which include his abduction of a bride at her wedding, travels to the desert, and an encounter with mountain-dwelling trolls. The most famous image from the text comes from its final act, Act V, in which Peer, now an old man, peels layers of skin off an onion, which he regards as emblematic of his life. Addressing himself as the onion, Peer says, "Why you're simply an onion / and now, my good Peer, I'm going to peel you / and tears and entreaties won't help in the least." With each layer of onion skin that he removes, Peer narrates one episode of his life. Frustrated finally with the task, he asks himself,

---

[16] A rare negative review illustrates Fuller's choice to omit any real plot development: "There is no story development aside from the effects of some nightgowns. Barefoot little girls dressed in long white tunics, go, come, run, appear, disappear; one might think oneself in a boarding school dormitory lost in a forest, after two minutes of this, the lack of signification overwhelms" (Jean Chantavoine, review of Loie Fuller, Collection Rondel).

[17] "Le Nouveau spectacle de Miss Loie Fuller," 22 May 1914, Collection Rondel.

[18] Lista, *Danseuse*, 459.

"Don't we get to the heart of it soon?" And the answer comes: no, there is no heart, no solid core to the onion or to life: "No . . . Right down to the centre / There's nothing but layers—smaller and smaller . . . / Nature is witty!"[19]

The onion might just as easily serve as model for the entirety of Ibsen's text. Unlike the more structured plots of his later works, *Peer Gynt* consists of slightly disconnected scenes that come and go with only minimal exposition. Characters appear as if by magic; settings range over the whole world; the plot has little linearity. Like onion skins, the episodes hang together only loosely, each falling off to reveal a new one, which gives the text a distinctly dreamlike quality. Such an onion of a play would have appealed to Loie Fuller, whose own performances often resembled dreams as well. And in choosing excerpts for her version of *Peer Gynt*, Fuller followed her usual method of focusing specifically on some of the more mystical moments of the text.[20] But however mystical *Peer Gynt* was, it was nevertheless deeply connected to Ibsen's later work; and understanding *Peer*'s relationship to its author's more realist works will illuminate Loie Fuller's own proximity to Ibsen's social realism, as well as lead us into a discussion of Fuller and the naturalist developments of Strindberg.[21]

It is precisely *Peer Gynt*'s dreamlike meditations on identity and the self that place it in line with the later Ibsen and with Strindberg. We can even find glimmers of the more absurdist and experimental works of Beckett and Pirandello in these elements of *Peer*.[22] We see this clearly in Act V's moment of revelation with the onion, for it is here that Peer achieves the kind of

[19] Henrik Ibsen, *Peer Gynt* (first published in Christiania [Oslo], Norway: Gyldendalske Boghandel, 1867; references are to *Peer Gynt*, trans. Peter Watt, New York: Penguin Books, 1966), 191.

[20] A review from the *Toledo Blade* writes, "One of the most striking dances which Loie Fuller illustrates in her remarkable act is that of scenes from *Peer Gynt*. These comprise Ase's death with three mystic forms of the past, present, and future; the soul of woman appealing to the mystic three; the dance of Anitra; the Arab dance; the storm; Solveig's song and morning. Through these dances the evolution of the soul of woman is the dominant theme, all fitting into the weird and mystical meaning of the strange poem" (*Toledo Blade*, 9 October 1909 NYPLPA).

[21] Fuller demonstrated interest in social realism as early as 1893, when she shared a bill at New York's Garden Theater with Carl Edvard Brandes's play, *A Visit*. The Danish Brandes was a colleague and admirer of Ibsen's and his play was very inspired by Ibsen's work. Unfortunately, the New York cabaret audience in attendance did not appreciate the slightly gloomy, complicated plot of the play and literally booed its leading lady, Olga Brandon, off the stage. The *New York Times* later referred to the "ill-bred crowd" that evening. Brandon left the stage in tears and refused to return despite the specific entreaties of Fuller herself who had encouraged producers to include Brandes's play (unsigned review, *New York Times*, 17 August 1893). Also see Current and Current, *Loie Fuller*, 67.

[22] Beckett's *Krapp's Last Tape*, in which the protagonist considers his multiple past selves, as preserved on tape, offers a good example of the development of the shedding, coreless "onion self" in modern drama.

ontological epiphany that so many later playwrights will reckon with; Peer recognizes the instability of the self, the mutability of social roles. Like the onion, he is but a series of skins, a series of sequential roles that exist only within specific contexts, devoid of foundational meaning. As Rolf Fjelde writes, "Here certainly is one of the earliest and most arresting images of the new existential picture of man as simply the history of his acts, an inventory of roles abandoned, of selves outlived and discarded."[23] In *Peer Gynt*, Ibsen sums up this existential angst with the onion allegory. Later, he will have his protagonists question, struggle against, and try to shed their own skins, albeit in more realistic fashion. Nora Helmer and Hedda Gabler, for example, will both strive to peel away their own social roles, their own onion skins, in an attempt to liberate some sort of essential yet elusive core self.

Versions of the "onion self" exist as well in the naturalism of Strindberg, who, in his famous manifesto of naturalism, the 1888 preface to *Miss Julie*, explains his rejection of the concept of a unified self or "character"—a notion he dismisses as bourgeois:[24]

> I have made the people in my play fairly "characterless" for . . . I do not believe in simple stage characters . . . the persons in my play are . . . unstable, . . . torn and divided . . . conglomerations from various stages of culture, past and present, walking scrapbooks, shreds of human lives, tatters torn from former fancy dresses. . . . I have even made use of "waking suggestion" (a variation of hypnotic suggestion).[25]

Miss Julie comes close to achieving Strindberg's goal of the "characterless" play. The personalities of its two protagonists, the aristocrat Julie and her servant lover, Jean, break down and reconstitute themselves continually as the characters take turns dominating, desiring, and humiliating each other. Neither Julie nor Jean retains a consistent personality over the course of the play. Instead, they acquire and then quickly shed contradictory roles, repeatedly exchanging the stances of master and servant, predator and prey. More than anything else, the play is a treatise on the unknowable mutability of the human psyche.[26]

---

[23] Rolf Fjelde, "*Peer Gynt*, Naturalism and the Dissolving Self," *The Drama Review* 13, no. 2 (Winter 1968): 39.

[24] "The middle-class conception of character was transferred to the stage, where the middle class has always ruled. A character there came to mean someone who was always one and the same."(August Strindberg, "Preface to *Miss Julie*" [1888] in *Miss Julie and Other Plays* [New York: Oxford University Press, 1998], 58.)

[25] Strindberg, "Preface to *Miss Julie*," 60.

[26] The experimental decomposition of a "self" in Strindberg's naturalism was later developed by the playwright in his *A Dream Play*, in which "scenes dissolve into others without anything

It is worth noting also that Strindberg intensifies *Miss Julie*'s atmosphere of dangerous instability by setting the action during a celebration of Midsummer's Eve—the night when the ghosts of the dead are believed to walk the earth. Like Shakespeare before him (and Loie Fuller afterward), Strindberg uses this charged festival to establish a sense of dreamlike liminality: all lines may be crossed on this night, even that between the living and the dead. Indeed, in the first moments of the play, we learn that Julie has been transgressing sexual and social boundaries by celebrating the festival with her servants, dancing wildly with her gamekeeper and with Jean. We do not see that inappropriate dance, but at the play's midpoint, Strindberg makes specific, visible use of dancing: as Julie leads Jean offstage to consummate their relationship, a group of peasants enters to perform a circle dance while singing a suggestive song.[27] The play's pivotal moment—which will brutally reverse the power between Jean and Julie—is figured then not by dialogue, but via deflection through dance.[28]

Harold Segel rightly points to the Midsummer's Eve dance in *Miss Julie* as evidence of the influence of modern dance on drama. And as we have seen, Loie Fuller would herself make use of the same disorienting night in her adaptation of Shakespeare's play. But more remains to be said about the relationship between classic naturalism and Fuller's work, which are bound by more than the mere fact of dance.

Fuller also shared with the naturalists her profound fascination with scientific detail, with peering beneath surfaces. As we know, Fuller consistently staged dramatic revelations of interiors, and of normally unseeable spectacles: human organs, microscopic creatures, heavenly bodies. In much the same spirit, Strindberg, along with French director André Antoine (who produced *Miss Julie* in 1893 at the Théâtre-Libre), opened the stage not only to psychological secrets, but also to an array of intimate daily actions normally hidden

---

intervening, [in] a most cinematic action. . . . Time moves backward and forward, [and] characters change into their older or younger selves." (Richard Gilman, *The Making of Modern Drama* [New Haven: Yale University Press, 1999], 109).

[27] The stage directions make clear what is happening: "Miss Julie hurries off . . . Jean follows her eagerly. The peasants enter, led by a fiddler. They are in holiday clothes, with flowers in their hats. . . . they take hands and dance in a circle, singing. . . . At the end, they dance out singing. Miss Julie comes in alone . . . she takes out a powder puff and powders her face . . . " (Strindberg, *Miss Julie*, in *Three Plays* [London: Penguin Books, 1958], 94).

[28] "*Miss Julie* is not strictly speaking a naturalistic work—partly because of the ballet, mime, and musical interlude Strindberg introduces in the middle," writes Robert Brustein ("Male and Female in August Strindberg," *Tulane Drama Review* 7, no. 2 [Winter 1962]: 155). As Harold Segel writes, "The ill-starred relationship between Julie . . . and . . . Jean cannot be separated from the context of the midsummer's eve dance" (Segel, *Body Ascendant*, 93).

from spectators: Jean changes his shirt within view of the audience; the cook, Kristin, curls her hair before a mirror; she prepares food.[29] Strindberg also famously banished the usual painted, *trompe l'oeil* scenery and stage properties, replacing them with actual walls and doors, pots and pans. Such items enhanced the spectators' impression of transgressing into intimate, domestic realms—of peeking under the veils of life. The effect was deliberate: "Our inveterately curious souls are no longer content to see a thing happen, we want to see how it happens," wrote Strindberg, "we want to see the strings, look at the machinery, examine the double-bottom drawer."[30] He might have been describing the curious, scientific mind of Loie Fuller, who, despite her apparent lack of naturalism, loved to incorporate into performances anything that "can bring to our vision those things we cannot see"—images produced by X-rays, telescopes, microscopes, and, especially, radium.[31] While Fuller may have turned these images into abstract fantasies, they were, in fact, born of a spirit very close to that of the naturalists.

Theatrical naturalism involved a change in acting technique as well. Strindberg yearned for an acting style that would replace the self-conscious, declamatory style of earlier theater, with a more natural demeanor: "is it too much to hope that crucial scenes could be played where the author indicated and not in front of the prompter's box as if they were duets demanding applause?" he wrote.[32] Dramatist Jean Jullien, another naturalist collaborator of Antoine's at the Théâtre-Libre, advocated a similar turn away from self-consciousness and toward an apparent unawareness of being onstage, of "acting." Actors should perform, he wrote, "as if at home, ignoring the emotions they arouse in the public." Jullien argued that the proscenium opening needed to become "a fourth wall, transparent for the public, opaque for the actor."[33]

This famous pronouncement about the transparent fourth wall leads us back, rather strikingly, to Loie Fuller, for one great constant of her performances was always their apparent "unconsciousness." And in 1898 Fuller even

---

[29] In this, the theatrical naturalists are following Zola's theories, put forth in his manifesto "Le Naturalisme au théâtre," about the need for stage artists to emulate scientists and seek to reveal unvarnished truth through exact, methodical analysis (see Emile Zola, "Le Naturalisme au théâtre" [1880] in *Le Roman expérimental* [Paris: Garnier-Flammarion, 1971]: 137–173).

[30] Strindberg, "Preface to *Miss Julie*," 64. Indeed, *Miss Julie*'s subplot of Julie's having "inherited" a degenerate nature from her round-heeled mother strongly recalls Zola's reliance on pseudo-Darwinian notions of genetic personality types and moral failings.

[31] Fuller, "Radium," NYPLPA.

[32] Strindberg, "Preface," *Miss Julie*, 67.

[33] Jean Jullien, *Le Théâtre vivant* (Paris: G. Charpentier et E. Fasquelle, 1892–1896), 11, qtd. in Marvin Carlson, *Theories of the Theatre* (Ithaca, NY: Cornell University Press, 1984), 280.

went so far as to literalize Jullien's metaphor; that is, she created an actual "fourth wall"—the glass panels that she erected as part of her "vitrine" construction. When the house was completely darkened and her glass box lit brilliantly from the interior, the glass became a perfect reflecting surface, a mirror for Fuller performing within, and a transparent window for spectators. (see chapter 1). We have already discussed the way in which this "glass box" contraption constructed a transgressive gaze for audience members; here we must also acknowledge how closely this theatrical setup—of a one-way mirrored glass wall and the attendant prurience of the crowd—recalls and literalizes the prime desideratum of naturalist theater: staged unconsciousness.[34]

Unconsciousness, of course, was Fuller's stock in trade. We have seen how she delighted in claiming and staging unknowingness. She routinely spoke of her stagecraft, her dancing, even her scientific experiments as just so many accidental discoveries. These claims were an important part of Fuller's lifetime pose as the guileless Yankee, the accidental genius. Fuller relied heavily on this persona, which protected her from all manner of unwanted attention, from homophobia to professional envy. It also encouraged wealthy patrons to support her; and much of Fuller's correspondence with her benefactors smacks of a slightly strained naiveté, which she had evidently cultivated.[35]

But unconsciousness was not just a convenient pose for Fuller. It reinforced a very powerful element of her performances: their ability to provoke the projection of audience fantasies upon her dancing person, and later, upon her students.[36] Fuller understood that her curiously hypnotic power depended partly on her disengaging from the audience, on not acknowledging their gaze. For the naturalists, such detachment was intended to add verisimilitude to emotional exchanges onstage; eliminating self-conscious "acting" was meant to free spectators to react beyond the confines of official prompting. In Fuller's

---

[34] I am not claiming that Fuller consciously reproduced Jullien's dictum, only that her work strikingly responds to this tenet of naturalism. Fuller did, though, know André Antoine personally and worked with him on at least one occasion. He asked her and her company to contribute a ballet to his production of *Faust*. Her "ballet des sylphes" was, however, more high Romantic than naturalist.

[35] Her many letters to Queen Marie of Romania address the monarch as "my dearest fairy princess." Writing to Rodin, whose august position in the art world she regularly exploited, she refers to him as "my very very dearest master." Letters to wealthy patrons of the arts such as the American Alma Spreckels abound with similar reverential, even worshipful remarks (undated letters, NYPLPA and Musée Rodin archives).

[36] That Fuller directed her students to enact "unconsciousness" onstage is borne out by reviews, such as this one of her 1914 production of *A Children's Corner*, with music by Debussy: "These are not actresses, but children, laughing and cavorting, knowing no one is watching them" (Vauxcelles, "L'Art de Loie Fuller," 10 May 1914, Collection Rondel).

case, the content differed but the desired effect was the same. Her apparent detachment from the crowd helped transform her into both a literal and figurative projection screen, the emotional equivalent of her white veils. Fuller needed to be a neutral, *unknowing* template receiving not only the colored lights and images she shone deliberately upon her white veils, but also the desires and interpretations of her spectators.

Fuller was acutely aware of her role as projection screen. We see this at once if we recall her account of that fateful performance of *Quack, M.D.* Fuller, as we know, attributed the discovery of her trademark technique to this vaudeville play during which, she claimed, the *spectators* told *her* what she was doing—unwittingly—onstage. As we saw in chapter 2, according to Fuller, while playing the role of a hypnotized woman, Imogene Twitter, she actually fell into a hypnotic state herself, reproducing in "reality" what her character experienced within the play's fiction: "Mechanically . . . transfixed in a state of ecstasy, I let myself drop . . . completely enveloped in a cloud of light material." In this meta-theatrical trance, Fuller stumbles upon her life's work. Unknowingly, she begins sculpting her costume into decorative shapes in which audience members—like sky-gazers seeing shapes in the "clouds" of her robes—discern various pleasing images. "It's a butterfly!" "It's an orchid!" they cry out, thus sparking an entire career.[37]

It is worth pausing to revisit this anecdote because of how clearly it positions Loie Fuller in the development of naturalism as well as later, more experimental modern drama. The *Quack, M.D.* story underscores Fuller's striking link to the naturalists by highlighting her penchant for staged unconsciousness. She foregrounds her unwitting genius by suggesting that she was, herself, hypnotized. Hypnosis, of course, produces the most extreme case of staged unconsciousness. Like an actor behind Jullien's mythical transparent fourth wall, a hypnotized person reveals himself while remaining completely oblivious to those who watch. Strindberg would famously make use of hypnosis in his final scene of *Miss Julie* in which Jean seems to put Julie into a trance, compelling her to commit suicide.[38]

Fuller's *Quack, M.D.* anecdote also reveals her connection to the still more modern work of Luigi Pirandello. As we have noted, Fuller's explanation of this seminal moment in her career suggests that the fiction of the play winds up overpowering reality—that the make-believe hypnotist, Dr. Quack, man-

---

[37] Fuller. *Fifteen Years*, 31.

[38] In the final scene of *Miss Julie*, Jean, having managed to hypnotize Julie, places a razor in her hand, and suggests that she use it to kill herself. She exits the stage in a trance, apparently intending to carry out this suicidal plan. Strindberg was very interested in hypnosis, not least for its ostensible capacity to uncover the secret mechanisims of the mind.

ages to hypnotize the actress Fuller, not her character, Imogene. The wall between actor and character has been breached. Such a "cross-contamination" between actors and characters, this "bleeding" of levels of fiction, is precisely what Pirandello investigates in his revolutionary 1922 play, *Six Characters in Search of an Author*, in which author-less characters, unmoored from their fictional "home," wander into a theater and beg the actors to tell their story. These nameless characters are successful in that the actors are forced to engage with them, to allow them to tell their story, and finally to be, at least emotionally, overtaken by them.

That premise unsettled audiences, as did Pirandello's staging, which pushed to extremes naturalism's tenets about "showing the seams" by staging the *preparation* for a play rather than the play itself. The house lights remained up; the actors appeared in rehearsal clothes, sitting on a bare stage. They "rehearsed" with their "director," while various electricians and technical crew members worked onstage. Richard Gilman offers this very clear explanation of the play's power:

> *Six Characters* . . . is a play *about* a play, or rather, about playing, about the stage, the human impulse to construct replicas of ourselves and most centrally, the choices we make or avoid between imagination and reality. . . . [The play contains] a story within a play and two sets of "characters" between whom the destiny of this story moves back and forth in an unresolved tension which corresponds to the one we feel in our own lives between "truth" and fiction.[39]

Loie Fuller's anecdote about her life-changing performance in *Quack, M.D.* clearly partakes of a Pirandellesque aesthetic of collapsed levels of fiction, suggesting her predisposition for such theatrical experiments. Indeed, looking at her career, we must acknowledge that, from her earliest performances, Fuller always evinced a powerful interest in shaking loose the connection between "character" and "actor"—or in her case "visionary image" and "human body beneath"—in staging a version of that "unresolved tension" that Gilman finds in Pirandello. We see this interest, for example, in her lifelong obsession with self-replication and identity games of all kinds.[40]

---

[39] Gilman, *The Making of Modern Drama*, 174.

[40] A letter from an audience member in 1896 suggests Fuller's curious power to suggest a disjunction between herself and her dance. Maisie Ludlow Thomas, twenty-three, wrote to her fiancé, Jonathan Lanman, "I never felt the same toward you as toward other men. Isn't it nice we neither of us have had other 'affaires?' I saw Loie Fuller dance the Serpentine Dance ever so long ago, and thought it (not her) very fascinating" (private correspondence from the archives of Sarah Ludlow Blake, 3 April 1896). I reproduce the initial lines of the letter because they demonstrate a

Onstage, of course, mirrors, tricks of light, and eventually, her army of look-alike young dancers helped multiply and divide Fuller's image. Audiences were often unsure of whether they were seeing Loie, a reflection, or someone else altogether. In 1922, one perceptive journalist took specific note of this phenomenon, seeing fit to include it in his review of *Ombres gigantesques* (thereby suggesting that it was actually part of the performance):

> The *ballets fantastiques* of Miss Loie Fuller have set light dancing . . . silhouettes grew and leapt beneath a giant hand. . . . One lady, fresh from the provinces, leaned in toward her companion as one of the taller dancers was performing, asking if that was she, was that *la Loie*? And he, without blinking, said, yes of course. Yet all the while, off to one side of the stage, dressed in a dark suit, there she was, the woman who had invented these phantasmagoric dances, giving her last directions to the dancers.[41]

Offstage, Fuller evinced a similar tendency; she loved, that is, the notion of being present and absent at the same time, of having doppelgangers, of being able somehow to separate from her own performing self. Her autobiography abounds with anecdotes revealing this side of Fuller. In one, an entranced little girl is introduced to Fuller after a performance, but shrinks away, visibly upset. "What is the matter, dear? This is Miss Fuller," says the child's mother; and the girl responds, "No, no. That isn't her. I don't want her. This one here is a fat lady, and it was a fairy I saw dancing." Fuller resolves the situation by telling the child, "Yes, my dear you are right. I am not Loie Fuller. The fairy has sent me to tell you how much she loves you and how sorry she is not to be able to take you to her kingdom."[42] As the story clearly tell us, Fuller relished being at once herself and not, the fat lady and the dancing fairy.

We have already seen to what extent Fuller's basic technique onstage enacted a similar kind of doubling and separation—her physical self giving rise

---

seamless train of thought from Maisie's appreciation of her own and her fiancé's "purity" (lack of "affaires") to her appreciation for Loie Fuller.

[41] Guy-Noël, review of Loie Fuller, 18 June 1922, Collection Rondel.

[42] Fuller, *Fifteen Years*, 141–42. Even when she wrote plays for others, Fuller relied on themes of masquerade and self-doubling. Her pantomime-melodrama for Sada Yacco, *The Little Japanese Girl*, for example, is a tragic tale of mistaken identity in which a young servant girl decides to dress up in the clothes of the princess she serves. The princess's husband, the prince, enters and, seeing the girl only from behind, mistakes her for his wife. Embarrassed and afraid of being punished, the maid remains silent and refuses to turn around to face the prince. Becoming enraged at his "wife's" coldness, the prince finally plunges a dagger into the girl's back, killing her. The real princess and the girl's husband, a palace valet, then enter and the prince realizes his horrible mistake.

to a second, fabric effigy that separates from its creator, rising into the air above her. We have likened this technique to the actions of the male *danseur* with his ballerina; but at an even more basic level, it is simply a performance of theatrical transformation at its purest. A performer takes on a new shape, a new identity, only to let it fall and rise again in a new guise. Fuller's continual onstage transformations—the interaction of her veil-self and human-self— may be read as an analogue for Pirandello's confrontation between "actors" and "characters." In this we can see yet again how much Fuller's work participated in the investigations of modern dramatists.[43] As Ted Merwin has written, "the apparent unmooring of her own body and her own identity . . . lends itself well to contemporary approaches that glorify the free play of signifiers."[44]

Fuller's proximity to the unsettling performances of modern drama was clear from her earliest years. Let us recall the lawsuit Fuller lodged (unsuccessfully) against imitator Minnie Bemis in 1892. In that case, the judge's ruling addressed specifically the problematic nature of "character" in Fuller's work, denying her claim of copyright infringement because, to his mind, "A stage dance . . . telling no story, portraying no character, and depicting no emotion, is not a 'dramatic composition' within the meaning of the copyright act."[45] Although he ruled against her, this judge wound up essentially describing half of the modernist theater to come. Ionesco and Beckett, one imagines, would have fared just as badly as Fuller in this judge's courtroom.

Tristan Tzara's *Mouchoir de Nuages*

Fuller became a full-fledged participant in avant-garde theater in 1924 when she was hired by Comte Etienne de Beaumont to design the lighting and many of the sets for Les Soirées de Paris, a springtime festival of the arts featuring

[43] Fuller's relationship to her costume also recalls the innovations of Alfred Jarry with his 1896 *Ubu Roi*, performed initially with some actors in outsized "body mask" costumes, and later entirely by puppets. On the famously shocking opening night of that performance, Jarry explained his philosophy to the audience. The goal of these exaggerated masks, he said, was to highlight the doubleness at the heart of all acting, to allow the actor "to become precisely the interior man and the soul of the life-sized marionettes you are about to see." (Jarry, *Tout Ubu* [Paris, 1898; repr. Paris: Librairie Générale Française, 1962], 20). For its astute observations about Jarry's use of the body mask, I am endebted to an unpublished paper written in 2001 by Elisa Legon.

[44] Ted Merwin, "Loie Fuller's Influence on Filippo Marinetti's Futurist Dance," *Dance Chronicle* 21, no.1 (1998): 85.

[45] *Fuller v. Bemis*, 50 *The Federal Reporter* 929 (New York Circuit Court) (18 June 1892) (#5929).

dance, drama, music, painting, and cabaret shows.[46] Mounted in Paris's famous music hall Le Théâtre de la Cigale, Les Soirées brought together some of the most talented modernist artists of the 1920s. Massine choreographed a series of light ballets; Darius Milhaud and Erik Satie provided original scores; Ida Rubenstein danced; Picasso and Braque designed some of the sets and costumes; Toulouse-Lautrec exhibited his lithographs. De Beaumont told the press that his goal was "to transform the music hall, by gathering together all its major elements, and displaying the blossoming of our poetry, our painting, our music, and our dance . . . entrusting finally the lighting of the entire thing to that goddess of light who is Miss Loie Fuller."[47]

Of all the Soirées performances she worked on, Fuller received the most acclaim for her participation in *Mouchoir de nuages*, a play by Tristan Tzara (collaborating with Sonia Delaunay), directed by Marcel Herrand, and costumed by the great Jeanne Lanvin. It was performed for four consecutive evenings in May during the festival. *Mouchoir* was a self-consciously modernist piece, as Tzara's article about it in *Le Gaulois* makes very plain:

> *Mouchoir de nuages* is an ironic tragedy or a tragic farce in fifteen short acts, separated by fifteen commentaries. The action, which comes from the world of serial novels and cinema, takes place on a platform erected in the middle of the stage. The commentaries are delivered from the two sides of this platform. The play unfolds from beginning to end without interruption. The commentaries, which start off slow and disorganized, gradually take on greater length and importance until they form a second play, parallel to the one taking place on the platform.
>
> Only three characters keep a single identity throughout the play: Mlle Andrée Pascal, and Mssrs. Marcel Herrand et Dapoigny. The six commentators play seventeen different roles among them, they apply their makeup and dress on stage. They will use onstage their actual, offstage names [the names they use in town]. The whole play, furthermore, is based on the fiction of theater. For this reason, Miss Loie Fuller's electricians will remain onstage with their projectors, and the technician will unroll the backdrops in full view of everyone. The set is not there to give the illusion of a reality, but to indicate the place where the action occurs. Each act corresponds to one of the images onscreen, which are

---

[46] The title of the festival was borrowed from Apollinaire's journal by the same name.

[47] Etienne de Beaumont, qtd. in review article, *Nouvelles littéraires*, 10 May 1924, Collection Rondel on Les Soirées de Paris, Ro 12581. (Unless otherwise noted, all references to contemporary reviews or press clippings about Les Soirées are found in this collection.)

blowups of picture postcards. . . . *Mouchoir de nuages* is a poetic work; it stages the relativity of things, feelings and events.[48]

The play's "first level" or primary story resembled countless melodramas, but with some curious twists toward the end: A beautiful woman, neglected by her wealthy banker husband, confides her troubles to the Poet, who tries to help her by instructing the Banker in the importance of love. The Banker regrets his callousness, but by that time, the woman has fallen in love with the Poet. The Poet tries to flee the situation, traveling to the tropics, only to realize he has feelings for the woman. He returns to Paris to win the woman back, but she has reconciled with her husband. The plot becomes complicated and vague when the Poet enacts several scenes of *Hamlet* (in French translation) in order to trap the Banker into realizing his (the Poet's) love for the woman. Soon thereafter the Banker is inexplicably murdered by Apaches (urban gang members in France). Twenty years pass, at which time, the Poet commits suicide, his soul is auctioned off (in an actual auction scene), and he ascends dramatically to heaven.[49]

Between the play's acts were the "commentaries"—meta-critiques of the action delivered from the sides of the stage by the actors, who in this capacity were called only by the letters A through F.[50] At least two reviewers referred to these commentators as "a modernized Greek chorus."[51] The following bits of dialogue demonstrate the flavor of these exchanges:

B: Have you got any lipstick?
C: I really like this play.
A: I wouldn't be surprised if it's a hit.

D: Since this is the middle of the play, don't you think we should have an intermission here?
C: No, the author said he doesn't want an intermission. He says that intermissions have killed the theater.

[48] Tristan Tzara, "Le Secret de *Mouchoir de nuages*," *Le Gaulois*, 17 May 1924.
[49] Tristan Tzara, *Mouchoir de nuages, tragédie en 15 actes*, illustrations by Juan Gris (Paris: Editions Galerie Simon, 1925), Getty Research Institute Special Collections. While translations from Tzara's play are my own, Aileen Robbins has done a fine job of translating the entire text into English. See Tristan Tzara, *Handkerchief of Clouds*, trans. Aileen Robbins, *Drama Review* 16, no. 4 (December 1972): 112–29.
[50] Interpolated meta-commentary of this sort appears in Diderot's *Supplément to the Voyage of Bougainville*, as well as in a number of ancient philosophical texts.
[51] René Crevel, "Les Soirées de Paris," *Nouveautés littéraires*, 10 May 1924. Also Louis Schneider, "La Cigale: Les Soirées de Paris," qtd. in Carlo Ippolito, "Une Américaine à Paris: Loie Fuller," *Ligeia* 7–8 (October–December 1990): 83.

F to B: The fact that you're playing Andrée's lover on the platform does not give you the right to think you are her lover in reality.[52]

Summing up his desired effect, Tzara wrote, "The entire play is based on the fiction of theater. I do not want to hide from the spectator that what he is seeing is theater."[53] We might mistake the remark for Pirandello's; and in fact, *Mouchoir*'s indebtedness to *Six Characters* (which had premiered in France one year earlier) is unmistakable. Tzara never mentioned the Italian playwright, but certainly critics noted the resemblance, sometimes with irritation:

> M. Tristan Tzara wishes to surprise and mystify us. In the case of *Mouchoir de nuages*, he has surprised no one and become the victim of his own mystification. He hoped to appear revolutionary. But he found his revolution ready made in the work of Pirandello.[54]

But the originality of *Mouchoir de nuages* lay not in Tzara's meta-theatricality, but in Loie Fuller's set design. The set consisted of a large white cube into which poured sky-blue light from above. The backdrops were created by virtue of multicolored, changing light projections beamed onto the rolling screen of images that unfurled behind the actors. The picture-postcard settings included Paris, Venice, Monte Carlo, a slave plantation on a tropical island, a forest, the ramparts of Elsinore Castle (for the *Hamlet* section, naturally), and a still from Fuller's film, *Le Lys de la vie*.[55] Fuller also employed certain staging ideas lifted directly from her dance productions. In some scenes, for example, the actors performed while standing behind a white tulle curtain that slightly blurred their forms for the audience.[56] In the final scene, in which the Poet dies, a white shroudlike cloth falls over him (possibly the "*mouchoir de nuages*" of the title) as he rises above the stage under a shimmering silver light. "Disembodiment," one critic pronounced it, "We have never before seen onstage an operation as delicate as this one, when the poet's soul rises slowly to heaven."[57]

---

[52] Tzara, *Mouchoir*, passim.

[53] Tzara, "Le Secret."

[54] Gabriel Boissy, "*Mouchoir de Nuages*," 20 May 1924, Collection Rondel.

[55] Tzara, "Le Secret"; Louis Schneider wrote, "In the center of the stage, bathed in azure blue, rises a hill that the artists climb. Behind, multicolored vistas, magnified postcards, synthesize the décor" (Schneider, qtd. in Ippolito, "Une Américaine à Paris," 83).

[56] "A tulle curtain placed between the actors and the spectators creates an atmosphere that is somewhat vaporous, almost unreal, softening contours, [and] placing the silhouettes in a sort of fog that can become a halo under the glow of the projectors" ("Divertissement à la Cigale," 8 June 1924).

[57] Qtd. in David Whitton, "Tristan Tzara's *Mouchoir de Nuages*," *Theatre Journal* 14, no. 3 (Fall 1989): 279.

In the case of *Mouchoir de nuages*, the success of Fuller's lighting depended, as it always did, upon spectators' being moved by the confluence of solid flesh and the ethereal light projections that, with the help of screens and fabrics, seemed to dissolve that flesh into ephemeral, colorful images—into spiritual images. And here we can see why the play's final scene—the Poet's ascension to heaven—was particularly striking: it intensified, even literalized what was already a very powerful element of Fuller's work. That is, the scene depicted a soul rising from the body, the separation of flesh and spirit—and this may be, at some level, what audiences saw every time Fuller's floating, weightless veil shapes rose up and out of her earthbound body. It is fair to say, then, that *Mouchoir*'s final scene actually helps us understand another aspect of Fuller's appeal: her tendency to mime the ascension of the soul from the body. The Poet's flying up to heaven—accomplished via this very recognizably Fulleresque stage technique—reveals to us that, when onstage herself, Fuller may well have conjured visions of the body's soulful emanations, of a religious *exstasis*.

Tzara's *Hamlet*

According to one critic, watching *Mouchoir de nuages* was like "visiting a play-producing factory, or . . . watching, while at that factory, the fabrication of detached pieces of plays.[58] Such an impression resulted, of course, from Tzara's self-conscious use of all the meta-theatrical tricks we have already seen: exposing the actors dressing and undressing, having them use their real names, staging those "commentaries," and of course keeping Loie Fuller's technical crew and lighting equipment in full view of the audience.

But Tzara's zeal to expose the "seams" of theater did not stop with these (heavily Pirandello-inspired) techniques. If spectators could feel they were in a "factory" producing pieces of plays, it was not least because of *Mouchoir*'s somewhat clunky pastiche of literary allusions. By making overt use of myriad other texts, Tzara turned the play into more of a collage than a coherent drama. He liberally sprinkled *Mouchoir* with references to Symbolist poetry, nineteenth-century melodrama, Huysmans's novel *Là-Bas*, and of course Shakespeare.[59] Act XII of *Mouchoir* consists entirely of three condensed scenes from *Hamlet*.

---

[58] Boissy, "*Mouchoir de Nuages*."

[59] For a list of literary allusions in *Mouchoir*, see Aileen Robbins, "Tristan Tzara's *Handkerchief of Clouds*," *Drama Review* 16, no. 4 (December, 1972): 110–111.

The plot explanation for *Mouchoir*'s interpolation of *Hamlet* is a bit hard to follow: The Poet, seeking to gain the Woman's love, decides to mount an abbreviated production of *Hamlet* with himself in the lead role. Inviting the Woman and her husband, the Banker, to the theater, he performs for them his chosen scenes from *Hamlet*—scenes, he believes, bound to goad the Banker into acknowledging the Poet's sincere love for the Woman, and then into stepping aside and turning his wife over to this rival.

Of course, Tzara borrows doubly from Shakespeare here. In addition to the actual quoted scenes (which are lifted and translated verbatim), Tzara reproduces also the play-within-a-play conceit from *Hamlet*. In Shakespeare's play, Hamlet arranges for a court production of the revenge tragedy, *The Murder of Gonzago* (which he refers to as "The Mousetrap"), hoping that its plot of fratricide will shock or "trap" Claudius into an admission of guilt in the murder of his own brother, King Hamlet. Within *Mouchoir de nuages*, *Hamlet* holds the place of *The Murder of Gonzago*, a fact overtly admitted by Commentator C, who informs the audience, "*Hamlet* is playing. . . . This production is a mousetrap."

To add still a third level of *mise-en-abîme*, the specific selections from *Hamlet* quoted in *Mouchoir* come from the very moments when Hamlet begins feigning madness in preparation of his plot to trap Claudius. In other words, at this self-referentially theatrical moment in *Mouchoir de nuages*—when a character produces a play in order to provoke a powerful reaction in another character—Tzara reproduces precisely those moments from his own play within a play—*Hamlet*—when a character is about to produce a play in order to elicit a powerful reaction from another character.[60]

If this explanation seems hard to follow, it represents accurately the vertiginous, logic-defying game of mirrors Tzara meant to create, perhaps returning to his Dadaist roots. To make matters more confusing, the specific scenes from *Hamlet* quoted in *Mouchoir de nuages* are not particularly well suited either to revealing the Poet's feelings for the Woman or for prompting the Banker to renounce his wife. The Poet performs sections from *Hamlet*, Act II, scenes 1 and 2, in which Polonius and Ophelia discuss Hamlet's apparent madness, and in which Hamlet speaks cryptically to Polonius about honesty and keeping

---

[60] "I'll have these players / Play something like the murder of my father / Before mine uncle . . . / If he do blench, / I know my course. . . . / The play's the thing / Wherein I'll catch the conscience of the King"; *Hamlet*, 2.2.623–634 (ed. Barbara A. Mowat and Paul Werstine, New Folger Library [New York: Simon and Schuster, 2000]).

Ophelia from sin.[61] In the latter conversation, the prince obliquely suggests that he may be suicidal—Polonius: "Will you walk / out of the air, my Lord?" Hamlet: "Into my grave."[62]

In the end Tzara makes ungainly and only partially successful use of *Hamlet*; and *Mouchoir* is, admittedly, a minor work that seems never to have been mounted again after its four-day run in May of 1924. Yet, there remains one portion of the interpolated *Hamlet* that bears further inquiry here. The last section of *Mouchoir*, Act XII, reproduces a famous bit of dialogue between Polonius and Hamlet which, as we shall see, leads us back to Fuller, and to a new, better understanding of her cultural power.

Reading the Clouds: Shakespeare, Freud, and Fuller

Act XII of *Mouchoir* closes with an exact reproduction of *Hamlet* 3.2, lines 404–413, in which Polonius and Hamlet have the following curious exchange. Hamlet's nonsequiturs may be intended to convince Polonius that he (Hamlet) is indeed mad:

> *Polonius*: My Lord, the Queen would speak with you, and presently.
> *Hamlet*: Do you see yonder cloud that's almost in shape of a camel?
> *Polonius*: By the mass, and 'tis like a camel, indeed.
> *Hamlet*: Methinks it is like a weasel.
> *Polonius*: It is backed like a weasel.
> *Hamlet*: Or like a whale.
> *Polonius*: Very like a whale.
> *Hamlet*: Then I will come to my mother by and by. . . .

Let us put aside for the moment Tzara's (somewhat incoherent) use of this passage and turn instead to Shakespeare's. Hamlet ignores Polonius's urging that he speak with his mother, and instead of a reply, proffers his musings on the clouds. As Hamlet reads different animal shapes in the clouds, Polonius follows his lead and agrees that he sees each in turn. As Hamlet changes his reading, so does Polonius, with no acknowledgment of either the strangeness of the situation or the multiple reversals of opinion. He is either humoring the prince, believing him to have lost his senses, or going along with the game, deeming it best not to anger Hamlet or upset his plans.

---

[61] "O my lord, my Lord, I have been so affrighted! . . . Pale as his shirt, his knees knocking each other, / And with a look so piteous in purport, / As if he had been loosed out of hell . . ." (2.1.85, 91–93).

[62] *Hamlet*, 2.2, 224–225.

In either case, Hamlet exercises power over Polonius—not by direct force, but by appearing lost in his own thoughts. That is, Hamlet goads Polonius into total acquiescence of what has to be a purely subjective matter (what clouds look like) not by aggressively imposing his opinion, but by feigning contemplative musing. By ignoring for the moment Polonius's insistence that he visit Gertrude, and by appearing lost in childlike meditation on clouds, Hamlet succeeds in bending Polonius's conversational will, forcing him to see (or appear to see) camel, weasel, and whale where he (Polonius) presumably had not before. He succeeds furthermore in drawing out a truth about their relationship: Polonius accedes to Hamlet's will here, for Hamlet is still his prince.

What can we make of this dense little scene? First, it is a kind of microcosm of the essential "Mousetrap" plan, soon to be executed. Hamlet plans to pro-voke Claudius to a particular confession via an apparently innocent staging of a play (although this plan will not go as hoped). And here, in similar fashion, by affecting an innocent oblivion toward Polonius's wishes, Hamlet prompts his interlocutor to reveal the hierarchical relation between them, to echo (Hamlet's) every passing thought. In both cases, Hamlet behaves like a knowing theater director, staging unknowingness in order to provoke his audience, or perhaps to provoke his *actors*—since Claudius and Polonius both are expected to follow a desired script.

And let us consider Hamlet's specific choice of diversionary tactics with Polonius: he reads the clouds; he finds fanciful shapes in indistinct, floating forms. Imposing sense and shape onto amorphous phenomena is an ancient human impulse—as old at least as the naming of the constellations. Hamlet makes a show of projecting his own imagined images onto clouds in order to elicit certain responses from Polonius.[63] And this brings us back to Loie Fuller.

According to Fuller, when she danced her role as the hypnotized Imogene Twitter, the audience grew excited reading shapes into the swirling forms of her skirts. Their pleasure in espying the ephemeral shapes of butterflies and orchids is akin to the pleasure we feel finding pictures in the clouds. It is the delight of finding the familiar in the unfamiliar, in bringing order to chaos,

---

[63] Hamlet's show of reading the clouds should also remind us of that other floating form whose presence engenders much of the play's action: the ghost of Hamlet I. Furthermore, in Act III, scene 4, Hamlet will once again impose a shape upon an indistinct form, this time with deadly consequences: While in Gertrude's chamber, he will mistake Polonius (who hides behind the arras) for Claudius. Without bothering to look, Hamlet will thrust his dagger through the fabric, killing Polonius. The scene remains mysterious, for Hamlet seems less horrified by his fatal mis-take than one might assume, evincing only impatience and anger upon addressing Polonius's dead body, "Thou wretched rash, intruding fool, farewell" (3.4.38).

finding confirmation of our internal references in the external world. Fuller must have known this at some level, for clouds creep into her account of the *Quack* performance: "I let myself drop, completely enveloped in a *cloud* of light material."

In her *Quack, M.D.* anecdote, Fuller implied that she was herself the passive recipient of her spectators' interpretations. In her recounting of this foundational tale of her career, she denied her own agency, preferring to tell a story about the projection of the audience's visions. Later she would devote her life to turning her own body into an apparently unknowing projection screen. Like Hamlet "lost" to his cloud meditations, Fuller projected images onto her own cloudlike veils (sometimes even images *of* clouds) and in so doing provoked spectators to project onto her. Tristan Tzara must have understood this aspect of Fuller's work, for he embedded into his play—lit and designed by Fuller—a fragment of Shakespeare devoted precisely to this phenomenon.

It is this "cloud picture"-quality that allowed Fuller to elicit the passionate yet completely contradictory responses we have seen repeatedly. Watching her turn her own whirling body into various images, spectators were prompted to revelations of their own desired relationship with the spectacle they witnessed. They were excited by the erotic Loie, or reassured by the chaste Loie, inspired by an Art Nouveau icon, bemused by the Yankee scientist, and so on. In the end, Loie Fuller may have been theater history's most successful Rorschach test. For nearly thirty years, audiences read pictures in her clouds—an exercise that led inevitably back to the spectators' interior selves and cultural framework. Indeed, of all the "secret landscapes" Fuller liked to uncover—the cancer cells, the fish skeletons, the surface of the moon—the most important interior belonged, ultimately, to the audience.

In this, Fuller's relationship to her audience resembled the psychoanalytic transference, that powerful love that develops between analyst and patient, which Freud referred to as both a *Tummelplatz* (playground) and a *Zwischenreich* (in-between realm)—a safe place to reenact troubling relationships and work through them.[64] Transference results from the patient's displacement of desires from his "real" life onto the analyst, who must maintain a studied neutrality (or a "staged unconsciousness"). The analyst, Freud wrote, "must take care not to steer away from the transference-love, or to repulse it, or to make it distasteful to the patient; but he must just as resolutely withhold any

[64] See Sigmund Freud, "Zur Dynamik der Übertragung" (1912), *Gesammelte Werke*, vol. 8 (Frankfurt: Fischer Verlag), 364–65.

response to it."[65] Freud famously said that transference was crucial to analysis because "when all is said and done, it is impossible to destroy anyone in absentia or *in effigie*."[66] The phrase contradicts itself, since the transference actually creates a kind of effigy or substitutive relationship. As Peter Brooks has observed, "it is precisely 'in effigy'—in the symbolic mode—that the past and its ghosts may be destroyed, or laid to rest in analysis."[67] And so, in his justification for the transference, in insisting on its "realness," Freud actually conjures it as a ghost. He denies its ghostliness while forcing us to think about it, thereby reinforcing the implied liminality of the transference relationship.

At once solid and ghostlike, the transference is a deeply metaphorical concept. As such, it suggests slippage far more than permanence. It is a dialogic relationship but constructed expressly with the goal of being dismantled. The transference, then, offers us a particularly fine model for the relationship between Fuller and her audience. At its most basic level, Fuller's work continually conjured effigies—spectral, disembodied beings that rose and fell onstage, enthralling generations of spectators, prompting them to seemingly infinite interpretations. Fuller's power lay precisely in this ability to engage this very primal and very personal urge to interpret, to read in the clouds, to lend meaning to specters—as Hamlet does with his father's ghost. But her spectral effigies, like clouds and like the effigies implicit in the transference, were necessarily ephemeral, and while she clearly partook of many major art movements of her time, Fuller was never firmly associated with any one of them. For these reasons, despite her worldwide celebrity and hypnotic effect on old and young, Loie Fuller just evaporated from cultural consciousness. Her curious aptitude for embodying the Zeitgeist in myriad art forms did not, in the end, serve her well. My hope here has been to resurrect her with enough interpretive force to reposition her in performance history. Like Horatio encountering Hamlet's ghost, I have called to her, across time, "Stay, illusion!"[68]

---

[65] Freud, "Observations on Transference-Love: Further Recommendations on the Technique of Psychoanalysis" (1915), in *The Standard Edition of the Complete Psychological Works of Sigmund Freud*, vol. 12, trans. Alix Strachey (London: Hogarth Press, 1958): 166–67.

[66] Freud, "The Dynamics of Transference," *Standard Edition*, vol. 12, 108.

[67] Peter Brooks, "The Idea of a Psychoanalytic Literary Criticism," *Critical Inquiry* 13, no. 2 (Winter 1987): 344–45.

[68] *Hamlet*: 1.1.139.

Afterword

Thoughts on Contemporary Traces of Fuller

WHILE LOIE FULLER EFFECTIVELY VANISHED from our cultural radar after her death, traces of her spirit certainly remain.[1] We can find the most overt of these in the work of Jody Sperling, who openly incorporates recreations of Fuller's work into her own choreography (fig. A.1). Sperling describes her style as "nouveau-retro," and with her company Time Lapse Dance, brings classical and modern dance as well as acrobatics to her adaptations of Fuller. Using "magic lantern" projections, provided by Terry Borton, founder of the American Magic-Lantern Theater, Sperling recreates classic pieces by Fuller, including *Night*, *Fire*, and *Le Firmament*. Like Fuller, she projects slides of stars, flames, and flowers onto voluminous, glittering robes (fig. A.2). (Unlike Fuller, she displays balletic grace and often allows glimpses of her leotard-clad body beneath the veils.) Although one hundred years have passed, critics continue to thrill to this combination of fabric, music, and lights: "Encased in a silken costume," writes Jack Anderson, "Ms. Sperling summoned up spirits of earth, water, wind, fire, and ether by manipulating the fabric so its folds swirled, billowed, and soared in delightful metamorphoses."[2] Elizabeth Zimmer echoes these sentiments: "This postmodern choreographer-critic transforms . . . the spectacular work of modern-dance pioneer Loie Fuller into her own hypnotic spectacle.[3]

[1] Jennifer Tipton, for example, is an award-winning lighting designer whose work for ballet and modern dance companies is highly influenced by Fuller. "It is a wonderfully juicy thing to 'paint' with colored light," she has written (Jennifer Tipton, "Light, Like Music, Can Help Establish the Rhythm," *New York Times*, 26 January 2003).

[2] Jack Anderson, "An Evening of Solos with a Shimmering Tribute: Jody Sperling," *New York Times*, 27 March 2002, Arts section.

[3] Elizabeth Zimmer, "Jody Sperling/Time Lapse Dance," *Village Voice*, 26 March 2002.

Figure A.1. Jody Sperling in *The Serpentine Dance*, photograph © Julie Lemberger

Figure A.2. Jody Sperling in "Ether" from *Dance of the Elements*, photograph
© Julie Lemberger

Sperling has also created more postmodern dances that develop and render
explicit some of Fuller's underlying thematic elements. In her witty duet
Cheaper, for example, Sperling and another dancer (Ashley Sowell) perform
tumbling gymnastics and yoga poses while "borrowing" each other's limbs.
That is, they interweave their arms and legs in such a way that spectators,
looking at a two-woman "handstand," for example, cannot discern whose legs
are flying up into the air and whose arms are bearing their combined body
weights. Costumed in horizontally striped cotton suits (a kind of cross between
the "onesies" babies wear and cartoon prison garb), the dancers tumble and
cavort like characters from a Buster Keaton movie, while occasionally moving
through intimate, twisting embraces that suggest a lesbian erotics. In this way,
Cheaper overtly develops a number of tacit themes in Fuller's work: the broad
comedy of vaudeville and cabaret, the notion of "prosthetically" extending
the capacity of a dancer's limbs (achieved here via the use of a second dancer's
limbs rather than batons), and a subtle blend of childlike innocence (the
women clown around with each other in their absurd costumes) and a woman-
centered sexuality.

In her very thoughtful *Symptomatic*, Sperling again uses some other Fuller-esque techniques to draw out Fuller's frequent mise-en-scène of medical or scientific interiority. The piece is set in a doctor's office where a woman "pa-tient" is to receive an onstage consultation with her physician. While a boom-ing male voice from offstage asks questions about her health, the patient gazes at her own body, which begins to tremble with increasing violence. The dancer is unperturbed by the shaking, regarding her disobedient limbs with disinterested calm and clinical detachment. The "doctor" (played as a man but by a female dancer) then appears silhouetted behind a screen. His giant, shadowed "hand" then looms toward the patient to examine her. The patient's body responds to the outsized hand, writhing under its "touch," as a hypnotized subject might respond to the hypnotizer. The patient's relationship to the shadow hand also suggest that of a disconnected puppet still guided by a phan-tom version of its puppeteer's hand.

Here, of course, Sperling plays not only with Fuller's scientific and medical themes, but uses her *Ombres gigantesques* technique to investigate the relation-ship between doctor and patient, patient and patient's body, flesh and shadow, and ultimately, self and other. *Symptomatic* ends with Sperling's body gradually being overtaken completely by the shaking.

While there are other periodic recreations of Loie Fuller's dancing, most notably by German choreographer Brygida Ochaim, what interests me most in this *postscriptum* is an art form that has received virtually no critical atten-tion but which clearly relies on the same powerful processes that drove Fuller's fame: I am referring to "flag dancing," or "flagging" (also known as "spinning linen," "rag dancing," and "fanning").

Although its official, scholarly history has yet to be written, flagging emerged in the gay nightclubs of Chicago and San Francisco, most likely in the late 1970s and early 1980s. At its most basic, it consists of groups of dancers (mostly but not all gay men) rhythmically waving large squares of weighted silk around their bodies, as lights dance over them. Often, the fabrics are tie-dyed in brilliant colors, which creates patterns that undulate wildly when agitated (fig. A.3).

While flagging styles and equipment vary, it seems that all dancers agree on one point: flagging has the capacity to provoke states of deep, hypnotic trance in participants and even in spectators. As the fabric whirls into the air—forming the same kind of ephemeral sculptural shapes that Fuller wielded so well—participants speak of feeling lifted out of their bodies and daily prob-lems, finding normally inaccessible emotions and thoughts rising effortlessly to consciousness. Although the art form tends to be associated with the heavy use of "club drugs," including Ecstasy and crystal methamphetamine, the most

Figure A.3. Dancer George Jagatic, flagging at Merce Cunningham Studio, 2002, © George Jagatic and Brad Carpenter (photographer)

thoughtful practitioners say that the dance itself is somewhat hallucinatory, obviating any need for mind-altering chemicals.

Choreographer and psychotherapist George Jagatic first encountered flagging as a club-going young man in San Francisco who, he admits freely, took a lot of drugs. He soon realized, though, that flagging made him feel not only sober, but clearheaded in an unaccustomed way: "The experiences I had doing this were so profound that I had to figure out what it was. It was so profoundly healthy. I was high as a kite and it would ground me, pull me out of my high. I felt clear." Jagatic (who gave up drugs completely) describes flagging as "a transfixing experience that takes you out of your body, while pulling you into the moment without baggage." Having studied dance formally, Jagatic decided to codify the flagging movements. He broke down what he was watching into basic building blocks with names such as "butterfly" and "windmill." After moving to New York, Jagatic made flagging the basis of the dance company he founded, Axisdanz. Inspired also by the psychological liberation he experienced in flagging, he decided to pursue a second career as a dance therapist, incorporating flagging into his practice.[4]

One of the few women involved in flagging, Candida Scott Piel, both practices and teaches the art. Often called the "godmother of flagging," she sees it as a kind of sacred guild, in which older "tribe members" pass on their art form to younger men. "It's a piece of gay culture," she says, "that takes you very deep, like any movement-based spiritual practice, such as Tai Chi." After a performance, she says, "people understand what the word 'mesmerized' means." Piel prefers to refer to the art form as "fanning," citing its obvious connection to Chinese fan dancing—a woman's art. The semantic choice is deliberate; for Piel, despite its connection to gay male culture, "fanning" has a deeply feminine side, depending as it does on the use of flowing fabrics. "Flags," says Piel, are associated with "parades and the military"; she sees the term "flagging" as an attempt by men to masculinize a form of dance that is threateningly female. In fact, Piel attributes the frequent use of hallucinogenic drugs that accompany flagging to a desire to avoid some of this gender ambiguity. "You need permission to get up there as a man and flit around with pink fabric," she says dryly. Like Jagatic, Piel believes that flagging produces an "altered state of consciousness, in which the left and right sides of the brain are synchronized." "It's going to unlock things," she adds.[5] Like Jagatic, Piel is also planning a career in psychotherapy, although she does not intend to make fanning part of her clinical practice. (Piel is also aware of the faintly

---

[4] Personal interview with George Jagatic, New York City, 2 February 2006.
[5] Personal interview with Candida Scott Piel, New York City, 4 February 2006.

Japanese undertones in flagging, which she situates in its gender ambiguity: "In a flick of a wrist, you go from Madame Butterfly to a samurai," she notes.)

I include this brief mention of the art of flagging not because I think the flaggers are consciously recreating any aspect of Loie Fuller's work, but because their dance confirms the hypnotic power inherent in the graceful manipulation of lights and fabric around a dancing human body. The rhapsodic descriptions of flagging, the testimonies of its mind-altering force, resemble nothing so much as they do the reviews of Loie Fuller—written one hundred years ago. The transferential relationship that I suspect underlies Fuller's power seems to live on in this gay art form, which is at once deeply personal and highly social. Fixing one's gaze on the swirling silk seems liberating to many people, freeing them to use that fabric as a screen on which (and through which) to view themselves and others. While I would resist labeling Fuller's work uniquely "queer," the proximity of her work to flagging does remind us that those whose erotic self-expression brings with it the risk of social ostracism feel especially drawn to this form of dance at once revealing and obscuring, in which bodies are both bare and covered, and no one spinning shape stays visible for very long.

Selected Bibliography

〰️

EXHIBITION CATALOGUES AND DOCUMENTS

Commisariat de l'Exposition Coloniale. *Guide illustré de l'Exposition Coloniale Française au Trocadéro en 1900*. Paris: Cambrai, 1900.

Guy, Camille. *Exposition Universelle de 1900: Publication de la commission*. Paris: Augustin Challamel, 1901.

Le Figaro. *Guide bleu de Figaro à l'Exposition de 1900*. Paris: Le Figaro, 1900.

Librairie Hachette. *Guide Hachette à l'Exposition Universelle*. Paris: Librairie Hachette, 1900.

Ministère du Commerce et de L'Industrie. *Compte des recettes et des dépenses: Exposition Universelle Internationale de 1900 à Paris*. Paris: Imprimerie Nationale, 1909.

Ministère du Commerce et de l'Industrie, de Poste, et des Télégraphes. *Exposition internationale des arts décoratifs et industriels à Paris, avril-octobre, 1925*. Paris: Imprimerie Nationale, 1925.

PUBLIC COLLECTIONS

Musée Rodin archives, Paris. Letters, programs, press clippings.

Collection Rondel on *Les Soirées*. Programs, reviews, press clippings. Bibliothèque de l'Arsenal, Paris.

Collection Rondel on Loie Fuller. Bibliothèque de L'Arsenal, Paris. Programs, reviews, press clippings.

Fuller, Loie. Papers. Unpublished manuscripts, articles, reviews, programs. New York Public Library for the Performing Arts (NYPLPA).

Getty Research Institute, Special Collections, Los Angeles, California.

Robinson Locke Collection. Theater Arts materials. Papers, reviews, articles, many dealing with Loie Fuller. New York Public Library for the Performing Arts.

PRIVATE COLLECTIONS

Blake, Sarah Ludlow. Personal archives.

Néagu, Philippe. Personal archives of the late curator. Musée d'Orsay, Paris.

FILMS, VIDEOS, AND RECORDINGS OF LIVE PERFORMANCES

Fuller, Loie, and Gab Sorère [Gabrielle Bloch]. *Le Lys de la Vie* (1921). Paris: Cinémathèque de la Danse.

Loie Fuller's Fire Dance: Reconstruction and Performance. Produced by John Mueller. Performed by Jessica Lindberg. Columbus: Dance Film Archive, Ohio State University, 2003.

Trailblazers of Modern Dance. Produced and directed by Merrill Brockner and Judy Kinber. Bloomington: Indiana University, 1977.

BOOKS AND ARTICLES

Alloula, Malek. *The Colonial Harem*. Translated by Myrna Godzich and Wlad Godzich. Minneapolis: University of Minnesota Press, 1986.

Anderson, Jack. *Ballet and Modern Dance*. Princeton, NJ: Princeton University Press, 1986.

———. "An Evening of Solos with a Shimmering Tribute: Jody Sperling." *New York Times*, 27 March 2002.

Appia, Adolphe. *Texts on Theatre*. Edited by Richard Beacham. New York: Routledge, 1993. Reprinted 2002.

Apter, Emily. *Continental Drift: From National Characters to Virtual Subjects*. Chicago: University of Chicago Press, 1999.

Aschengreen, Erik. "The Beautiful Danger: Facets of Romantic Ballet." Translated by Patricia N. McAndrew, *Dance Perspectives* no. 58 (1974).

Au, Susan. *Ballet and Modern Dance*. London: Thames & Hudson, 1988.

Bablet, Denis. *Esthétique générale du décor du théâtre de 1870 à 1914*. Paris: Editions du Centre de la Recherche Scientifique, 1965.

Balanchine, George, and Francis Mason. *Complete Stories of the Great Ballets*. 1954. Reprint, Garden City, NY: Doubleday, 1977.

Banes, Sally. *Writing Dancing in the Age of Postmodernism*. Hanover, NH: University Press of New England, 1994.

Baril, Jacques. *La Danse moderne*. Paris: Editions Vigot, 1977.

Beacham, Richard. *Adolphe Appia, Theatre Artist*. Cambridge: Cambridge University Press, 1987.

Becker-Leckrone, Megan. "Salome: The Fetishization of a Textual Corpus." *New Literary History* 26, no. 2 (1995): 239–60.

Benjamin, Walter. *The Arcades Project*. Translated by Howard Eiland and Kevin McLaughlin. New York: Belknap Press, 2002.

———. *Charles Baudelaire: A Lyric Poet in the Era of High Capitalism*. Translated by Harry Zohn. London: Verso, 1983.

Bentivoglio, Leonetta. "Danza e futurismo in Italia 1913–1933." *La Danza Italiana*, no. 1 (Autumn 1984): 61–82.

Bentley, Eric. *In Search of Theatre*. New York: Applause Theater Book Publishers, 1947.

Bentley, Toni. *Sisters of Salome*. New Haven, CT: Yale University Press, 2002.

Bergeret, Gaston. *Journal d'un nègre à l'exposition de 1900*. Paris: Librarie L. Conque; L. Carteret et Cie, Successeur, 1901.

Bizot, Richard. "The Turn of the Century Salome Era." *Choreography and Dance* 2, pt. 3 (1992): 71–87.

Blair, John G. "First Steps toward Globalization: Nineteenth-Century Exports of American Entertainment Forms." In *Here, There and Everywhere: The Foreign Politics of American Popular Culture*, edited by Reinhold Wagnleitner and Elaine Tyler May. Hanover, NH: University Press of New England, 2000.

Blumenthal, Henry. *American and French Culture, 1800–1900*. Baton Rouge: Louisiana State University Press, 1975.

Brooks, Peter. "The Idea of a Psychoanalytic Literary Criticism." *Critical Inquiry* 13, no. 2 (Winter 1987): 344–45.

Brown, Bill. "Science Fiction, the World's Fair, and the Prosthetics of Empire, 1910–1915." In *Cultures of United States Imperialism*, edited by Amy Kaplan and Donald E. Pease. Raleigh, NC: Duke University Press, 1993.

Brown, Sarah Graham. *Images of Women: The Portrayal of Women in Photography of the Middle East 1860–1950*. New York: Columbia University Press, 1988.

Brustein, Robert. "Male and Female in August Strindberg." *Tulane Drama Review* 7, no. 2 (Winter 1962): 130–74.

Buck-Morss, Susan. *The Dialectics of Seeing: Walter Benjamin and the Arcades Project*. Cambridge, MA: MIT University Press, 1989.

Buckle, Richard. *Diaghilev*. New York: Atheneum, 1984.

Buonaventura, Wendy. *Something in the Way She Moves: Dancing Women from Salome to Madonna*. New York: Da Capo Press, 2004.

Carlson, Marvin. *Theories of the Theatre*. Ithaca, NY: Cornell University Press, 1984.

Carrouges, Michel. *Les Machines célibataires*. Paris: Editions du Chêne, 1976.

Castle, Terry. *The Apparitional Lesbian*. New York: Columbia University Press, 1993.

Çelik, Zeynep, and Leila Kinney. "Ethnography and Exhibitionism at the Expositions Universelles." *Assemblage* 13 December 1990: 35–59.

Chiba, Yoko. "Japonisme: East-West Renaissance in the Late Nineteenth Century." *Mosaic* 31, no. 2 (June 1998): 1–20.

Cixous, Hélène, and Catherine Clément. *The Newly Born Woman*. Translated by Betsy Wing. Minneapolis: University of Minnesota Press, 1986.

Cocteau, Jean. *Souvenirs*. Paris: Editions Flammarion, 1935.

Coffman, Elizabeth. "Women in Motion: Loie Fuller, and the Interpenetration of Art and Science." *Camera Obscura*. 17, no. 1 (2002): 73–105.

Coleman, Bud. "The Electric Fairy: The Woman behind the Apparition of Loie Fuller." In *Staging Desire: Queer Readings of American Theater History*, edited by Kim Marra and Robert A. Schanke. Ann Arbor: University of Michigan Press, 2002.

Cueto-Asin, Elena. "The Chat Noir's Théâtre d'Ombres." In *Montmartre and the Making of Mass Culture*, edited by Gabriel Weisberg. New Brunswick, NJ: Rutgers University Press, 2001.

Current, Richard, and Marcia Ewing Current. *Loie Fuller: Goddess of Light*. Boston: Northeastern University Press, 1997.

Décoret-Ahiha, Anne. *Les Danses exotiques en France 1880–1940*. Paris: Centre National de la Danse, 2004.

Dementev, Igor. *Imperialists and Anti-Imperialists*. Translated by David Skvirsky. Moscow: Progress Publishers, 1979.

de Morinni, Claire. "Loie Fuller: The Fairy of Light." In *Chronicles of the American Dance: From the Shakers to Martha Graham*, edited by Paul Magriel. New York: Da Capo, 1984.

Dempster, Elizabeth. "Women Writing the Body: Let's Watch a Little How She Dances." In *The Routledge Dance Studies Reader*, edited by Alexandra Carter. New York: Routledge, 1998.

Diderot, Denis. *Selected Writings on Art and Literature*. Translated by Geoffrey Bremer. London: Penguin, 1994.

Dorfman, Ariel. *The Empire's Old Clothes*. New York: Pantheon Books, 1983.

Duncan, Isadora. "The Freedom of Woman." In *Isadora Speaks*. Chicago: Charles Kerr Publishing, 1994. Originally published 1922.

Dyer, Richard. *Heavenly Bodies: Film Stars and Society*. New York: St. Martin's Press, 1986.

Eagleton, Terry. *Walter Benjamin Or Towards a Revolutionary Criticism*. London: Verso Press, 1981.

Erdman, Jean. "The Dance Theater Pieces of the 1940s: A Conversation with Jean Erdman and Erich Hawkins." *Choreography and Dance* 5, pt. 2 (1999). Special issue on Martha Graham edited by Alice Helpern.

Esslin, Martin. "Max Reinhardt: High Priest of Theatricality." *Drama Review* 21, no. 2 (June 1977): 3–27.

Ferrell, Robyn. *Passion in Theory: Conceptions of Freud and Lacan*. London: Routledge, 1996.

Fjelde, Rolf. "*Peer Gynt*, Naturalism and the Dissolving Self." *The Drama Review* 13, no. 2 (Winter 1968): 28–43.

Foster, Susan Leigh. "The Ballerina's Phallic Pointe." In *Corporealities*, edited by Susan Leigh Foster. New York: Routledge, 1996.

———. *Choreography and Narrative*. Bloomington: Indiana University, 1998.

Foulkes, Julia. *Modern Bodies: Dance and American Modernism from Martha Graham to Alvin Ailey*. Chapel Hill: University of North Carolina Press, 2002.

Franko, Mark. *Dancing Modernism/Performing Politics*. Bloomington: Indiana University Press, 1995.

Freedman, Russell. *Martha Graham: A Dancer's Life*. New York: Clarion Books, 1998.

Freud, Sigmund. "Fetishism." In *Collected Papers*, authorized translation under the supervision of Joan Rivière. New York: Basic Books, 1959.

———. "Observations on Transference-Love: Further Recommendations on the Technique of Psychoanalysis." In *The Dynamics of Transference*, vol. 12 of *The Standard Edition*. Originally published 1915.

———. *An Outline of Psychoanalysis*. Translated by Alix Strachey. 1949. Reprint, New York: W.W. Norton & Co., 1969.

———. "Zur Dynamik der Übertragung" (1912). In *Gesammelte Werke*, vol. 8. Frankfurt: Fischer Verlag, 1940.

Fuller, Loie. *Fifteen Years of a Dancer's Life*. With an introduction by Anatole France. Boston: Small, Maynard & Co., 1913.

Gallagher, Fiona. *Christie's Art Nouveau*. New York: Watson-Guptill Publications, 2000.

Garafola, Lynn. "Dance, Film, and the Ballets Russes." *Dance Research* 16, no. 1 (Summer 1998): 3–25.

———. *Diaghilev's Ballets Russes*. New York: Da Capo Press, 1989.

———. *Legacies of Twentieth Century Dance*. Middletown, CT: Wesleyan University Press, 2005.

Garber, Marjorie. *Vested Interests: Cross-Dressing and Cultural Anxiety*. New York: Routledge, 1992.

Garelick, Rhonda. "Electric Salome." In *Imperialism and Theatre*, edited by Ellen Gainor. New York: Routledge, 1995.

———. *Rising Star*. Princeton, NJ: Princeton University Press, 1998.

Geddes, Patrick. "The Closing Exhibition—Paris 1900." *The Contemporary Review* 78 (November 1900): 653–68.

Gilman, Richard. *The Making of Modern Drama*. New Haven: Yale University Press, 1999.

Girard, René. "Scandal and the Dance: Salome in the Gospel of Mark." *New Literary History* 15, no. 2 (Winter 1984): 116–18.

Girardet, Raoul. *L'Idée coloniale en France de 1871 à 1962*. Paris: La Table Ronde, 1972.

Goodall, Jane. *Performance and Evolution in the Age of Darwin: Out of the Natural Order*. New York: Routledge, 2002.

Gordon, Rae Beth. "From Charcot to Charlot: Unconscious Imitation in French Cabaret." *Critical Inquiry* 27, no. 3 (Spring 2001): 515–49.

Graham, Martha. *Blood Memory*. New York: Macmillan, 1991.

Greenhalgh, Paul. *Ephemeral Vistas*. Manchester, UK: Manchester University Press, 1988.

Griffith, Mrs. M. "Loie Fuller: The Inventor of the Serpentine Dance." *Strand Magazine*, Winter 1984, 540–45.

Grunfeld, Frederic V. *Rodin: A Biography*. New York: Henry Holt, 1987.

Hale, Dana S. "French Images of Race on Product Trademarks during the Third Republic." In *The Color of Liberty: Histories of Race in France*, edited by Sue Peabody and Tyler Stovall. Raleigh, NC: Duke University Press, 2003.

Hallays, André. *En flânant: A Travers l'expo de 1900*. Paris: Perrin, 1901.

Hamon, Philippe. *Expositions*. Paris: José Corti, 1989.

Haraway, Donna. *Simians, Cyborgs, and Women: The Reinvention of Nature*. New York: Routledge, 1991.

Hardy, Georges. *Les Eléments de l'histoire coloniale*. Paris: Renaissance du Livre, 1920.

Harris, Margaret Haile. "Loie Fuller: The Myth, the Woman and the Artist." *Arts in Virginia* 20, no. 1 (1979): 16–29.

Hastings, Baird. "Hide and Seek: Illusion and Fantasy in the Scenic Design of Pavel Tchelitchev." *Ballet Review* 23, no. 5 (Fall 1995): 91–96.

Hoganson, Kristin. *Fighting for American Manhood: How Gender Politics Provoked the Spanish-American and Philippine-American Wars*. New Haven: Yale University Press, 2000.

Ibsen, Henrik. *Peer Gynt*. Translated by Peter Watts. New York: Penguin Books, 1966. Originally published 1867.

Ippolito, Carlo. "Une Américaine à Paris: Loie Fuller." *Ligeia* 4, no. 7–8 (1990): 59–85.

Jameson, Fredric. "Modernism and Imperialism." In *Nationalism, Colonialism, and Literature*. Minneapolis: University of Minnesota Press, 1990.

———. "Modernism and Its Repressed." In *The Ideologies of Theory*. Minneapolis: University of Minnesota Press, 1988.

Jarry, Alfred. *Tout Ubu*. Paris: Librairie Générale Française, 1962.

Jouhet, Serge. "Quand Loie Fuller flottait ses longs voiles." *Danser* no. 2 (May 1983): 14–46.

Jowitt, Deborah. "In Pursuit of the Sylph." In *The Routledge Dance Studies Reader*, edited by Alexandra Carter. New York: Routledge, 1998.

———. *Time and the Dancing Image*. Berkeley: University of California Press, 1988.

Jullian, Philippe. *Esthètes et magiciens*. Paris: Perrin et Cie., 1969.

———. *Jean Lorrain*. Paris: Flammarrion, 1950.

———. *The Triumph of Art Nouveau*. Translated by Stephen Hardman. New York: Larousse, 1974.

Kahane, Martine, and Delphine Pinasa. *Le Tutu: Petit Guide*. Paris: Flammarion/Opéra National de Paris, 1997.

Kendall, Elizabeth. "1900: A Doorway to Revolution." *Dance Magazine*, January 1999, 80–83.

Kermode, Frank. "Loie Fuller and the Dance before Diaghilev." *Salmagundi*, nos. 33–34 (Spring–Summer 1976): 23–47.

———. *Romantic Image*. London: Routledge and Kegan Paul, 1957.

Kern, Stephen. *The Culture of Time and Space 1880–1918*. Cambridge, MA: Harvard University Press, 1983.

Kevles, Bettyann. *Naked to the Bone: Medical Imaging in the Twentieth Century*. New York: Perseus, 1998.

Kirstein, Lincoln. *Tchelitchev*. New York: Twelvetrees, 1994.

Kochno, Boris. *Diaghilev and the Ballets Russes*. Translated by Adrienne Foulke. New York: Harper & Row, 1970.

Kurth, Peter. *Isadora: A Sensational Life*. New York: Little Brown, 2001.

Kuryluk, Ewa. *Salome and Judas in the Cave of Sex*. Evanston, IL: Northwestern University Press, 1987.

Latimer, Tirza True. "Loie Fuller: Butch Femme Fatale." In *Proceedings of the Society of Dance History Scholars: 22nd Annual Conference*. Albuquerque: University of New Mexico Press, 1999.

Lee, Sang-Kyong. "Edward Gordon Craig and Japanese Theatre." *Asian Theatre Journal* 17, no. 2 (Fall 2000): 215–35.

Legrand-Chabrier. "La Loie Fuller: D'Une Exposition à l'autre." *L'Art Vivant* 1 (April–December, 1925): 26–29.

———. "Les Fêtes." In *Exposition des Arts Décoratifs et Industriels*, edited by L'Art Vivant. Paris: Librarie Larousse, 1925.

Léon, Paul. "Art du théâtre." In *Encyclopédie du théâtre*, section 10: *Photographie et Cinématographie*. Paris: Editions Larousse, 1955.

Leprun, Sylviana. *Le Théâtre de colonies: scénographie, acteurs et discours imaginaires dans les Expositions 1855–1937*. Paris: Editions l'Harmattan, 1986.

Levinson, André. *André Levinson on Dance: Writings from Paris in the Twenties*. Edited by Joan Acocella and Lynn Garafola. Middletown, CT: Wesleyan University Press, 1991.

Lista, Giovanni. *Danseuse de la Belle Epoque*. Paris: Editions Somogy, 1995.

———. "Prampolini scenografia." Introduction to *Prampolini: Dal futurismo all'informale*, by Enrico Prampolini. Rome: Edizioni Carte Segrete, 1992.

"Loie Fuller." In *Encyclopedia dello spettacolo*, vol. 5. Rome: Unione Editorale, 1954.

Lorrain, Jean. *Poussières de Paris*. Paris: Société d'Editions Littéraires et Artistiques, 1902.

Mallarmé, Stéphane. "Les Fonds dans le ballet." In *Oeuvres complètes*. Paris: Editions Gallimard, 1979.

Mandel, Richard D. *Paris 1900: The Great World's Fair*. Toronto: University of Toronto Press, 1967.

Mannoni, Octave. *Clefs pour l'imaginaire de l'autre scène*. Paris: Seuil, 1985.

Marcus, Jane. "Salome: The Jewish Princess Was a New Woman." *Bulletin of the New York Public Library* 78 (1974): 95–113.

Marinetti, Filippo. "Manifesto of the Futurist Dance." http://futurism.org.uk/manifestos/index.htm. Originally published as F. T. Marinetti, "La danza futurista (Danza dello shrapnel—Danza della mitragliatrice—Danza dell'aviatore)—MANIFESTO FUTURISTA," in *L'Italia Futurista* (8 July 1917): 1–2.

Martin, John. "Isadora Duncan and Basic Dance." In *Nijinsky, Pavlova, Duncan: Three Lives*, edited by Paul Magriel. New York: Da Capo Press, 1978.

Mauclair, Camille. *Idées vivantes*. Paris: Librairie de l'Art Ancien et Moderne, 1904.

Mazo, Joseph. *Prime Movers: The Makers of Modern Dance in America*. New York: Morrow, 1977.

McCarren, Felicia. *Dance Pathologies*. Stanford, CA: Stanford University Press, 1998.

———. *Dancing Machines*. Stanford, CA: Stanford University Press, 2003.

———. "The Symptomatic Act." *Critical Inquiry* 21, no. 1 (1995): 748–61.

McClintock, Anne. *Imperial Leather: Race, Gender, and Sexuality in the Colonial Contest*. New York: Routledge, 1995.

Meltzer, Françoise. *Salome and the Dance of Writing*. Chicago: University of Chicago Press, 1977.

Merwin, Ted. "Loie Fuller's Influence on Filippo Marinetti's Futurist Dance." *Dance Chronicle* 21, no. 1 (1998): 73–92.

Miller, J. Scott. "Dispossessed Melodies: Recordings of the Kawakami Theater Troupe." *Monumenta Nipponica* 53, no. 2 (Summer 1998): 225–35.

Miller, Richard H. "Introduction." In *American Imperialism in 1898: The Quest for National Fulfillment*, edited by Richard H. Miller. New York: John Wiley and Sons, 1970.

Miomandre, Francis. *Danse*. Paris: Flammarion, 1935.

Mitchell, Timothy. "Orientalism and the Exhibitionary Order." In *Colonialism and Culture*, edited by Nicholas Dirks. Ann Arbor: University of Michigan Press, 1992.

Morand, Paul. *1900 A.D.* Translated by Rollilly Feden. New York: William Farquhar Payson, 1931.

Morris, Gay. "La Loie." *Dance Magazine* 51, no. 8 (August 1977): 36–41.

Moynet, G. "Le Pavillon national des Etats-Unis." In *L'Encyclopédie du siècle*. Paris: Montgredien et Cie, 1900

Mulvey, Laura. "Some Thoughts on Theories of Fetishism in the Context of Contemporary Culture." *October* 65 (Summer 1993): 3–20.

Musée de l'Ecole de Nancy. *Loie Fuller: Danseuse de l'Art Nouveau*. Paris: Editions de la Réunion des Musées Nationaux, 2002.

Ninkovich, Frank. *The United States and Imperialism*. New York: Blackwell, 2000.

Ochaim, Brygida. "Loie Fuller, The Soloist of the Dancing Color." *Parkett* 9 (1986): 115–19.

Phelan, Peggy. *Unmarked: The Politics of Performance*. New York: Routledge, 1993.

Picard, Alfred. *Le Bilan d'un siècle*. Paris: Imprimerie Nationale, 1906.

Pinet-Cheula, Hélène. *Ornement de la durée: Loie Fuller, Isadora Duncan, Adorée Villany*. Paris: Musée Rodin, 1987.

Polcari, Stephen. "Martha Graham and Abstract Expressionism." *Smithsonian Studies in American Art* 4, no. 1 (Winter 1990): 2–7.

Porter, Jacques. *Une Fascination réticente: Les Etats-Unis dans l'opinion française*. Nancy: Presses Universitaires de Nancy, 1990.

Prampolini, Erico. "Futurist Scenography." Translated by V. N. Kirby. In Michael Kirby, *Futurist Performance*, edited by Michael Kirby. New York: E.P. Dutton, 1971. Originally published as "Scenografia e coreografia," 1915.

Praz, Mario. *The Romantic Agony*. Translated by Angus Davidson. Oxford: Oxford University Press, 1974.

Reynolds, Nancy, and Malcolm McCormick. *No Fixed Points: Dance in the Twentieth Century*. New Haven: Yale University Press, 2003.

Roach, Joseph. *Cities of the Dead*. New York: Columbia University Press, 1996.

———. *The Player's Passion: Studies in the Science of Acting*. Newark: University of Delaware Press, 1985.

Robbins, Aileen. "Tristan Tzara's *Handkerchief of Clouds*." *Drama Review* 16, no. 4 (December 1972): 110–11.

Roger-Marx, Claude. *La Loie Fuller*. Paris: Editions Société des Cent Bibliophiles, 1904.

———. "Loie Fuller." *Les Arts et la Vie*, January–June 1905, 265–352.

———. "Une Rénovatrice de la danse." *Le Musée* March 1907: 91–104.

Roose-Evans, James. *Experimental Theatre: From Stanislavksy to Peter Brook*. London: Routledge, 1970.

Said, Edward. *Culture and Imperialism*. New York: Alfred A. Knopf, 1993.

Schechner, Richard. *Between Theatre and Anthropology*. Philadelphia: University of Pennsylvania Press, 1985.

Schulzinger, Robert D., ed. *A Companion to American Foreign Relations*. New York: Blackwell, 2003.

Segel, Harold B. *Body Ascendant: Modernism and the Physical Imperative*. Baltimore: Johns Hopkins University Press, 1998.

Seltzer, Mark. *Bodies and Machines*. New York: Routledge, 1992.

Severi, Rita. "Oscar Wilde, La Femme Fatale and the Salome Myth." In *Proceedings of the Tenth Congress of the International Comparative Literature Association, 1982*, edited by Anna Balakian. New York: Garland Publishing, 1985.

Shakespeare, William. *Hamlet*. Edited by Barbara A. Mowat and Paul Werstine. New Folger Library. New York: Simon & Schuster, 2000

Shewan, Rodney. "The Artist and the Dancer in Three Symbolist Salomes." *Bucknell Review* 30, no. 1 (1986): 102–30.

Showalter, Elaine. *Sexual Anarchy*. New York: Viking, 1990.

Siegel, Marcia. *The Shapes of Change: Images of American Modern Dance*. Boston: Houghton Mifflin, 1979.

Silvagni. "L'Etonnante vie de la fée de la lumière." *Pour Tous* (Paris), 20 September 1953.

Silverman, Debora. *Art Nouveau in Fin-de-Siècle France*. Berkeley: University of California Press, 1991.

Slotkin, Richard. "Buffalo Bill's 'Wild West' and the Mythologization of the American Empire." In *Cultures of United States Imperialism*, edited by Amy Kaplan. Raleigh, NC: Duke University Press, 1993.

Solomon-Godeau, Abigail. "The Legs of the Countess." *October* 39 (Winter 1986): 65–108.

Sommer, Sally. "Loie Fuller." *Drama Review* 19, no. 1 (1975): 53–67.

———. "Loie Fuller." In *International Encyclopedia of Dance*, vol. 3, edited by Selma Jeanne Cohen. New York: Oxford University Press, 1998.

———. "Loie Fuller's Art of Music and Light." *Dance Chronicle*, 4, no. 4 (1981): 389–401.

Sowell, Debra Hickenlooper. "Marinetti's Manifesto of Futurist Dance. In *Proceedings of the Eight Annual Conference of Dance History Scholars*. Albuquerque: University of New Mexico Press, 1985.

Strindberg, August. *Miss Julie*, translated by Peter Watt. In *Three Plays*. London: Penguin Books, 1958. Originally published in 1888.

Strindberg, August. "Preface to *Miss Julie*." In *Miss Julie and Other Plays*, translated by Michael Robinson. New York: Oxford University Press, 1998. Originally published in 1888.

Thomas, Helen. *Dance, Modernity, and Culture*. New York: Routledge, 1995.

Townsend, Julie. "Alchemic Visions and Technological Advances: Sexual Morphology in Loie Fuller's Dance." In *Dancing Desires: Choreographing Sexualities on and off the Stage*, edited by Jane C. Desmond. Madison: University of Wisconsin Press, 2001.

Tzara, Tristan. *Handkerchief of Clouds*. Translated by Aileen Robbins. *The Drama Review*, 16, no. 4 (December 1972): 112–129.

———. *Mouchoir de nuages: tragédie en 15 actes*. Paris: Editions Galerie Simon, 1925.

———. "Le Secrète de *Mouchoir de Nuages*." *Le Gaulois* (Paris), 17 May 1924.

Ullman West, Martha. "Fuller, Rosenthal, and Tipton." *Dance Magazine* 70, no. 2 (February 1996): 88–93.

Van Vechten, Carl. "Terpsichorean Souvenirs." *Dance Magazine* (January 1957): 16–17.

Veroli, Patrizia. *Baccanti et dive dell'aria: Donne danza et società in Italia, 1900–1945*. Perugia: Edimond, 2001.

Wallace, Chris. *Character: Profiles in Presidential Courage*. New York: Ruggedland Press, 2003.

Whitton, David. "Tristan Tzara's *Mouchoir de Nuages*." *Theatre Journal* 14, no. 3 (Fall 1989): 271–87.

Wiley, John. *A Century of Russian Ballet*. Oxford: Oxford University Press, 1991.

Williams, Rosalind. *Dream Worlds: Mass Consumption in Late Nineteenth-Century France*. Berkeley: University of California Press, 1982.

Wyndham, Donald. "The Stage and Ballet Design of Pavel Tchelitchev." *Dance Index* 3 (1944): 4–32.

Zimmer, Elizabeth. "Jody Sperling/Time Lapse Dance." *Village Voice*, 26 March 2002.

Zola, Emile. "Le Naturalisme au théâtre," in *Le Roman experimental*. Paris: Garnier-Flammarion, 1971.

Zornitzer, Amy. "Revolutionaries of the Theatrical Experience: Fuller and the Futurists." *Dance Chronicle* 21, no. 1 (1998): 95–105.

Index

CPSIA information can be obtained at www.ICGtesting.com
Printed in the USA
BVOW08s0115200913

331700BV00002B/13/P

9 780691 141091